France
**Belgium, Luxembourg
and the Netherlands**

France
**Belgique, Luxembourg
et les Pays-Bas**

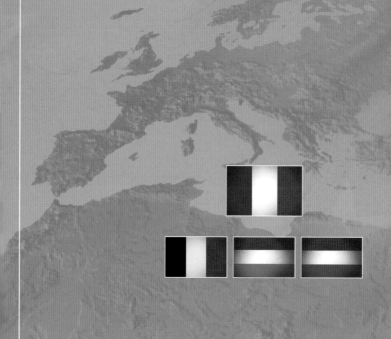

Table of contents/Table des matières

Key to map pages/Vue d'ensemble des cartes	3
Channel Ferries/Ferries de la Manche	4 - 5
Legend/Légende	6
Significant points of interest/Sites remarquables	7
Maps/Atlas routier 1:800 000	8 - 73
Regions of France/Région française	74
Key to map pages/Vue d'ensemble des cartes; Legend/Légende; City maps/Atlas des villes	75
Amsterdam 1:100 000	76 - 77
Brussels/Bruxelles 1:100 000	78 - 79
Luxembourg 1:100 000	80 - 81
Paris 1:150 000	82 - 83
Index of place names/Index des localités	84 - 104

© Kunth Verlag GmbH & Co. KG 2018
St.-Cajetan-Straße 41, D-81669 München,
phone +49-89-458020-0, fax +49-89-458020-21
e-mail: info@kunth-verlag.de
www.kunth-verlag.de

© AA Media Limited 2018
Fanum House, Basing View,
Basingstoke, Hampshire RG21 4EA, UK
ISBN 978 0 7495 7987 6
A05635

Hill shading 1:800 000:
Produced using SRTM data from Heiner Newe,
GeoKarta, Altensteig

Printed in China

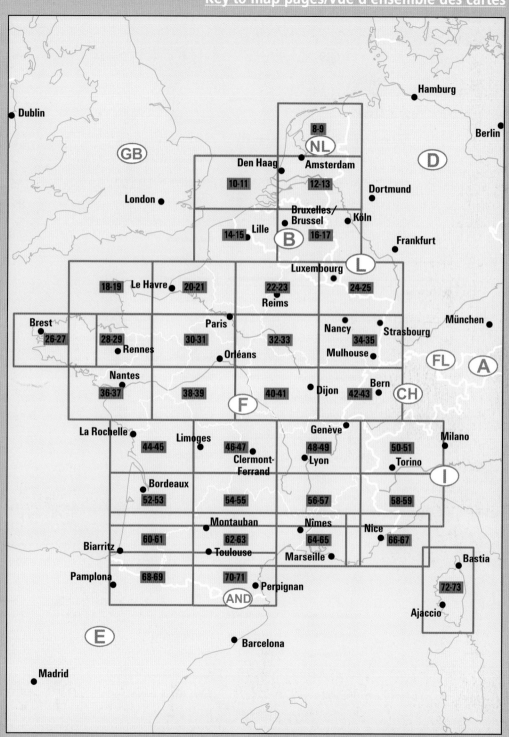

	GB	F
Motorway/under construction		Autoroute/en construction
Toll motorway		Autoroute à péage
Tunnel motorway		Tunnel autoroute
Dual carriageway/under construction		Double chaussée/en construction
Tunnel dual carriageway		Tunnel double chaussée
Primary route/under construction		Route primaire/ en construction
Tunnel primary road		Tunnel route primaire
Important main road/under construction		Route principale importante/en construction
Main road		Route principale
Secondary road		Route secondaire
Touristic/historic route		Route touristique
Railway		Chemin de fer
Distances in kilometres (within UK in miles)	25	Distances kilométriques (au sein du RU en miles)
Steep gradient/Mountain pass height in metres	Col de la Schlucht / 9 % / (1361)	Indication de la pente/ Col et sa cote d'altitude
Motorway number	4 2 A22	Numéros des autorutes
European road number	E54	Numéro des routes européennes
Other road numbers	34 28 N22 322	Autre numéro de routes
Motorway junction number/Access only in the direction of arrow	22	Numéros d'échangeurs/Accessible seulement dans le sens de la flèche
Junction		Échangeur
Not suitable/closed for caravans		Non adapté/ Fermé aux caravanes
Filling station/Restaurant		Station-service/Restaurant
Restaurant with motel		Hôtel-Restaurant
Major airport		Grand aéroport
Airport		Aéroport
Airfield		Aérodrome
Ferry		Ferry
Border crossing		Douane
International boundary		Frontière de l'État
Administrative boundary		Limite administrative
Restricted area		Zone restreinte
National or nature park		Parc national, parc naturel
Mountain summit with height in metres	Grand 1424 Ballon ▲	Sommet avec cote d'altitude
Place of interest	COLMAR	Ville très intéressante

GB / F

GB	F
Major tourist route	Circuit touristique important
Major tourist railway	Ligne ferroviaire touristique
Highspeed train	Train à Grande Vitesse
Shipping route	Itinéraire de navigation
UNESCO World Natural Heritage	Patrimoine naturel de l'humanité de l'UNESCO
Mountain landscape	Paysage de montagne
Rock landscape	Paysage rocheux
Ravine/canyon	Gorge/canyon
Glacier	Glacier
Extinct volcano	Volcan éteint
Cave	Grotte
River landscape	Paysage fluvial
Waterfall/rapids	Cascade/ Rapide
Lake country	Paysage de lacs
Fossil site	Site fossilifère
Nature park	Parc naturel
National park (landscape)	Parc national (paysage)
National park (flora)	Parc national (flore)
National park (fauna)	Parc national (faune)
Biosphere reserve	Réserve de biosphère
Botanical garden	Jardin botanique
Wildlife reserve	Réserve animale
Protected area for sea-lions/seals	Rés. naturelle d'otaries/de phoques
Zoo/safari park	Zoo/ Parc Safari
Coastal landscape	Paysage côtier
Beach	Plage
Island	Île
Underwater reserve	Réserve sous-marine
Spring	Source
UNESCO World Cultural Heritage	Patrimoine culturel de l'humanité de l'UNESCO
Pre-and early history	Préhistoire et protohistoire
Prehistoric rockscape	Peintures rupestres préhistoriques
Etruscan site	Civilisation étrusque
Roman antiquity	Antiquité romaine
Places of Jewish cultural interest	Site d'intérêt culturel juif
Places of Christian cultural interest	Site d'intérêt culturel chrétien
Romanesque church	Église romane
Gothic church	Église gothique
Renaissance church	Église Renaissance
Baroque church	Église baroque
Byzantine/Orthodox church	Église byzantine/ orthodoxe
Christian monastery	Monastère chrétien
Cultural landscape	Paysage culturel
Historical city scape	Cité historique
Impressive skyline	Gratte-ciel impressionnant

GB	F
Castle/fortress/fort	Château/forteresse/remparts
Castle ruin	Château ruine
Worth seeing tower	Tour intéressante
Striking building	Bâtiment remarquable
Palace	Palais
Technical/industrial monument	Monument technique/industriel
Mine (in service)	Mine en activité
Disused mine	Mine fermée
Dam	Barrage
Impressive lighthouse	Très beau phare
Windmill	Moulin à vent
Notable bridge	Pont remarquable
Tomb/grave	Tombeau
Monument	Monument
Memorial	Mémorial
Theatre of war/battlefield	Champs de bataille
Space telescope	Télescope astronomique
Market	Marché
Festivals	Fêtes et festivals
Museum	Musée
Open-air museum	Musée de plein air
Theatre	Théâtre
Tourist information centre	Information
World exhibition/World Fair	Exposition universelle
Olympics	Site olympique
Arena/stadium	Arène/stade
Race track	Circuit automobile
Golf	Golf
Horse racing	Centre équestre
Skiing	Station de ski
Sailing	Port de plaisance
Wind surfing	Planche à voile
Surfing	Surf
Diving	Plongée
Canoeing/rafting	Canoë/rafting
Waterskiing	Ski nautique
Beach resort	Station balnéaire
Mineral/thermal spa	Station hydrothermale
Leisure pool	Piscine plein air
Leisure park	Parc de loisirs
Casino	Casino
Aerial tramway	Téléférique
Hiking region	Zone de randonnées
Lookout point	Point de vue
Deep-sea fishing	Pêche en eau profonde
Seaport	Port

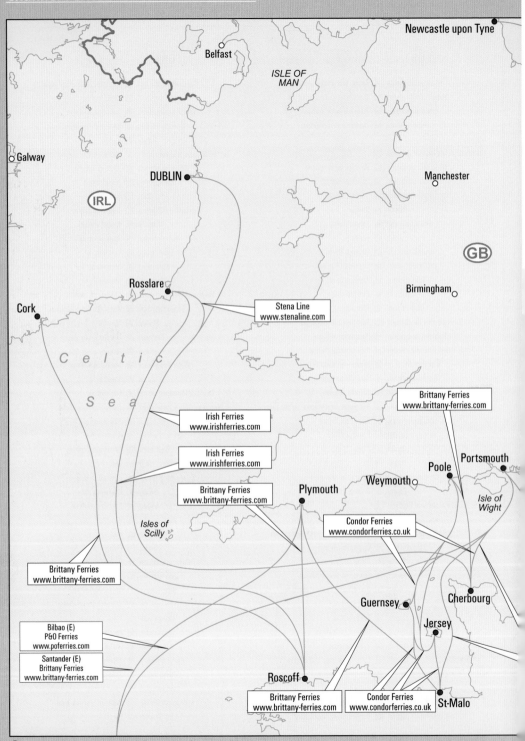

Newcastle upon Tyne

Belfast

ISLE OF MAN

Galway

DUBLIN

IRL

Manchester

GB

Rosslare

Birmingham

Cork

Stena Line
www.stenaline.com

C e l t i c

S e a

Brittany Ferries
www.brittany-ferries.com

Irish Ferries
www.irishferries.com

Portsmouth

Poole

Irish Ferries
www.irishferries.com

Weymouth

Isle of Wight

Brittany Ferries
www.brittany-ferries.com

Plymouth

Condor Ferries
www.condorferries.co.uk

Isles of Scilly

Brittany Ferries
www.brittany-ferries.com

Guernsey

Cherbourg

Jersey

Bilbao (E)
P&O Ferries
www.poferries.com

Santander (E)
Brittany Ferries
www.brittany-ferries.com

Roscoff

Brittany Ferries
www.brittany-ferries.com

Condor Ferries
www.condorferries.co.uk

St-Malo

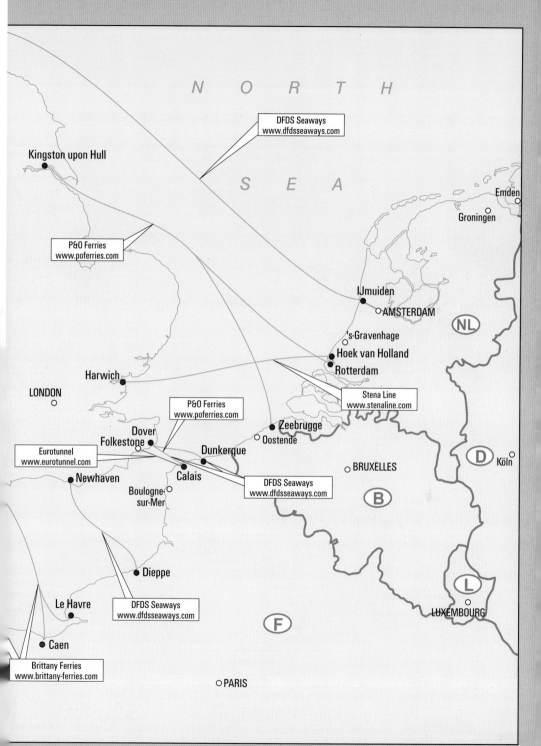

NORTH SEA

DFDS Seaways
www.dfdsseaways.com

Kingston upon Hull

Emden

Groningen

P&O Ferries
www.poferries.com

IJmuiden

AMSTERDAM

NL

's-Gravenhage

Hoek van Holland

Rotterdam

Harwich

LONDON

Stena Line
www.stenaline.com

P&O Ferries
www.poferries.com

Dover

Zeebrugge

Folkestone

Oostende

Eurotunnel
www.eurotunnel.com

Dunkerque

BRUXELLES

D

Köln

Newhaven

Calais

DFDS Seaways
www.dfdsseaways.com

B

Boulogne-
sur-Mer

L

Dieppe

LUXEMBOURG

Le Havre

DFDS Seaways
www.dfdsseaways.com

F

Caen

Brittany Ferries
www.brittany-ferries.com

PARIS

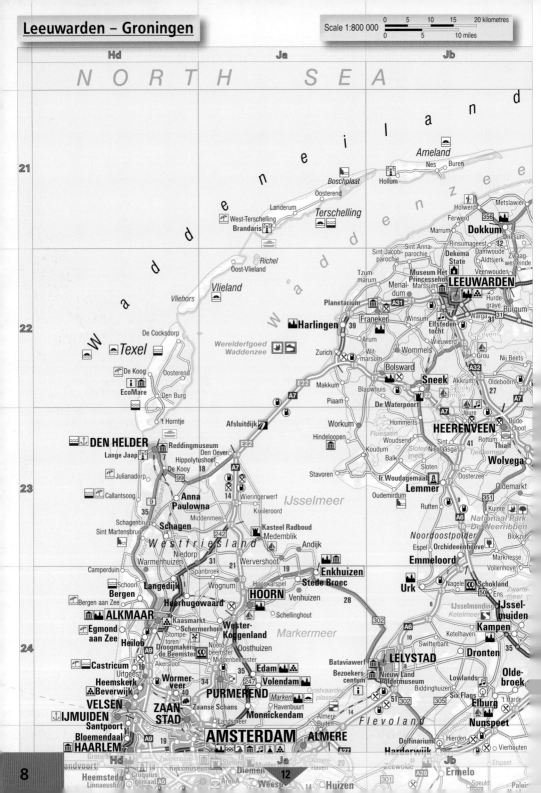

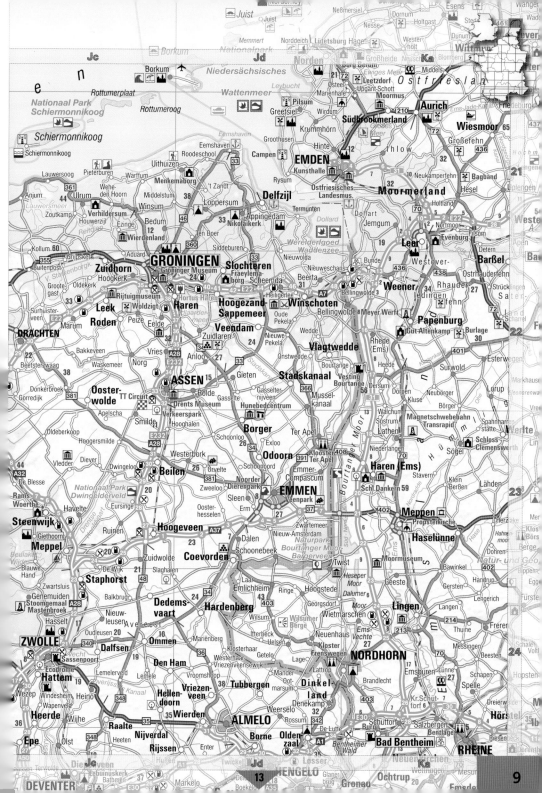

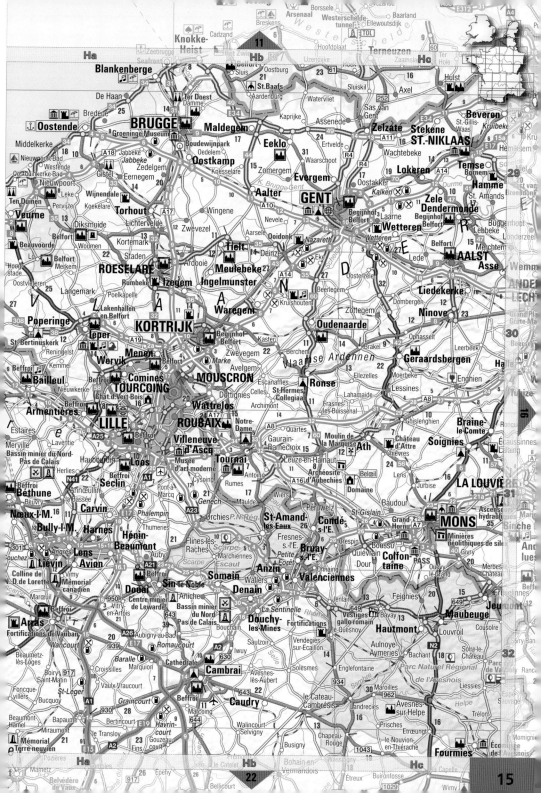

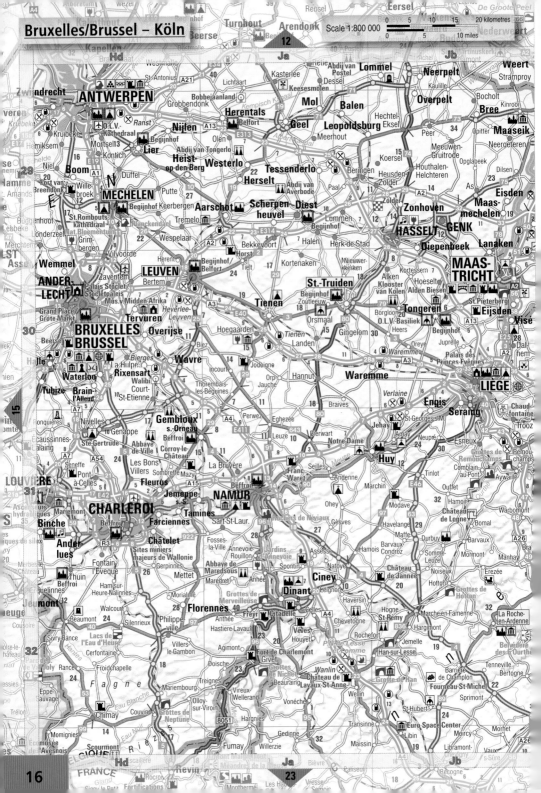

Scale 1:800 000

| 0 | 5 | 10 | 15 | 20 kilometres |
| 0 | | 5 | | 10 miles |

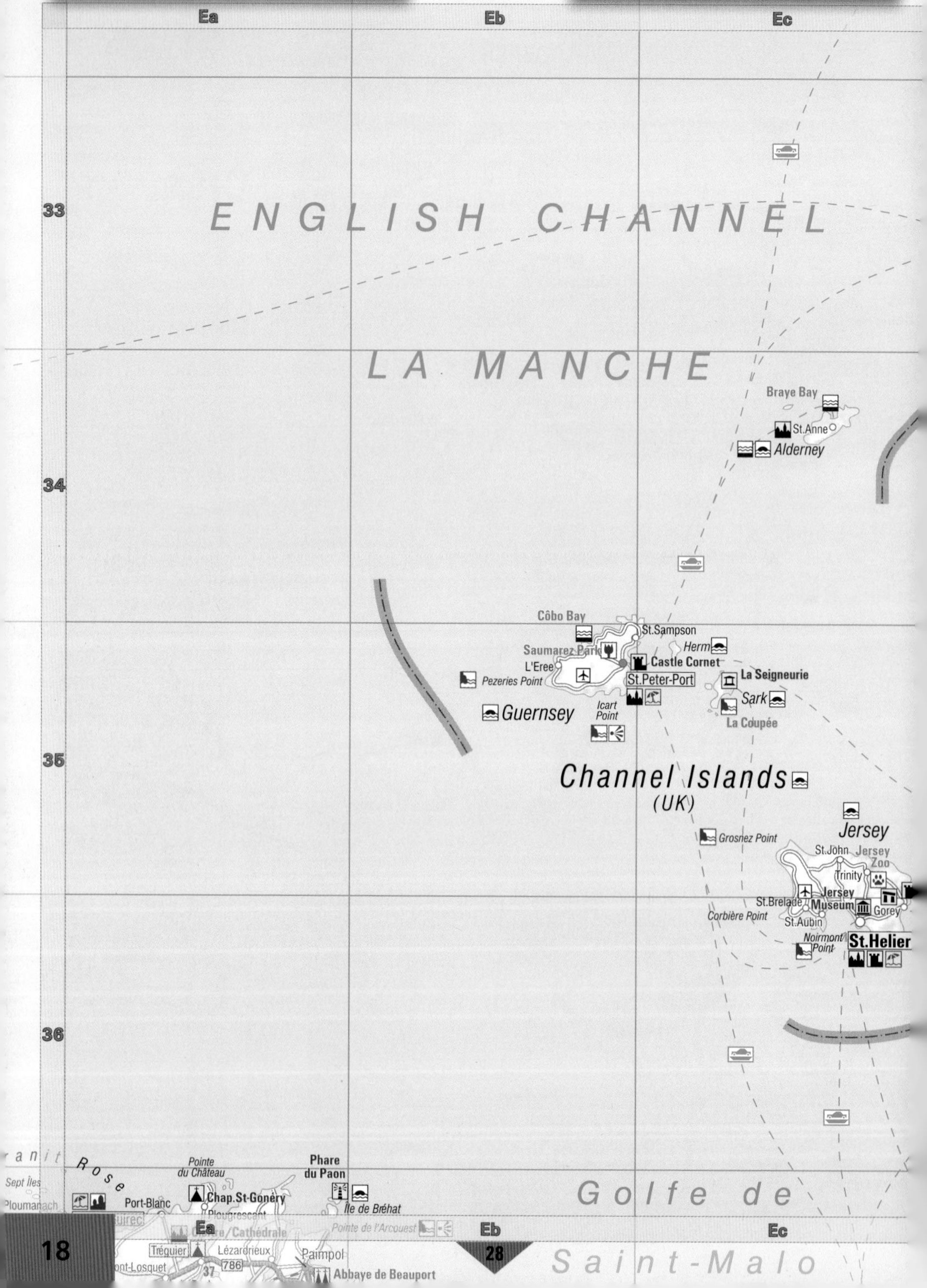

Ea   Eb   Ec

E N G L I S H   C H A N N E L

33

L A   M A N C H E

Braye Bay
St.Anne
Alderney

34

Côbo Bay   St.Sampson
Saumarez Park   Herm
L'Eree   Castle Cornet
Pezeries Point   St.Peter-Port
    La Seigneurie
Guernsey   Sark
Icart   La Coupée
Point

35

Channel Islands
(UK)

Grosnez Point   Jersey
St.John   Jersey
Zoo
Trinity
St.Brelade   Jersey
Museum
Corbière Point   St.Aubin   Gorey
Noirmont
Point   St.Helier

36

Golfe de

28

S a i n t - M a l o

ranit Rose
Sept Îles
Ploumanach   Pointe   Phare
du Château   du Paon
Port-Blanc   Chap.St-Gonéry
Ploungrescant   Île de Bréhat
re/Cathédrale   Pointe de l'Arcouest
Ea   Eb   Ec
Tréguier   Lézardrieux   Paimpol
ont-Losquet   37   (786)   Abbaye de Beauport

Scale 1:800 000

0   5   10   15   20 kilometres

0   5   10 miles

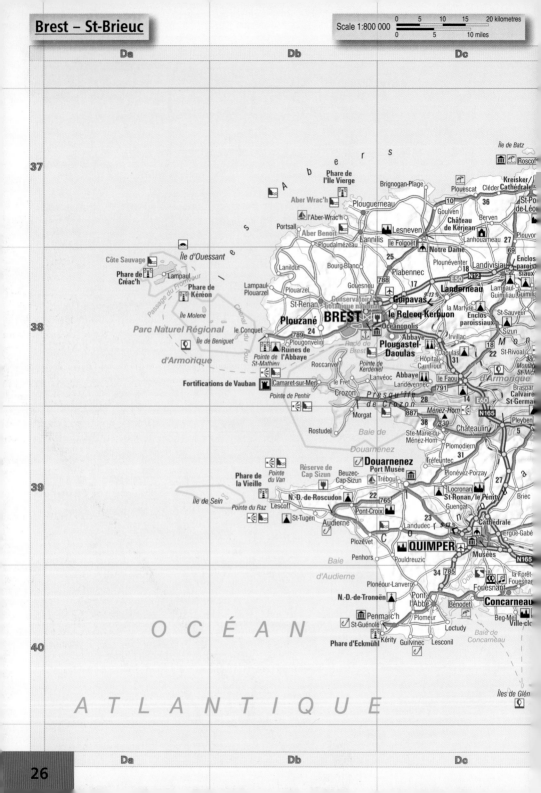

| | Da | Db | Dc |

37

Abers

Île de Batz

Roscoff

Phare de l'Île Vierge

Brignogan-Plage

Plouescat   Cléder

Kreisker Cathédrale

St-Pol-de-Léon

Aber Wrac'h

l'Aber-Wrac'h

Plouguerneau

10

Goulven   Berven

36

Plouvorn

Château de Kerjean

Portsall

Aber Benoit

Lannilis

Lesneven

Le Folgoët

Notre Dame

Lanhouarneau

27

69

Ploudalmézeau

Côte Sauvage

Île d'Ouessant

Lanildut

Bourg-Blanc

25

Plounéventer

Landivisiau

Enclos paroissiaux

Phare de Créac'h

Lampaul

Plouarzel

Gouesnou

Plabennec

17

788

E50   N12

18

Lampaul-Guimiliau

Guimiliau

Lampaul Plouarzel

St-Renan

Conservatoire botanique national

Guipavas

Landerneau

la Martyre

St-Sauveur

Île Molene

Plouzané

BREST

le Relecq-Kerhuon

Enclos paroissiaux

Sizun

38

Parc Naturel Régional

Île de Beniguet

le Conquet

789

24

Océanopolis

Rade de Brest

Abbaye

Plougastel-Daoulas

(Daoulas)

Irvillac

31

22

St-Rivoal

Mor

d'Armorique

Plougonvelin

Hôpital-Camfrout

18

Mont St-Mic

Ruines de l'Abbaye

Pointe de Kerdéniel

791

Abbaye

le Faou

Braspar

Calvaire

St-Germa

Pointe St-Mathieu

Roscanvel

Lanvéoc

Landévennec

E60

Fortifications de Vauban   Camaret-sur-Mer

le Fret

Crozon

Presqu'île de Crozon

28

14

Pleyben

Pointe de Penhir

Morgat

887

Ménez-Hom

N165

Châteaulin

5

330

38

Rostudel

Baie de Douarnenez

Ste-Marie-du-Ménez-Hom

Plomodiern

Réserve de Cap Sizun

Tréfuentec

31

a

39

Phare de la Vieille

Pointe du Van

Beuzec-Cap-Sizun

Douarnenez   Port Musée

Tréboul

Plonévez-Porzay

Locronan

27

Île de Sein

N.-D.-de-Roscudon

22

765

St-Ronan/le Pénity

Guengat

Briec

Pointe du Raz

Lescoff

Pont-Croix

Cathédrale

St-Tugen

Audierne

23

Landudec

Ergué-Gabé

Plozévet

C

QUIMPER

Musées

N165

Penhors

Pouldreuzic

Baie d'Audierne

34   785

la Forêt-Fouesnan

Plonéour-Lanvern

Odet

Fouesnant

N.-D.-de-Tronoën

Pont-l'Abbé

Bénodet

Concarneau

Plomeur

Beg-Meil

Ville-clo

Penmarc'h

Loctudy

Baie de Concarneau

St-Guénolé

Guilvinec

Lesconil

40

Phare d'Eckmühl

Kérity

O C É A N

Îles de Glén

A T L A N T I Q U E

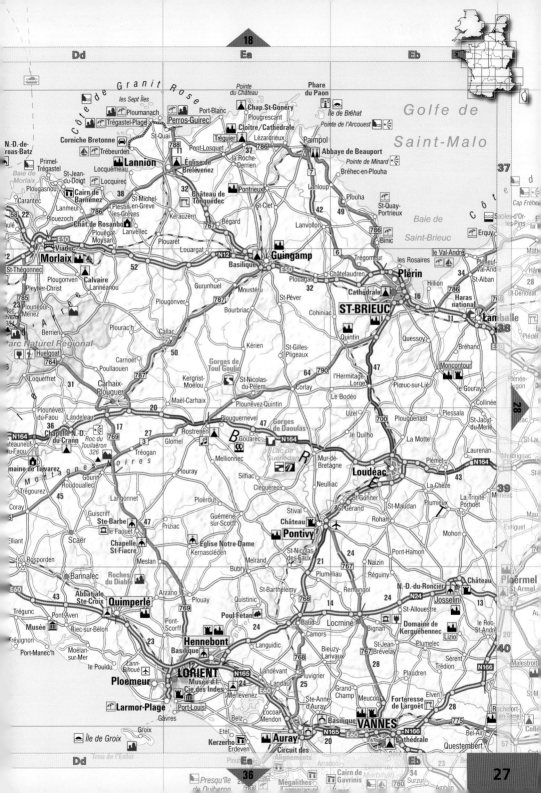

St-Brieuc – Rennes

Golfe de

Saint-Malo

Côte d'Émeraude

Granit Rose
les Sept Îles
Ploumanach
astel-Plage
Port-Blanc
Perros-Guirec
St-Quai
788
Pont-Losquet
Lannion
37
Église de
Brélévenez
St-Michel-
stin-en-Grève
Grèves
Lanvellec
Ploua et
32
Château de
Tonquédec
Kerauzern
767
Bégard
Louargat
N12
Basilique
Gurunhuel
Moustéru
Plougonver
787
Bourbriac
rach
38
Callac
50
Gorges de
Toul Goulic
Kergrist-
Moëlou
Maël-Carhaix
Plounévez-Quintin
27
Rostrenen
Glomel
Mellionnec
Plouray
Ploërdut
39
gonnet
Priziac
Guémené-
sur-Scorff
Église Notre-Dame
Kernascléden
be
aouët
pelle
fiacre
Meslan
hes
able
Arzano
imperlé
Plouay
769
Poul-Fétan
Pont-
Scorff
40
Hennebont
Basilique
Lorient
Musée d.l.
Cie.des Indes
oemeur
Port-Louis
Gâvres
mor-Plage
Groix

Pointe
du Château
Chap.St-Gonéry
Plougrescant
Île de Bréhat
Cloître / Cathédrale
Tréguier
Lézardrieux
786
la Roche-
Derrien
Pontrieux
7
37
St-Clet
42
Lanvollon
786
Binic
6
Trégomeur
Châtelaudren
Plouagat
32
St-Péver
Cohiniac
Quintin
St-Gilles-
Pligeaux
64
790
L'Hermitage-
Lorge
Corlay
Le Bodéo
Uzel
700
Plouguenast
le Quilho
N164
Gouarec
Lac de
Guerlédan
Mur-de-
Bretagne
Silfiac
Cléguérec
Neulliac
Stival
Château
Pontivy
St-Nicolas-
des-Eaux
Melrand
Bubry
St-Barthélémy
Quistinic
Languidic
Landévant
25
Landaul
Merlevenez
Belz
Etel
Kerzerho
Erdeven
Auray
Circuit des
Alignements

Phare
du Paon
Pointe de l'Arcouest
Paimpol
Abbaye de Beauport
Pointe de Minard
Bréhec-en-Plouha
Lanloup
Plouha
St-Quay-
Portrieux
49
Baie de
Saint-Brieuc
Plérin
Cathédrale
ST-BRIEUC
16
Quessoy
Bréhand
47
Ploeuc-sur-Lié
le Gouray
Collinée
Plessala
La Motte
Plémet
N164
Loudéac
St-Gonner
St-Gérand
St-Maudan
Plumieux
La-Chèze
43
La Trinité-
Porhoët
Rohan
Pont-Hamon
Mohon
24
767
Naizin
Réguiny
Pluméliau
Remungol
24
N24
14
Locminé
768
Baud
Camors
Bignan
Bieuzy-
Lanvaux
767
Plumelec
28
Plaudren
Forteresse
de Largoët
Domaine de
Kerguéhennec
St-Jean-
Brévelay
Sérent
Trédion
Grand-
Champ
Ste-Anne-
d'Auray
Locoal
Mendon
Meucon
Pluvigner
20
Elven
Basilique
VANNES
Cathédrale
N166
N165
E60
Questembert

le Val-André
le Val-André
34
786
Haras
national
11
Lamballe
Moncontour
Plénée-
Jugon
36
Broons
Éréac
St-Launeuc
Merdrignac
Laurenan
Ménéac
Évriguet
Mauron
34
Concoret
Forêt de Paimpont
Paimpont
N24
Beignon
Campénéac
Augan
Montemeuf
les Pierres
Droites
Malestroit
47
La Gacilly
St-Martin
St-Gravé
Rochefort-
en-Terre
Collégiale
775
Redon
Caden
Berric
Limerzel

les Rosaires
Plérin
Hillion
St-Alban
Pléneuf-
Val-André
Hénanbihen
Matignon
Erquy
Sables-d'Or-
les-Pins
Fort
la Latte
Fréhel
Cap Fréhel
Phare
St-Cast-
le-Guildo
St-Jacut-
de-la-Mer
768
St-Denoual
Plancoët
St-Lunaire
Dinard
St-Mal
Usine
marémotri
Mystères
de la Mer
14
Ploubalay
Pleslin-Trigavou
Vallée de la Rance
Corseul
Quévert
Château
Remparts
Dinan
37
766
Yvignac
24
Caulnes
Quédillac
10
Médréac
10
Abbatiale
St-Méen-le-Grand
Gaël
11
St-Maugan
Montauban-
de-Bretagne
Iffendic
Montfo
s.-M
St-Péran
Plélan-
le-Grand
Guer
Bruc-s.-Aff
Carentoir
Sixt-s.-Aff
873 177
Aves
St-Sauveur
26
Rieux
26

N176
E50
Jugon-
les-Lacs
N12
E50
11
790

873

St-Nicolas-
du-Pélem

Le Roc-
St-André
le Quilho

Pléneuf-Jugon

N166

le Roc-
St-André
20
Lizio

N.-D.-du-Roncier
Josselin
13
St-Allouestre

Château
St-Armel
Ploërmel
Château

Bel-Air
57

Vilaine

28

Plédéliac
Plélan-
le-Petit

Château de
la Hunaudaye

Pléneuf-
Val-André

Hillion

Ploubalay

Plémet

Plumélec

28

Ea   Eb   Ec

Presqu'île
de Quiberon
26
Carnac
Mégalithes
Cairn de
Gavrinis
Morbihan
23
Ambon
Muzillac
36
780

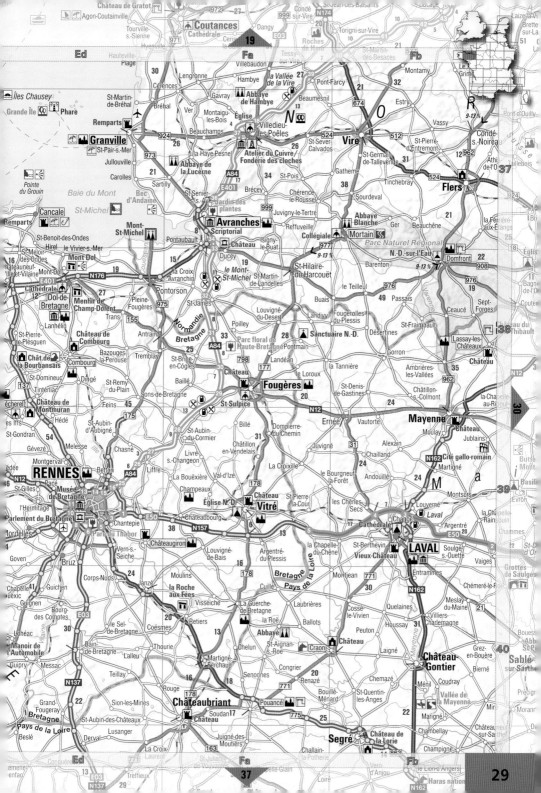

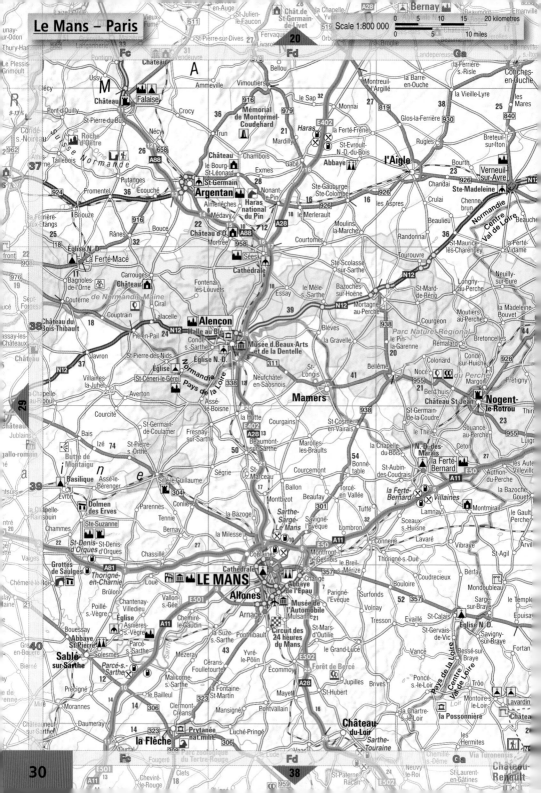

Scale 1:800 000

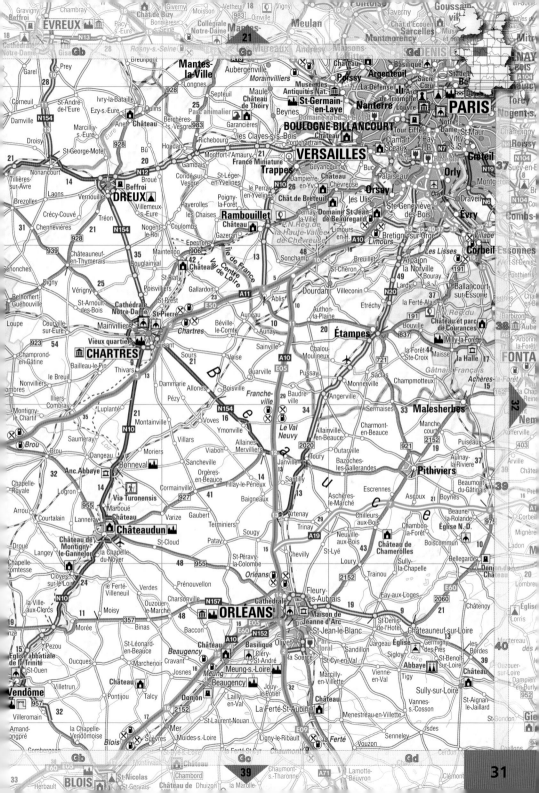

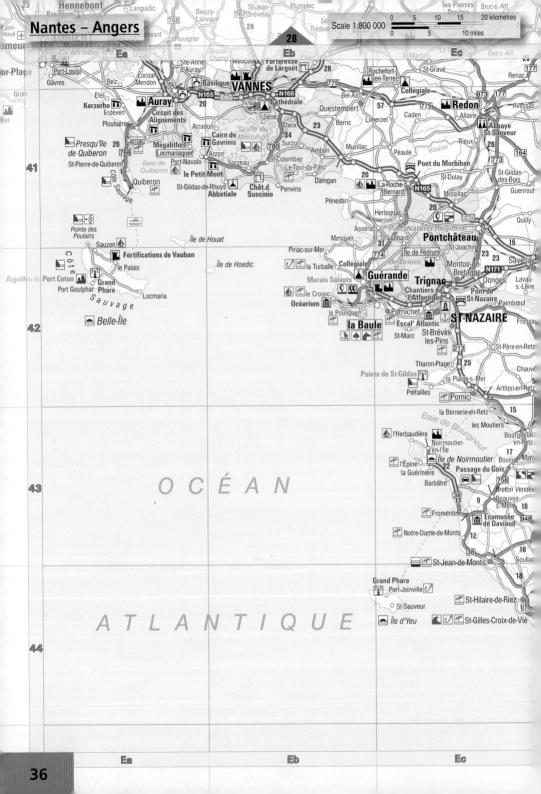

Scale 1:800 000

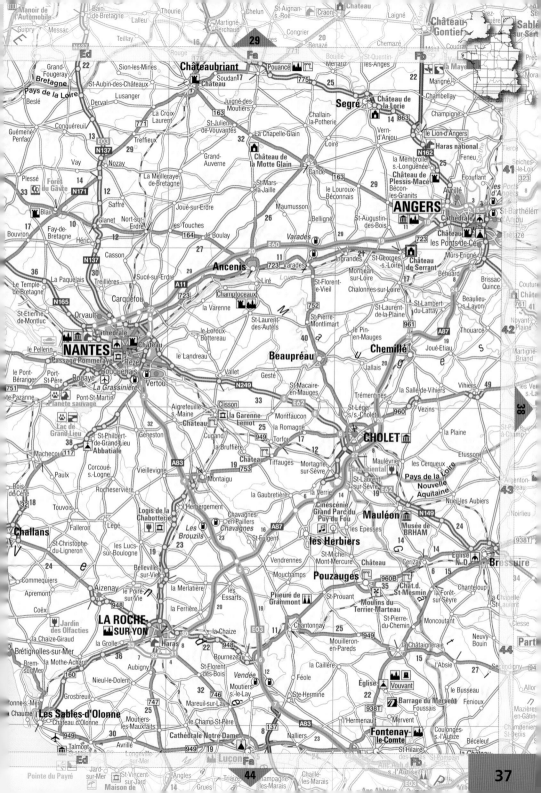

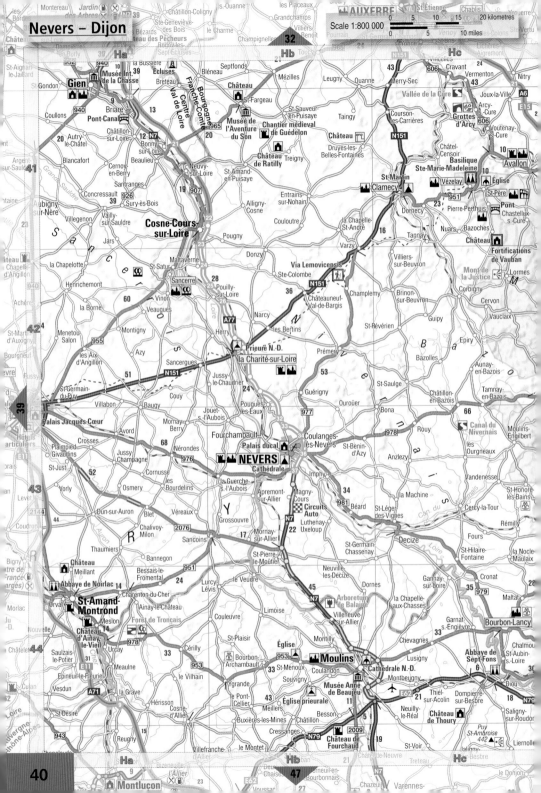

Scale 1:800 000

Scale 1:800 000

0   5   10   15   20 kilometres

0   5   10 miles

Ed   Fa   Fb

la Chaize-Giraud   la Grolle   Haras   948   22   948   Bournezeau   Mouilleron-en-Pareds   la Châtaigneraie   Bouin
80   Nieul-le-Dolent   12   St-Florent-des-Bois   Ste-Hermine   Église   Vouvant   la Busseau
Olonne-s.-Mer   Grosbreuil   747   Mareuil-sur-Lay   le Champ-St-Père   Fa   22   938T   Barrage du Mervent   Fenioux
la Chaume   Moutiers-les-Mauxfaits   le Champ-St-Père   8   137   A83   l'Hermenault   Mervent   Foussais   Coulonges-s.-l'Autize   Béceleuf
Les Sables d'Olonne   25   949   Cathédrale Notre-Dame   949   Nalliers   703   Fontenay-le-Comte   St-Hilaire-des-Loges   St-Pompain   la Châteaudrie
Avrillé   30   19   Luçon   5   24   71   Anc.Abb.d.Nieul-s.-l'Autise   A83
Talmont   St-Hilaire   Longeville-sur-Mer   Angles   Triaize   Champagne-les-Marais   Chaillé-les-Marais   Anc.Abbaye   E03   Oulmes   32 en-Plaine   Villiers-
Pointe du Payré   Jard-sur-Mer   St-Vincent-sur-Jard   14   Grues   Vix   Benet   648   Église N.-D.
Maison de G.Clemenceau   747   St-Michel-l'Herm   137   46   Maillé   Maillezais   Coulon   NIORT
la Tranche-sur-Mer   l'Aiguillon-sur-Mer   Pointe d'Aiguillon   Marans   la Ronde   Sansais   15   Donjon
Île de Ré   les Portes-en-Ré   Esnandes   Charron   E03   Andilly   St-Hilaire-la-Palud   12   Frontenay-Rohan-Rohan   650
Phare des Baleines   Fortifications de Vauban   48   E601   N11   Courcon   Mauzé-s.-le-Mignon   Beauvoir-sur-Niort   Usseau   32
St-Clément-des-Baleines   St-Martin-de-Ré   St-Xandre   Soulle   St-Sauveur-d'Aunis   Vouhé   Marsais   E05   44
Ars-en-Ré   la Couarde-s.-Mer   42   la Flotte   Dompierre-sur-Mer   Aigrefeuille-d'Aunis   20   Villeneuve-la-Comtesse
Ste-Marie-de-Ré   Quartier Ancien   Aquarium   Surgères   St-Félix   Loulay
les Ports   LA ROCHELLE   Aytré   Ciré-d'Aunis   Puydrouard   911   Nachamps   A10
Pertuis d'Antioche   Châtelaillon-Plage   32   Muron   27   Tonnay-Boutonne   36   739
Île d'Aix   137   E602   Ste-Denis-d'Oléron   St-Georges-d'Oléron   Fort Boyard   Fouras   31   Puydrouard
Domino   734   Boyardville   St-Pierre-d'Oléron   ROCHEFORT   Tonnay-Charente   A837   30   St-Jean-d'Angély   150
Île d'Oléron   36   Dolus-d'Oléron   Corderie Royale   733   Bords   St-Savinien   Fenioux   St-Hilaire-de-Villefranche   E602   le Douhet   Ecoyeux
le Château-d'Oléron   734   Remparts   Port-des-Barques   Soubise   Château de la Roche-Courbon   St-Porchaire   27   Saintes
Fort Louvois   Brouage   27   Pont-l'Abbé-d'Arnoult   22   St-Trojan-les-Bains   St-Jean-d'Angle   Soulignonne   Abbaye aux Dames
Marennes   733   Nancras   26   la Clisse   Les Arènes   Arc de Germanicus   St-Sauvant
Ronce-les-Bains   la Tremblade   Parcs à huîtres   728   Pisany   Rétaud   E05   22   20
Arvert   14   18   Saujon   Chaniers   26
Phare de la Coubre   la Palmyre   Zoo   N150   38   Église   A10   Tessor   Pérignac   23
la Grande-Côte   St-Palais-sur-Mer   Royan   Rioux   St-Léger   732
St-Georges-de-Didonne   Église N.-D.   16   Cozes   Donjon   Pons   137   Marignac
Phare de Cordouan   le Verdon-s.-Mer   Meschers-sur-Gironde   Gémozac   730   Hôpital des   St-Genies-de-Saintonge
Basilique N.-D.-de-la-Fin-des-Terres   Pointe de Grave   Ste-Radegonde   Moulin du Fâ   23   Plassac
Soulac-s.-Mer   Talmont-s-Gironde   Mortagne-s.-Gironde   Mirambeau
l'Amélie-s.-Mer   Talais   St-Fort-s.-Gironde   87
le Gurp   St-Vivien-de-Médoc   Port Maubert   St-Ciers-du-Taillon   Boisredon   30
Montalivet-les-Bains   37   Vensac   Valeyrac   Saugon
Vendays-Montalivet   1215   St-Christoly-Médoc   St-Ciers-du-Taillon
Lesparre-Médoc   St-Yzans-de-Médoc   Port des Callonges   St-Estèphe   Reignac
Artiguillon

OCÉAN   ATLANTIQUE   Pertuis Breton   Pertuis d'Antioche

P   O   I   T   O   U   Marais   Poitevin

S   A   I   N   T   O   N   G   E

M   É   D   O   C   G   I   R   O   N   D   E

Hourtin-Plage   Château Lafite Rothschild   Château Mouton Rothschild   Etauliers
Château Pichon-Longueville   Pauillac   A10

Scale 1:800 000

0   5   10   15   20 kilometres

0   5   10 miles

OCÉAN

ATLANTIQUE

BORDEAUX

Arcachon

Pauillac

Blaye

Château Lafite Rothschild

Château Mouton Rothschild

Château Pichon-Longueville

Château Maucaillou

Fortifications de Vauban

Château Margaux

Château Lascombes

Cussac-Fort-Médoc

Château

les Landes

Parc Naturel Régional des Landes de Gascogne

Dune du Pilat

Étang de Cazaux et de Sanguinet

Étang de Biscarrosse et de Parents

Bassin d'Arcachon

Lac de Lacanau

Lac d'Hourtin-Carcans

Ed   Fa   60   Fb

Scale 1:800 000

Hd | Ja | Jb

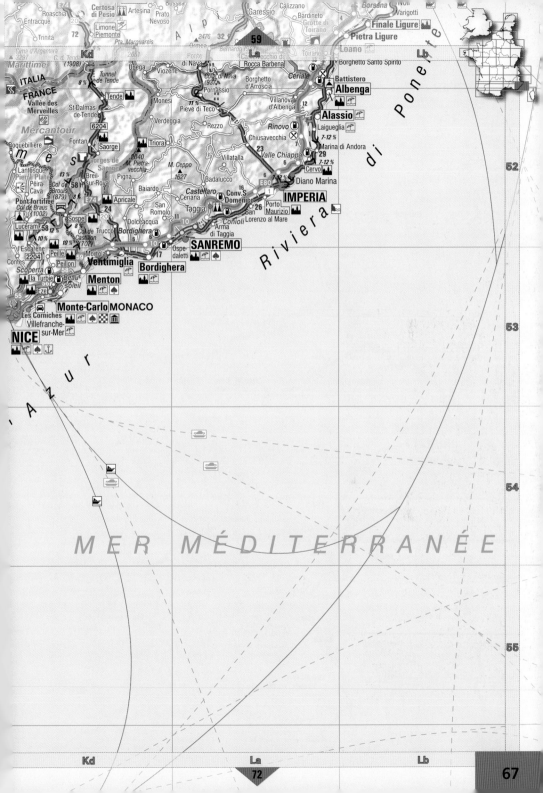

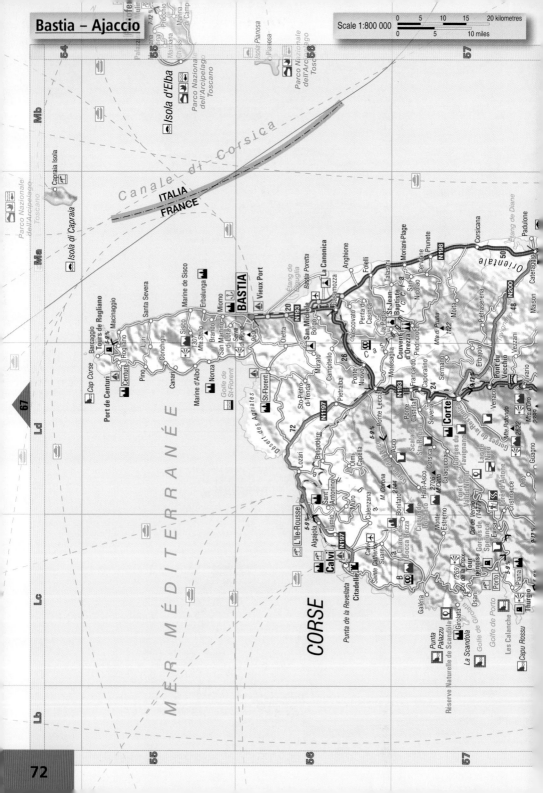

Scale 1:800 000

0 5 10 15 20 kilometres
0 5 10 miles

54 55 56 57

Mb

Procchio
Marina di Campo
Isola Pianosa
Isola di Pianosa

Isola d'Elba

Parco Nazionale
dell'Arcipelago
Toscano

Canale di Corsica

Ma

Parco Nazionale
dell'Arcipelago
Toscano

Capraia Isola

Isola di Capraia

ITALIA
FRANCE

Etang de Diane
Padulone

Corsicana

Ld

67

MER MÉDITERRANÉE

Cap Corse
Port de Centuri
Barcaggio
Tours de Rogliano
Centuri Rogliano
Pino
Canari
Marine d'Albo
Nonza

Santa Severa
Lur
Conchigliu
307
Mte Stello
Brando
San Martino
di Lota
Serra
di Pietra
960

Marine de Sisco
Sisco
Miomo
BASTIA
Erbalunga
Marine de Sisco
Vieux Port
Etang de Biguglia

San Michele
Borgo
Oletta
Murato
Campitello
Pietralba

Bakia Poretta
La Canonica
Anghione
Folelli
Moriani-Plage
Prunete
Cervione

N193
N193
20
Lucciana
N193
Casamozza
Vescovato
La Porta
Penta di Casinca
Morosaglia
Ponte
Nuovo
Ponte
Castirla
26
St-Jean-
Baptiste
Couvent
d'Orezza
Pedicroce
Caporalino
Francardo
Soveria
Scalad
Ste-Reale
Casorria
Corsica
Haut-Asco
M. Orto
Calacuccia
2144
M. Corona
2706

San
Nicolao
Mte di Pruno
1122
Sermano
Erbajolo
24
Corte
N200
50
48
Orientale
Talasani
Vezzani
Pont du
Pont du
Vecchio
Ivario
D.13
Venaco
Mte Rotondo
Pietraserena

Golfe de
St-Florent
St-Florent
Oletta
Sto-Pietro-
di-Tenda
N197
72
Désert des Agriates
Lozari
Belgodère
Olmi-
Capella
Asco
Ponte
Leccia
5-9 %

St-
Antonino
Sant'
Antonino
Muro
Calenzana
Bonifato
Monte
Estremo

Circuit de
Bonifato
M.
Corona

Forêt de
Valdu-Niellu
Golfe
Vergo
Lacde
Calacuccia

Gorges de la Restonica

L'Île-Rousse
Algajola
5-9 %
N197
Calvi
Calvi
Citadelle
Punta de la Revellata

CORSE

Lumio
Bocca Bozza
Suare
Sainte
Catherine
B
Galéria

Lac de
Nino
1472
Col de
Vergio
1477
(1289)
Sol de la Croix
Tour
Osani
Girolata
Girolata

Punta
Palazzu
La Scandola
Réserve Naturelle de Scandola

Capu Rossu
Les Calanche

Golfe de Girolata
Golfe de Porto
Porto
Piana
Thurgio

Gorges de
Spelunca
Ota
Evisa
5-9 %
9-13 %
Forêt d'Aïtone
Cristinacce
Guagno
Orto
Guagno-
les-Bains

Lc

Lb

55 56 57

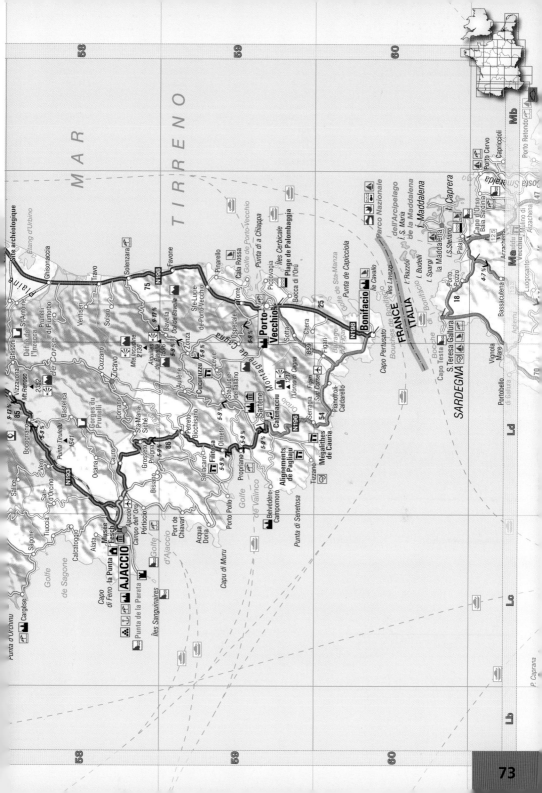

M A R

T I R R E N O

Site archéologique

Punta d'Urcinu

Cargèse

Golfe de Sagone

Sagone

Tiuccia

Calcatoggio

Capo di Feno, la Punta
Punta de la Parata
Îles Sanguinaires

Golfe d'Ajaccio

AJACCIO

Musée Fesch
Ajaccio
Campo dell'Oro
Porticcio

Port de Chiavari

Acqua Doria

Capu di Muru

Golfe de Valinco

Porto Pollo

Punta di Senetosa

Belvédère-Campomoro

N193

Salice

Sari-d'Orcino

Alata

Ocana

Cauro

Bisinao

Prugna

Bastelica

Gorges du Prunelli

Punta Triulelli 1641

Grosseto-Prugna

Ste-Maria-Siché

Petreto-Bicchisano

Sollacaro

Filitosa

Olmeto

Propriano

Tizzano

Mégalithes de Cauria

Alignements de Pagliaju

Sartène

Étang d'Urbino

Ghisonaccia

Defilé de St-Antoine l'Inzecca

Prunelli di Fiumorbo

Ghisoni

Venteseri

Solaro

Travo

Solenzara

Favone

75

N198

Vizzavona
Mt.Renoso
2352

Mte.Incudine
2136

Aiguilles de Bavella
1596

Bavella
Col de Bavella

Zonza

Levie

Ste-Lucie-de-Tallano

Cucuruzzu

Aullène

Zicavo

Cozzano

Corrano

Monte de Cagna

Serra-di-Scopamène

Catenacciu

N196

San Corse

Serragia

Pianottoli-Caldarello

Pinarello

Torre

Ste-Lucie-de-Porto-Vecchio

Cala Rossa

Punta di a Chiappa

Îles Cerbicale

Porto-Vecchio

Ospedale

Figari

Pertusato

Bonifacio

FRANCE
ITALIA

Capo Pertusato

Bouches de Bonifacio

Îles Lavezzi

Île Cavallo

Parco Nazionale dell'Arcipelago de la Maddalena

I.Razzoli
I.Budelli
I.Spargi

la Maddalena

I.S.Stefano

I.Caprera

SARDEGNA

S.Teresa Gallura
Capo Testa

Santa Maria

Porto Cervo

Capicciolo

Costa Smeralda

Arzachena

Bassacutena

Vignola Mare

Portobello di Gallura

Luogosanto

Palau

Mulino di Azzachena

P. Caprara

Regions of France/Région française

Region	Capital	km²	Inhabitants
Auvergne-Rhône-Alpes	Lyon	69 711	7 634 000
Bourgogne-Franche-Comté	Dijon	47 784	2 816 000
Bretagne	Rennes	27 208	3 237 097
Centre-Val de Loire	Orléans	39 151	2 556 835
Corse	Ajaccio	8 680	322 000
Grand Est	Strasbourg	57 433	5 545 000
Île-de-France	Paris	12 011	12 005 077
Nord-Pas-de-Calais-Picardie	Lille	31 813	5 960 000
Normandie	Rouen	29 906	3 315 000
Nouvelle Aquitaine	Bordeaux	84 061	5 773 000
Occitanie	Toulouse	72 724	5 573 000
Pays de la Loire	Nantes	32 082	3 601 113
Provence-Alpes-Côte d'Azur	Marseille	31 400	4 916 000

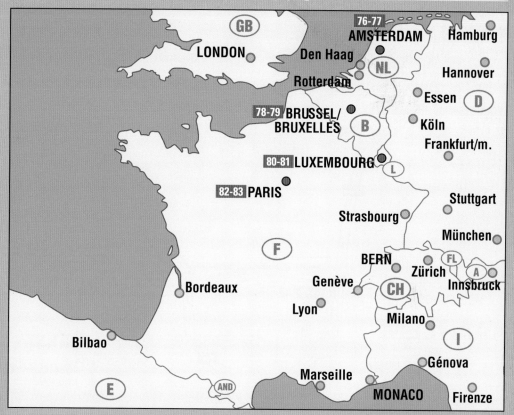

Legend suburban map/Légende région carte

	GB	F		GB	F
	Motorway	Autoroute	Church	Église
	Dual carriageway	Double chaussée	Monastery	Monastère
	Main road	Route principale	Castle/Palace	Palais/Château
	Secondary road	Route secondaire	Other point of intrest	Autres curiosités
	Railway	Chemin de fer	Museum	Musée
	Express train	Train rapide	Golf course	Terrain de golf
	Underground	Métro	Filling station	Station-service
	Motorway junction number	Numéros d'échangeurs	Motorway restaurant	Restoroute
	Stadium	Stade	Car-ferry	Car-ferry
	Exhibition Hall	Parc des expositions	Important Airport	Aéroport important
	Central station	Gare centrale	Airport	Aéroport

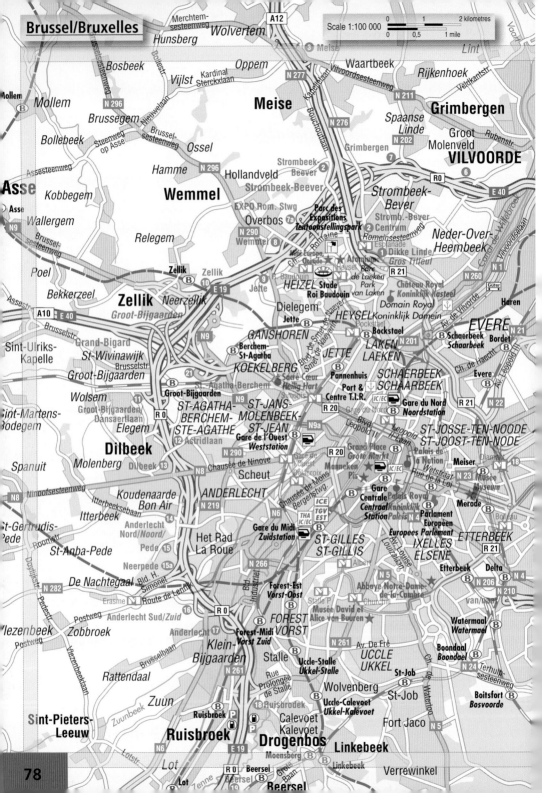

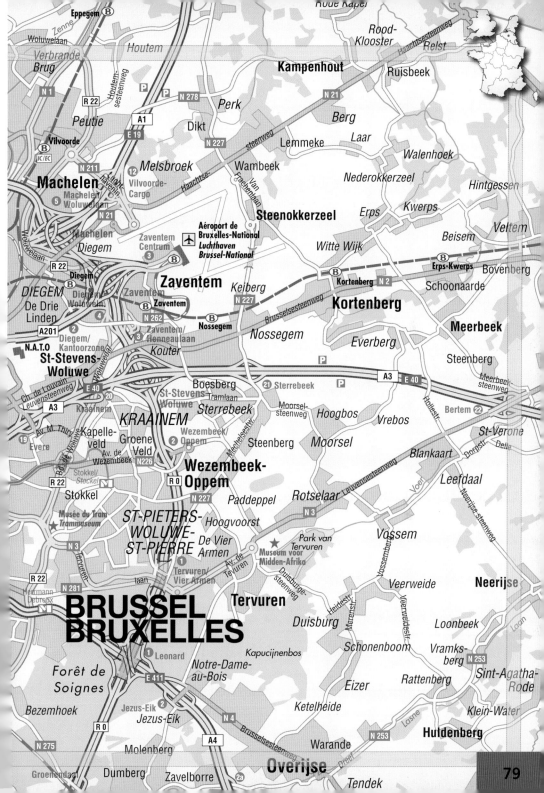

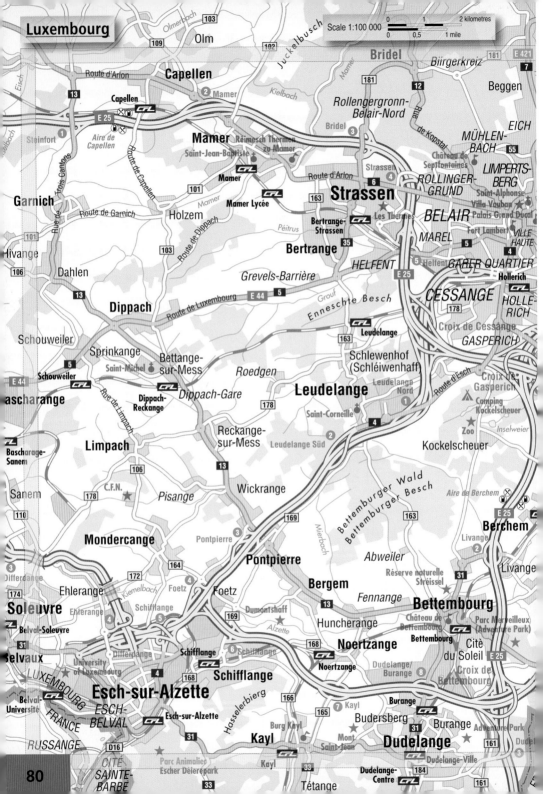

Luxembourg

Scale 1:100 000

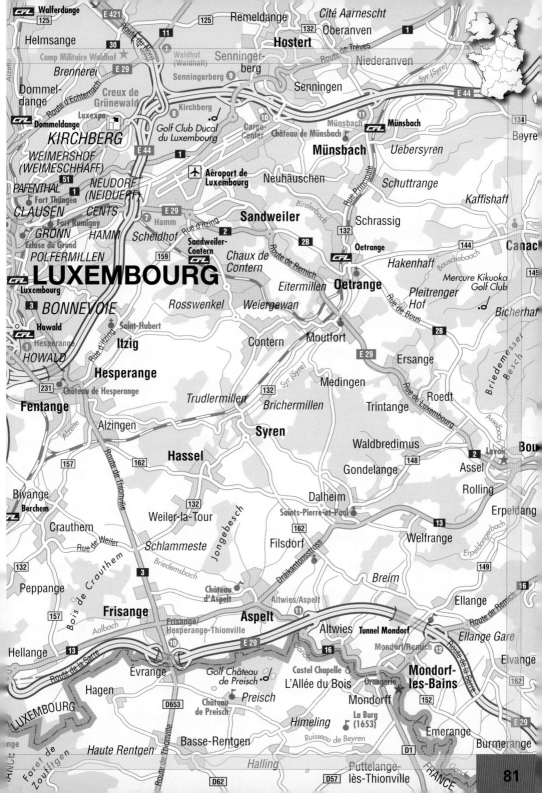

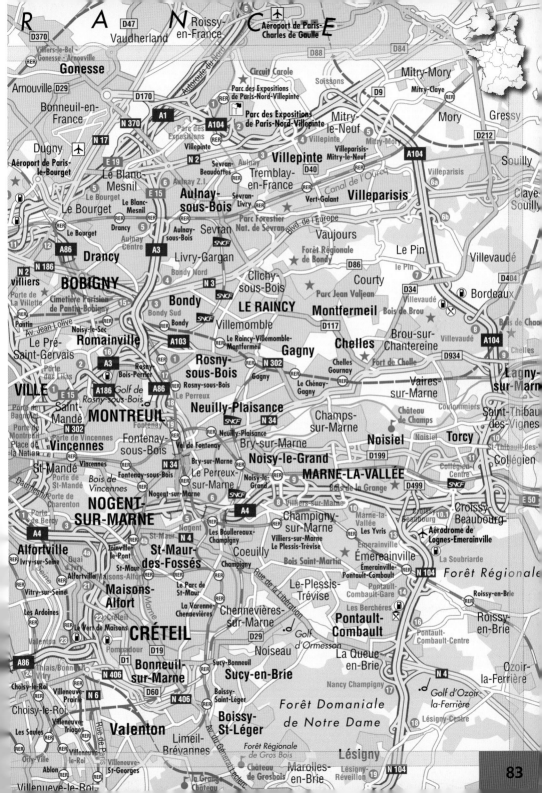

A

Aalburg NL 12 Ja27
Aalsmeer NL 12 Hd25
Aalst B 15 Hc30
Aalten NL 13 Jd26
Aalter B 15 Hb29
Aardenburg NL 15 Hb29
Aarschot B 16 Ja29
Aarsele B 15 Hb29
Abancourt F 21 Gc34
Abaucourt-Hautecourt F 23 Jb35
Abbeville F 21 Gc33
Ablis F 31 Gc38
Abondance F 50 Kb45
Abreschviller F 35 Kb37
Abriès F 58 Kb49
Achel B 12 Jb28
Achères F 40 Ha42
Achtkarspelen NL 8 Jb22
Acqua Doria F 73 Lc59
Acy-en-Multien F 22 Ha36
Adinkerke B 14 Gd29
Adriers F 45 Ga45
Aduard NL 9 Jc22
Affoux F 48 Ja46
Agay F 66 Kc54
Agde F 63 Hc55
Agen F 53 Ga52
Agimont B 16 Ja32
Agon-Coutainville F 19 Ed36
Aguessac F 55 Hb52
Ahun F 46 Gd46
Aignan F 61 Fd54
Aignay-le-Duc F 33 Ja40
Aigre F 45 Fc47
Aigrefeuille-d'Aunis F 44 Fa46
Aigrefeuille-sur-Maine F 37 Fa43
Aiguebelle F 49 Ka47
Aigueblanche F 49 Ka47
Aiguefonde F 63 Ha54
Aigueperse F 47 Hb46
Aigues-Mortes F 64 Ja54
Aigues-Vives F 63 Hb55
Aiguilles F 58 Kb49
Aiguillon F 53 Fd52
Aiguines F 65 Ka53
Aigurande F 46 Gc45
Ailefroide F 57 Ka49
Aillant-sur-Tholon F 32 Hb40
Aillas F 53 Fc51
Aillevillers-et-Lyaumont F 34 Jd39
Aillianville F 34 Jc38
Aillon-le-Jeune F 49 Jd47
Ailly-le-Haut-Clocher F 21 Gc33
Ailly-sur-Noye F 21 Gd34
Aimargues F 64 Ja54
Aime F 50 Kb47
Ainay-le-Château F 40 Ha44
Ainhoa F 60 Ed55
Airaines F 21 Gc33
Airel F 19 Fa36
Aire-sur-l'Adour F 61 Fc54
Aire-sur-la-Lys F 14 Gd31
Airvault F 38 Fc43
Aisey-sur-Seine F 33 Ja40
Aissey F 42 Jd41
Aisy-sur-Armançon F 33 Hd40
Aix-en-Othe F 32 Hc39
Aix-en-Provence F 65 Jc54
Aixe-sur-Vienne F 46 Gb47
Aix-les-Bains F 49 Jd47
Aizenay F 37 Ed44
Ajaccio F 73 Lc58
Ajain F 46 Gd46
Akersloot NL 8 Hd24
Akkrum NL 8 Jb22
Alata F 73 Lc58

Alban F 63 Ha53
Albas F 54 Gb51
Albens F 49 Jd46
Albert F 22 Ha33
Albertville F 49 Ka47
Albi F 62 Gd53
Albias F 54 Gc52
Alblasserdam NL 12 Hd26
Alboussière F 56 Jb49
Alby-sur-Chéran F 49 Jd46
Aldtsjerk NL 8 Jb22
Alençon F 30 Fd38
Aléria F 72 Ma57
Alès F 64 Hd52
Alet-les-Bains F 70 Gd56
Alexain F 29 Fb39
Algajola F 72 Lc56
Alise-Sainte-Reine F 41 Ja41
Alixan F 56 Jb49
Alken B 16 Jb30
Alkmaar NL 8 Hd24
Allaines-Mervilliers F 31 Gc39
Allainville-en-Beauce F 31 Gd39
Allaire F 36 Ec41
Allanche F 55 Hb49
Allasac F 54 Gc49
Allauch F 65 Jd55
Allemagne-en-Provence F 65 Ka53
Allemant F 32 Hc37
Allerborn L 17 Jc32
Allerey-sur-Saône F 41 Jb43
Alleuze F 55 Hb49
Allevard F 49 Jd48
Allex F 56 Jb50
Allibaudières F 33 Hd37
Alligny-Cosne F 40 Hb41
Allogny F 39 Gd42
Allones F 30 Fd40
Allones F 31 Gc38
Allonne F 38 Fc44
Allons F 53 Fc52
Allos F 58 Kb51
Alloue F 45 Ga46
Ally F 54 Gd49
Ally F 55 Hc49
Almelo NL 9 Jd24
Almenêches F 30 Fd37
Almere NL 12 Ja25
Almere-Buiten NL 12 Ja25
Almere-Haven NL 12 Ja25
Alphen NL 12 Ja28
Alphen aan de Rijn NL 12 Hd26
Altkirch F 35 Kb40
Alvignac F 54 Gc50
Alzon F 63 Hc53
Amagne F 23 Hd34
Amailloux F 38 Fc44
Amance F 33 Ja38
Amance F 34 Jd40
Amange F 42 Jc42
Amay B 16 Ja31
Ambarès et-Lagrave F 52 Fb50
Ambazac F 46 Gb46
Ambérieu-en-Bugey F 49 Jc46
Ambérieux-en-Dombes F 48 Jb46
Ambert F 47 Hc47
Ambialet F 63 Ha53
Ambierle F 48 Hd46
Ambiévillers F 34 Jd39
Amblainville F 21 Gd36
Ambleteuse F 14 Gd30
Ambleville F 21 Gc36
Amboise F 39 Gb42
Ambon F 36 Eb41
Ambrault F 39 Gd44
Ambrières-les-Vallées F 29 Fb38
Ambronay F 49 Jc46
Amel B 17 Jc31
Amélie-les-Bains-Palalda F 71 Ha58

Amerongen B 12 Jb26
Amersfoort NL 12 Jb25
Amiens F 21 Gd33
Amilly F 32 Ha40
Ammerzoden NL 12 Ja27
Ammeville F 20 Fd36
Amnéville F 24 Jd35
Amou F 60 Fa54
Amous F 66 Kb53
Amplepuis F 48 Ja46
Amplier F 14 Gd32
Amstelveen NL 12 Ja25
Amsterdam NL 12 Ja25
Ancelle F 57 Ka50
Ancenis F 37 Fa42
Ancerville F 33 Jc37
Anché F 45 Fd45
Ancy-le-Franc F 33 Hd40
Andance F 48 Jb48
Andelot-Blancheville F 33 Jb38
Andelot-en-Montagne F 42 Jd43
Andelst NL 12 Jb26
Andenne B 16 Ja31
Anderlecht B 16 Hd30
Anderlues B 16 Hd31
Andernos-les-Bains F 52 Fa50
Andijk NL 8 Ja23
Andlau F 35 Kb37
Andoins F 61 Fc55
Andon F 66 Kb53
Andorra la Vella AND 70 Gc58
Andouillé F 29 Fb39
Andrest F 61 Fd55
Andrésy F 21 Gd36
Andrézieux-Bouthéon F 48 Ja47
Anduze F 64 Hd52
Anet F 31 Gb37
Angé F 39 Gb42
Angerlo NL 13 Jc26
Angers F 37 Fb41
Angerville F 31 Gd38
Anghione F 72 Ma56
Anglards-de-Salers F 55 Ha49
Anglefort F 49 Jd46
Angles F 44 Fa45
Anglès F 63 Ha54
Angles-sur-l'Anglin F 38 Ga44
Angliers F 38 Fd43
Anglure F 32 Hc37
Angoulême F 45 Fd47
Anhée B 16 Ja32
Aniane F 63 Hc54
Aniche F 15 Hb32
Anizy-le-Château F 22 Hb34
Anjum NL 9 Jc21
Anloo NL 9 Jd22
Anna Paulowna NL 8 Hd23
Annecy F 49 Jd46
Annemasse F 49 Ka45
Annevoie-Rouillon B 16 Ja31
Annonay F 48 Ja48
Annot F 58 Kb52
Annœullin F 15 Ha31
Anost F 41 Hd42
Anould F 34 Ka38
Anoye F 61 Fc55
Ansac-sur-Vienne F 45 Ga46
Anse F 48 Ja46
Ansignan F 71 Ha57
Anthée B 16 Ja32
Anthéor F 66 Kc54
Anthy F 42 Ka44
Antibes F 66 Kc53
Antoing B 15 Hb31
Antraigues-sur-Volane F 56 Ja50
Antrain F 29 Ed38

Antwerpen B 16 Hd29
Anvin F 14 Gd31
Anzin F 15 Hb32
Anzat-le-Luguet F 47 Hb48
Anzy-le-Duc F 48 Hd45
Aouste F 23 Hd33
Apeldoorn NL 12 Jb25
Apelscha NL 9 Jc23
Appeltern NL 12 Jb26
Appingedam NL 9 Jd21
Appoigny F 32 Hc40
Apremont F 37 Ed44
Apremont-la-Forêt F 24 Jc36
Apremont-sur-Allier F 40 Hb43
Apt F 65 Jc53
Arâches F 49 Ka45
Aragnouet F 69 Fd57
Aramits F 68 Fb56
Aramon F 64 Jb53
Arbonne-la-Forêt F 32 Ha38
Arc F 42 Jc41
Arcachon F 52 Fa51
Arcen NL 13 Jc27
Arcenant F 41 Ja42
Arc-en-Barrois F 33 Jb39
Arcens F 56 Ja50
Arces-Dilo F 32 Hc39
Arc-et-Senans F 42 Jc42
Arcey F 34 Ka40
Archiac F 45 Fc48
Archiane F 57 Jc50
Archigny F 38 Ga44
Archimont B 15 Hb30
Arcins F 52 Fb49
Arcis-sur-Aube F 33 Hd38
Arcy-sur-Cure F 40 Hc41
Ardentes F 39 Gc44
Ardes F 47 Hb48
Ardooie B 15 Hb30
Ardres F 14 Gd30
Arèches F 49 Ka47
Arendonk B 12 Jb28
Arengosse F 60 Fb53
Arès F 52 Fa50
Arette F 68 Fb56
Argein F 70 Gb56
Argelès-Gazost F 69 Fc56
Argelès-Plage F 71 Hb57
Argelès-sur-Mer F 71 Hb57
Argentan F 30 Fd37
Argentat F 54 Gd49
Argenteuil F 21 Gd36
Argentière F 50 Kb45
Argenton-Château F 38 Fc43
Argenton-sur-Creuse F 39 Gc44
Argentré F 29 Fb39
Argentré-du-Plessis F 29 Fa39
Argent-sur-Sauldre F 39 Gd41
Argueil F 21 Gd34
Argy F 39 Gb43
Arinsal AND 70 Gc57
Arinthod F 42 Jc44
Arjuzanx F 60 Fb53
Arlanc F 47 Hc48
Arlempdes F 56 Hd50
Arles F 64 Jb53
Arles-sur-Tech F 71 Ha58
Arleuf F 41 Hd42
Arlon B 24 Jc33
Armentières F 15 Ha31
Arnac-Pompadour F 46 Gb48
Arnac-sur-Dourdou F 63 Hb54
Arnage F 30 Fd40
Arnay-le-Duc F 41 Ja42
Arnemuiden NL 11 Hb28
Arnhem NL 12 Jb26

Arpajon la Norville F 31 Gd38
Arques F 14 Gd30
Arques-la-Bataille F 21 Gb33
Arracourt F 34 Ka37
Arradon F 36 Eb41
Arrans F 33 Hd40
Arras F 15 Ha32
Arraute-Charritte F 60 Fa55
Arreau F 69 Fd56
Arrens F 69 Fc56
Arrien F 61 Fc55
Arrigny F 33 Ja37
Arromanches-les-Bains F 19 Fb35
Arrou F 31 Gb39
Ars-en-Ré F 44 Ed45
Arsague F 60 Fb54
Ars-sur-Formans F 48 Jb46
Ars-sur-Moselle F 24 Jc35
Artemare F 49 Jc46
Artenay F 31 Gc39
Arthez-de-Béarn F 60 Fb55
Arthies F 21 Gc36
Arthon-en-Retz F 36 Ec42
Arthonnay F 33 Hd39
Artiguelouve F 60 Fb55
Artiguillon F 52 Fb49
Artix F 60 Fb55
Arudy F 68 Fb56
Arum NL 8 Ja22
Arvant F 47 Hc48
Arvieux F 58 Kb50
Arville F 30 Ga39
Arville F 32 Ha39
Arzacq-Arraziguet F 60 Fb54
Arzano F 27 Dd40
Arzon F 36 Eb41
As B 16 Jb29
Asasp-Arros F 68 Fb56
Ascain F 60 Ed55
Aschères-le-Marché F 31 Gd39
Asco F 72 Ld57
Ascoux F 31 Gd39
Asfeld F 23 Hd34
Asnières-sur-Vègre F 30 Fc40
Asperen NL 12 Ja26
Aspet F 69 Ga56
Aspremont F 57 Jd51
Aspres-sur-Buëch F 57 Jd50
Assat F 61 Fc55
Asse B 15 Hc30
Assé-le-Bérenger F 30 Fc39
Assé-le-Boisne F 30 Fc38
Assen NL 9 Jc22
Assenede B 15 Hc29
Assenois B 23 Jb33
Assérac F 36 Ec41
Assesse B 16 Ja31
Assier F 54 Gd51
Asson F 69 Fc56
Astaffort F 61 Ga53
Asten NL 12 Jb28
Athée F 42 Jc42
Athesans F 34 Ka40
Athies F 22 Ha33
Athis-de-l'Orne F 29 Fb37
Attert B 24 Jc33
Attigny F 23 Hd34
Aubagne F 65 Jd55
Aubazine F 54 Gd49
Aubel B 17 Jc30
Aubenas F 56 Ja50
Aubenton F 23 Hd33
Aubepierre-sur-Aube F 33 Jb39
Aubergenville F 21 Gc36
Aubérive F 23 Hd35

Auberive F 33 Jb40
Aubeterre-sur-Dronne F 53 Fd49
Aubiat F 47 Hb46
Aubiet F 61 Ga54
Aubigné F 45 Fc46
Aubigny F 37 Ed44
Aubigny-au-Bac F 15 Hb32
Aubigny-en-Artois F 14 Gd32
Aubigny-sur-Nère F 39 Gd41
Aubin F 54 Gd51
Aubrac F 55 Hb51
Aubusson F 46 Gd46
Auby F 15 Ha31
Auch F 61 Ga54
Auchel F 14 Gd31
Auchy-au-Bois F 14 Gd31
Aucun F 69 Fc56
Audenge F 52 Fa51
Auderville F 19 Ed34
Audierne F 26 Db39
Audincourt F 42 Ka41
Audruicq F 14 Gc30
Audun-le-Roman F 24 Jc34
Audun-le-Tiche F 24 Jc34
Aufferville F 32 Ha39
Augan F 28 Ec40
Augé F 45 Fc45
Augerolles F 47 Hc47
Aullène F 73 Ld59
Aulnay F 45 Fc46
Aulnay-la-Riviere F 31 Gd39
Aulnay-sous-Bois F 21 Gd36
Aulnizeux F 32 Hc37
Aulnoye-Aymeries F 15 Hc32
Ault F 21 Gb33
Aulus-les-Bains F 70 Gb57
Aumale F 21 Gc34
Aumetz F 24 Jc34
Aumont F 42 Jc43
Aumont-Aubrac F 55 Hc50
Aunay F 31 Gc38
Aunay-en-Bazois F 40 Hc42
Aunay-sur-Odon F 19 Fb36
Auneau F 31 Gc38
Auneuil F 21 Gc35
Aups F 65 Ka53
Auray F 36 Ea41
Aurice F 60 Fb53
Aurignac F 61 Ga55
Aurillac F 55 Ha50
Auriol F 65 Jd55
Aurons F 65 Jc53
Auros F 53 Fc51
Aussonne F 62 Gb54
Auterive F 62 Gc55
Auteuil F 21 Gd35
Autheuil-Authouillet F 21 Gb36
Authon F 57 Ka51
Authon-du-Perche F 30 Ga39
Authon-la-Plaine F 31 Gc38
Autrans F 49 Jc48
Autrèche F 39 Gb41
Autrey F 42 Jc41
Autricourt F 33 Ja39
Autry-le-Châtel F 40 Ha41
Autun F 41 Hd43
Auverse F 38 Fd41
Auvers-sur-Oise F 21 Gd36
Auvillar F 61 Ga53
Auvillars-sur-Saône F 41 Jb42
Auvre F 23 Ja36
Auxerre F 32 Hc40
Auxi-le-Château F 14 Gd32
Auxon F 32 Hc39

Auxonne F 42 Jc42
Auxy F 41 Ja43
Auzances F 47 Ha46
Auzat-la-Combelle F 47 Hc48
Availles-Limouzine F 45 Ga46
Avallon F 40 Hc41
Avant-lès-Marcilly F 32 Hc38
Avant-lès-Remerupt F 33 Hd38
Avelgem B 15 Hb30
Avenas F 48 Ja45
Avereest NL 9 Jc24
Avernay-Val-d'Or F 23 Hd36
Averton F 30 Fc38
Avesnes-le-Comte F 14 Gd32
Avesnes-lès-Aubert F 15 Hb32
Avesnes-sur-Helpe F 15 Hc32
Avessac F 36 Ec41
Avignon F 64 Jb53
Avignonet-Lauragais F 62 Gc55
Avilley F 42 Jd41
Avion F 15 Ha31
Avirey F 33 Hd39
Avize F 22 Hc36
Avoine F 38 Fd42
Avord F 40 Ha43
Avoriaz F 50 Kb45
Avot F 33 Jb40
Avoudrey F 42 Ka42
Avranches F 29 Fa37
Avrillé F 44 Ed45
Avrillé F 37 Fb41
Axat F 70 Gd57
Axel NL 15 Hc29
Ax-les-Thermes F 70 Gd57
Ayen F 54 Gb49
Ayguesvives F 62 Gc55
Aynac F 54 Gc50
Ayron F 38 Fd44
Aytré F 44 Fa46
Aywaille B 16 Jb31
Azannes F 23 Jb35
Azay-le-Ferron F 39 Gb43
Azay-le-Rideau F 38 Fd42
Azé F 31 Gb40
Azincourt F 14 Gd31
Azur F 60 Fa53
Azy F 40 Ha42

B

Baak NL 13 Jc25
Baarland NL 11 Hc28
Baarle-Nassau NL 12 Ja28
Baarlo NL 13 Jc28
Baarn NL 12 Ja25
Baccarat F 34 Ka37
Baccon F 31 Gc40
Bach F 54 Gc52
Bachant F 15 Hc30
Bacquepuis F 21 Gb36
Badonviller F 34 Ka37
Bâge-le-Châtel F 48 Jb45
Bages F 71 Hb57
Bagnac-sur-Célé F 54 Gd51
Bagnères-de-Bigorre F 69 Fd56
Bagnères-de-Luchon F 69 Ga57
Bagneux-la-Fosse F 33 Hd39
Bagnoles-de-l'Orne F 30 Fc38
Bagnols F 47 Ha48
Bagnols-en-Forêt F 66 Kb54
Bagnols-les-Bains F 55 Hc51

Bagnols-sur-Cèze F 64 Jb52
Baigneaux F 31 Gc39
Baigneux-les-Juifs F 41 Ja41
Baillé F 29 Fa38
Bailleau-le-Pin F 31 Gb38
Bailleul F 15 Ha30
Bailly F 56 Hd49
Bains F 56 Hd49
Bains-les-Bains F 34 Jd39
Bais F 30 Fc39
Baix F 56 Jb50
Bakel NL 12 Jb27
Bakkeveen NL 9 Jc22
Balaruc-les-Bains F 64 Hd54
Balazuc F 56 Ja51
Balbigny F 48 Hd46
Baleix F 61 Fc55
Balen B 16 Ja29
Balizac F 52 Fb51
Balk NL 8 Jb23
Balkbrug NL 9 Jc24
Ballancourt-sur-Essone F 31 Gd38
Balleroy F 19 Fb36
Ballon F 30 Fd39
Ballots F 29 Fa40
Balsièges F 55 Hc51
Bandol F 65 Jd55
Bannalec F 27 Dd40
Bannegon F 40 Ha43
Bannes F 32 Hc37
Bannes F 33 Jb39
Bannoncourt F 23 Jb36
Banon F 65 Jd52
Bantheville F 23 Ja35
Bantzenheim F 35 Kc39
Banyuls-sur-Mer F 71 hb58
Bapaume F 15 Ha32
Baraque-Saint-Jean F 55 Ha52
Baraqueville F 55 Ha52
Barbaste F 53 Fd52
Barbâtre F 36 Ec43
Barbazan F 69 Ga56
Barbezieux-Saint-Hilaire F 45 Fc48
Barbières F 57 Jc49
Barbizon F 32 Ha38
Barbonne-Fayel F 32 Hc37
Barbotan-les-Thermes F 61 Fc53
Barcaggio F 72 Ld55
Barcelonne-du-Gers F 61 Fc54
Barcelonnette F 58 Kb51
Barchem NL 13 Jc25
Barcillonnette F 57 Jd51
Barcus F 60 Fb55
Bard-le-Régulier F 41 Hd42
Barèges F 69 Fd56
Barendrecht NL 12 Hd26
Barentin F 20 Ga34
Barenton F 29 Fb38
Barfleur F 19 Fa34
Bargème F 66 Kb53
Bargemon F 66 Kb53
Barisey-la-Côte F 34 Jc37
Barjac F 55 Ha51
Barjac F 56 Ja51
Barjols F 65 Ka54
Bar-le-Duc F 33 Jb37
Barles F 57 Ka51
Barnave F 57 Jc50
Barnay F 41 Hd42
Barneveld NL 12 Jb25
Barneville-Carteret F 19 Ed35
Baron F 22 Ha36
Baronville F 24 Ka36
Barr F 35 Kb37
Barrême F 65 Ka52
Barret-le-Bas F 57 Jd51
Barrière de Champlon B 16 Jb32

Barrou F 38 Ga43
Barsanges F 46 Gd48
Barst F 24 Ka35
Bar-sur-Aube F 33 Ja38
Bar-sur-Seine F 33 Hd39
Bartenheim F 35 Kc40
Barvaux B 16 Jb31
Barvaux-Condroz B 16 Jb31
Basilique de Hennebont F 27 Ea40
Bassac F 45 Fc47
Bassignac F 47 Ha48
Bassignac-le-Haut F 54 Gd49
Bassilac F 53 Ga49
Bassou F 32 Hc40
Bassoues F 61 Fd54
Bastelica F 73 Ld58
Bastia F 72 Ma56
Bastogne B 17 Jc32
Bathmen NL 13 Jc25
Baud F 27 Ea40
Baudour B 15 Hc31
Baudreville F 31 Gc38
Bauduen F 65 Ka53
Baugé F 38 Fc41
Baugy F 40 Ha42
Baume-les-Dames F 42 Ka41
Baume-les-Messieurs F 42 Jc43
Bavay F 15 Hc32
Bavella F 73 Ma59
Bavigne L 24 Jc33
Baye F 32 Hc37
Bayeux F 19 Fb35
Bayon F 34 Jd37
Bayonne F 60 Ed54
Bayons F 57 Ka51
Bazas F 53 Fc51
Bazicourt F 22 Ha35
Baziège F 62 Gc55
Bazoches F 40 Hc41
Bazoches-les-Gallerandes F 31 Gd39
Bazoches-sur-Hoëne F 30 Fd38
Bazolles F 40 Hc42
Bazoques F 20 Ga36
Bazouges-la-Perouse F 29 Ed38
Béard F 40 Hb43
Beaucaire F 64 Jb53
Beaucamps-le-Vieux F 21 Gб33
Beauchamps F 29 Fa37
Beauchamps F 21 Gd34
Beauchastel F 56 Jb50
Beauche F 30 Ga37
Beauchêne F 29 Fb37
Beaufay F 30 Fd39
Beaufort F 49 Ka46
Beaufort L 24 Jd33
Beaugency F 31 Gc40
Beaujeu F 48 Ja45
Beaujeu F 42 Jc41
Beaujeu F 57 Ka51
Beaulieu F 30 Ga37
Beaulieu F 40 Ha41
Beaulieu-sur-Dordogne F 54 Gc50
Beaumesnil F 29 Fa37
Beaumesnil F 20 Ga36
Beaumetz-lès-Loges F 15 Ha32
Beaumont B 16 Hd32
Beaumont F 24 Jc36
Beaumont-de-Lomagne F 62 Gb53
Beaumont-du-Gâtinais F 32 Ha39
Beaumont-du-Périgord F 53 Ga50
Beaumont-en-Argonne F 23 Ja34
Beaumont-Hague F 19 Ed34
Beaumont-Hamel F 22 Ha33

Beaumont-la-Ronce F 38 Ga41
Beaumont-le-Roger F 20 Ga36
Beaumont-lès-Valence F 56 Jb50
Beaumont-sur-Oise F 21 Gd36
Beaumont-sur-Sarthe F 30 Fd39
Beaumont-sur-Vingeanne F 41 Jb41
Beaune F 41 Ja42
Beaune-la-Rolande F 31 Gd39
Beaupréau F 37 Fa42
Beauquesne F 21 Gd33
Beauraing B 16 Ja32
Beaurainville F 14 Gc31
Beauregard F 54 Gc52
Beaurepaire F 48 Jb48
Beaurières F 57 Jc50
Beauvais F 21 Gd35
Beauval F 21 Gd33
Beauvezer F 58 Kb52
Beauvoir-sur-Mer F 36 Ec43
Beauvoir-sur-Niort F 44 Fb46
Beauzac F 48 Hd48
Beauzée-sur-Aire F 23 Jb36
Béceleuf F 44 Fb45
Bécherel F 29 Ed39
Bécon-les-Granits F 37 Fb41
Bédarieux F 63 Hb54
Bédarrides F 64 Jb52
Bédée F 29 Ed39
Bédenac F 53 Fc49
Bédoin F 65 Jc52
Bedous F 68 Fb56
Bedum NL 9 Jc21
Beek NL 17 Jc29
Beekbergen NL 13 Jc25
Beek en Donk NL 12 Jb27
Beerlegem B 15 Hc30
Beerse B 12 Ja28
Beerta NL 9 Jd22
Beesel NL 13 Jc28
Beetsterzwaag NL 9 Jc22
Bégard F 27 Ea37
Begles F 52 Fb50
Beg-Meil F 26 Dc40
Begnecourt F 34 Jd38
Beho B 17 Jc32
Béhuard F 37 Fb42
Beignon F 28 Ec40
Beilen NL 9 Jc23
Bekkevoort B 16 Ja29
Bélâbre F 39 Gb44
Bel-Air B 16 Eb41
Belcaire F 70 Gd57
Belcastel F 55 Ha51
Belfort F 34 Ka39
Belgodère F 72 Ld56
Belhade F 52 Fb51
Belhomert-Guéhouville F 31 Gb38
Belin-Béliet F 52 Fb51
Bellac F 46 Gb46
Bellechaume F 32 Hc39
Belle Croix B 17 Jc31
Belle-Eglise F 21 Gd35
Bellegarde F 31 Gd39
Bellegarde F 64 Ja53
Bellegarde-en-Marche F 46 Gd46
Bellegarde-sur-Valserine F 49 Jd45
Belleherbe F 42 Ka41
Bellême F 30 Ga38
Bellenaves F 47 Hb45
Bellencombre F 21 Gb34
Bellerive-sur-Allier F 47 Hc46
Belles-Forêts F 24 Ka36
Belleu F 22 Hb35
Bellevaux F 23 Ja33
Bellevesvre F 42 Jc43

Belleville F 48 Ja45
Belleville-sur-Vie F 37 Ed44
Bellevue-la-Montagne F 56 Hd49
Belley F 49 Jc46
Bellicourt F 22 Hb33
Belligné F 37 Fa41
Bellingwolde NL 9 Ka22
Belloc F 61 Fc54
Bellocq F 60 Fa54
Bellot F 32 Hb37
Bellou F 20 Fd36
Belmont-sur-Rance F 63 Hb53
Belœil B 15 Hc31
Belpech F 62 Gc55
Belvédère-Campomoro F 73 Ld59
Belvès F 54 Gb50
Belvèze-du-Razès F 70 Gd56
Belvezet F 56 Hd51
Belvoir F 42 Ka41
Belz F 27 Ea40
Bemmel NL 13 Jc26
Benassay F 38 Fd44
Beneden-Leeuwen NL 12 Jb26
Bénesse-lès-Dax F 60 Fa54
Benesse-Maremne F 60 Fa54
Bénestroff F 24 Ka36
Benet F 44 Fb45
Beneuvre F 33 Jb40
Bénévent-l'Abbaye F 46 Gc46
Benfeld F 35 Kc38
Bénodet F 26 Dc40
Bérat F 62 Gb55
Bercenay-le-Hayer F 32 Hc38
Berchem B 15 Hd30
Berchères-sur-Vesgre F 31 Gc37
Berck F 14 Gb32
Berck-Plage F 14 Gb32
Berd'huis F 30 Ga38
Berfay F 30 Ga40
Bergen NL 8 Hd24
Bergen aan Zee NL 8 Hd24
Bergen op Zoom NL 11 Hc28
Bergerac F 53 Fd50
Bergéres-lès-Vertus F 22 Hc36
Bergeyk NL 12 Jb28
Bergnicourt F 23 Hd34
Bergnicourt F 23 Hd35
Bergues F 14 Gd30
Beringen B 16 Ja29
Berkel NL 12 Hd26
Bernaville F 14 Gd32
Bernay F 30 Fc39
Bernay F 20 Ga36
Bernécourt F 24 Jc36
Bernin F 49 Jd48
Bernon F 33 Hd39
Berre-l'Étang F 65 Jc54
Berric F 36 Eb41
Berrien F 27 Dd38
Bertem B 16 Hd30
Bertincourt F 15 Ha32
Bertogne B 16 Jc32
Bertrix B 23 Jb33
Berven F 26 Dc37
Berville-sur-Mer F 20 Fd35
Berzé-la-Ville F 48 Ja45
Besançon F 42 Jd42
Beslé F 37 Fa41
Bessais-le-Fromental F 40 Ha44
Bessan F 63 Hc55
Bessans F 50 Kb48
Besse F 57 Ka49
Besse-et-Saint-Anastaise F 47 Hb48

Bességes F 64 Hd52
Bessenay F 48 Ja47
Bessé-sur-Braye F 30 Ga40
Bessières F 62 Gc53
Besson F 40 Hb44
Best NL 12 Jb27
Béthenville F 23 Hd35
Bétheny F 22 Hc35
Béthines F 38 Ga44
Béthisy-Saint-Pierro F 22 Ha35
Bethmale F 70 Gb56
Bethon F 32 Hc37
Béthune F 15 Ha31
Bettembourg L 24 Jc34
Betton F 29 Ed39
Betz F 22 Ha36
Beugneux F 22 Hb35
Beuil F 58 Kc52
Beuning NL 12 Jb26
Beuvron-en-Auge F 20 Fc36
Beuvry F 15 Ha31
Beuzec-Cap-Sizun F 26 Db39
Beuzeville F 20 Fd35
Beveren B 15 Hc29
Beverwijk NL 8 Hd24
Béville-le-Comte F 31 Gc38
Beynac-et-Cazenac F 54 Gb50
Beynat F 54 Gc49
Beynes F 31 Gc37
Bézaudun-sur-Bine F 57 Jc50
Bèze F 41 Jb41
Béziers F 63 Hc55
Biarritz F 60 Ed54
Biarrotte F 60 Fa54
Bias F 52 Fa51
Biddinghuizen NL 8 Jb24
Bierné F 29 Fb40
Bierwart B 16 Ja31
Biesles F 33 Jb39
Bieuzy-Lanvaux F 27 Ea40
Bièvre B 23 Ja33
Biez B 16 Hd30
Biganos F 52 Fa51
Bignan F 28 Eb40
Bigny F 39 Gd43
Biliat F 49 Jd45
Billé F 29 Fa39
Billom F 47 Hc47
Billy F 47 Hc45
Binarville F 23 Ja35
Binas F 31 Gb40
Binche B 16 Hd31
Binic F 28 Eb37
Biot F 66 Kc53
Biscarrosse F 52 Fa51
Biscarrosse-Plage F 52 Fa51
Bischheim F 35 Kc37
Bischwiller F 25 Kc36
Bisiano F 73 Ld58
Bissy-sur-Fley F 41 Ja44
Bitche F 25 Kb35
Biville F 19 Ed34
Bizeneuille F 47 Ha45
Bladel NL 12 Ja28
Blagnac F 62 Gb54
Blagon F 52 Fa50
Blain F 37 Ed41
Blainville-Crevon F 21 Gb35
Blainville-sur-l'Eau F 34 Jd37
Blaise F 33 Ja38
Blaisy-Bas F 41 Ja41
Blajan F 61 Ga55
Blâmont F 34 Ka37
Blan F 62 Gd54
Blancafort F 40 Ha41
Blangy-sur-Bresle F 21 Gc33
Blangy-sur-Ternoise F 14 Gd31

Blankenberge – Carlepont

Blankenberge B 11 Ha28
Blanquefort F 52 Fb50
Blanzac F 45 Fd48
Blanzy F 41 Ja44
Blauwe Hand NL 9 Jc23
Blauwhuis NL 8 Jb22
Blavozy F 56 Hd49
Blaye F 52 Fb49
Blaye F 55 Ha52
Blaye-les-Mines F 62 Gd53
Bléneau F 32 Ha40
Blénod-lès-Toul F 34 Jc37
Blérancourt F 22 Hb34
Bleré F 38 Ga42
Blesle F 47 Hd48
Blet F 40 Ha43
Bletterans F 42 Jc43
Bleurville F 34 Jd39
Bleury F 32 Hb40
Blévaincourt F 34 Jc39
Bléves F 30 Fd38
Bliesbruck F 25 Kb35
Bligny F 22 Hc35
Bligny F 33 Ja39
Bligny-sur-Ouche F 41 Ja42
Bloemendaal NL 12 Hd25
Blois F 39 Gb41
Blokzijl NL 8 Jb23
Blond F 46 Gb46
Bobigny F 21 Gc36
Bocca di l'Orú F 73 Ma59
Bocholt B 16 Jb29
Bocognano F 73 Ld58
Bodange B 24 Jc33
Bodegraven NL 12 Hd26
Boé F 53 Ga52
Boëge F 49 Ka45
Boekel NL 12 Jb27
Boekelo NL 13 Jd25
Boën F 48 Hd47
Bogny-sur-Meuse F 23 Ja33
Bohain-en-Vermandois F 22 Hb33
Bohan B 23 Ja33
Boiry-Saint-Matin F 15 Ha32
Boiscommun F 31 Gd39
Bois-de-Céné F 37 Ed43
Bois-le-Roi F 32 Ha38
Boismont F 24 Jc34
Boisredon F 44 Fb48
Boisseron F 64 Hd53
Boisson F 4a Ja52
Boisville F 31 Gc38
Bolandoz F 42 Jd42
Bolbec F 20 Fd34
Bollène F 64 Jb52
Bollezeele F 14 Gd30
Bologne F 33 Jb39
Bolsward NL 8 Jb22
Bomal B 16 Jb31
Bompas F 71 Hb57
Bona F 40 Hc43
Bonac F 70 Gb56
Bonboillon F 42 Jc41
Bonhomme F 35 Kb38
Bonifacio F 73 Ma60
Bonifato F 72 Lc57
Bonlieu F 42 Jd44
Bonnat F 46 Gc45
Bonne F 49 Ka45
Bonnebosq F 20 Fd36
Bonnétable F 30 Fd39
Bonneuil-Matours F 38 Ga44
Bonneval F 31 Gb39
Bonneval F 50 Kb47
Bonneval-en-Diois F 57 Jd50
Bonneuvaux F 42 Jd43
Bonnevaux F 42 Jc44
Bonneville F 49 Ka45
Bonneville-la-Louvet F 20 Fd35
Bonnières-sur-Seine F 21 Gc36

Bonnieux F 65 Jc53
Bonny-sur-Loire F 40 Ha41
Bonrepaux F 62 Gc53
Bons F 49 Ka45
Bonsecours F 21 Gb35
Boom B 16 Hd29
Boos F 21 Gb35
Borculo NL 13 Jd25
Bordeaux F 52 Fb50
Bordères-Louron F 69 Fd57
Bordessoule F 46 Gd45
Bords F 44 Fb47
Borger NL 9 Jd23
Borgloon B 16 Jb30
Borgo F 72 Ma56
Borkel NL 12 Jb28
Bormes les Mimosas F 66 Kb55
Born NL 17 Jc29
Borne F 56 Hd49
Borne NL 13 Jd25
Borrèze F 54 Gb50
Bort-les-Orgues F 47 Ha48
Boscamnant F 53 Fc49
Boskoop NL 12 Hd26
Bossée F 38 Ga42
Botrange B 17 Jc31
Bouaye F 37 Ed42
Bouce F 30 Fc37
Bouchain F 15 Hb32
Boucq F 34 Jc37
Boudin F 49 Ka46
Boudreville F 33 Ja39
Boueilho F 61 Fc54
Bouessay F 30 Fc40
Bouesse F 39 Gc42
Bouges-le-Château F 39 Gc43
Bouglainval F 31 Gb38
Bouguenais F 37 Ed42
Bouilland F 41 Ja42
Bouillargues F 64 Ja53
Bouillé-Ménard F 29 Fa40
Bouillon B 23 Ja33
Bouilly F 33 Hd39
Bouin F 36 Ec43
Boujailles F 42 Jd43
Boulay-Moselle F 24 Jd35
Bouligneux F 48 Jb46
Bouligny F 24 Jc35
Bouloc F 55 Hb52
Boulogne-Billancourt F 31 Gd37
Boulogne-sur-Gesse F 61 Ga53
Boulogne-sur-Mer F 14 Gc30
Bouloire F 30 Ga40
Bouniagues F 53 Ga50
Bouray sur-Juine F 31 Gd38
Bourbon-Lancy F 40 Hc44
Bourbon-l'Archambault F 40 Hb44
Bourbonne-les-Bains F 34 Jc39
Bourbourg F 14 Gd30
Bourbriac F 27 Ea38
Bourdeaux F 57 Jc50
Bourdeilles F 45 Ga48
Bourdon F 21 Gc33
Bourdons-sur-Rognon F 33 Jb39
Bouresse F 45 Ga45
Bourg F 52 Fb49
Bourg-Achard F 20 Ga35
Bourganeuf F 46 Gc46
Bourg-Archambault F 46 Gb45
Bourg-Argental F 48 Ja48
Bourg-Beaudouin F 21 Gb35
Bourg-Blanc F 26 Db38
Bourg-de-Péage F 56 Jb49

Bourg-des Comptes F 29 Ed40
Bourg-de-Visa F 54 Gb52
Bourg-d'Oueil F 69 Ga57
Bourg-en-Bresse F 48 Jb45
Bourges F 39 Gd43
Bourg-et-Comin F 22 Hc35
Bourg-Lastic F 47 Ha47
Bourg-Madame F 70 Gd58
Bourgneuf F 39 Gd42
Bourgneuf F 49 Ka47
Bourgneuf-en-Retz F 36 Ec43
Bourgogne F 23 Hd35
Bourgoin-Jallieu F 49 Jc47
Bourg-Saint-Andéol F 56 Jb51
Bourg-Saint-Maurice F 50 Kb47
Bourgthéroulde-Infreville F 20 Ga35
Bourgueil F 38 Fd42
Bournand F 38 Fd43
Bourneville F 20 Ga35
Bournezeau F 37 Fa44
Bournos F 61 Fc55
Bourriot-Bergonce F 53 Fc52
Bourron F 32 Ha38
Bourtange NL 9 Ka22
Bourth F 30 Ga37
Bousières F 42 Jd42
Boussac F 46 Gd45
Boussais F 38 Fc43
Boussens F 70 Gb56
Bousses F 53 Fd52
Boussière-Poitevine F 45 Ga45
Bousschoten B 15 Hc31
Bouvières F 57 Jc51
Bouville F 31 Gd38
Bouvron F 37 Ed41
Bouxwiller F 25 Kb36
Bouy F 23 Hd36
Bouzonville F 24 Jd35
Boves F 21 Gd33
Bovigny B 17 Jc32
Bovenau NL 13 Jc27
Boyardville F 44 Fa46
Boynes F 31 Gd39
Bozel F 50 Kb47
Bozouls F 55 Ha51
Bra B 17 Jc31
Brach F 52 Fa49
Bracieux F 39 Gc41
Bragayrac F 62 Gb54
Braine F 22 Hb35
Braine-le-Comte B 15 Hc31
Brain-l'Alleud B 16 Hd30
Braives B 16 Ja30
Brakel B 15 Hc30
Brakel NL 12 Ja26
Bram F 62 Gd55
Brancion F 41 Ja44
Brando F 72 Ma56
Brannay F 32 Hb39
Branne F 53 Fc50
Bransles F 32 Ha39
Brantôme F 45 Ga48
Brasparts F 26 Dc38
Brassac F 63 Ha54
Brasschaat B 12 Hd28
Brassempouy F 60 Fb54
Brassy F 41 Hd42
Bray-sur-Seine F 32 Hb38
Bray-sur-Somme F 22 Ha33
Brazey-en-Plain F 41 Jb42
Bréau F 32 Ha38
Brécey F 29 Fa37
Brecht B 12 Hd28
Breda NL 12 Hd27
Bredene B 15 Ha29
Bree B 16 Jb29
Bréhal F 29 Ed37

Bréhand F 28 Eb38
Bréhec-en-Plouha F 28 Eb37
Breidenbach F 25 Kb35
Breil F 38 Fd41
Breil-sur-Roya F 58 Kd52
Brem-sur-Mer F 37 Ed44
Brénaz F 49 Jd46
Brenod F 49 Jc46
Brény F 22 Hb35
Breskens NL 11 Hb28
Bresles F 21 Gd35
Bressuire F 37 Fb43
Brest F 26 Db38
Breteau F 32 Ha40
Bretenoux F 54 Gc50
Breteuil F 21 Gd34
Breteuil-sur-Iton F 30 Ga37
Brétignolles-sur-Mer F 37 Ed44
Bretigny-sur-Orge F 31 Gd37
Bretoncelles F 30 Ga38
Bretteville-sur-Ay F 19 Ed35
Bretteville-sur-Laize F 20 Fc36
Breuillet F 31 Gd38
Breuilpont F 21 Gb36
Breukelen NL 12 Ja25
Breuvannes-en-Bassigny F 34 Jc39
Brézins F 49 Jc48
Brezolles F 31 Gb37
Briançon F 58 Kb49
Briare F 40 Ha41
Briatexte F 62 Gd54
Bricon F 33 Jb39
Bricquebec F 19 Ec35
Bricqueville F 19 Fb35
Bridel L 24 Jc33
Briec F 26 Dc39
Brie-Comte-Robert F 32 Ha37
Brielle NL 11 Hc26
Brienne-la-Vieille F 33 Ja38
Briénon-sur-Armançon F 32 Hc39
Brieulles-sur-Bar F 23 Ja34
Briey F 24 Jc35
Brignais F 48 Jc47
Brignogan-Plage F 26 Dc37
Brignoles F 65 Ka54
Brignoud F 49 Jd48
Brigueuil F 45 Ga46
Brillon-en-Barrois F 33 Jb37
Brinon-sur-Beuvron F 40 Hc42
Brinon-sur-Sauldre F 39 Gd41
Brion F 39 Gc43
Brionne F 20 Ga36
Brion-près-Thouet F 38 Fc43
Brion-sur-Ource F 33 Ja39
Brioude F 47 Hc48
Brioux-sur-Boutonne F 45 Fc46
Briouze F 30 Fc37
Briscous F 60 Ed55
Brissac-Quince F 38 Fc42
Brive-la-Gaillarde F 54 Gc49
Brives F 30 Ga40
Brocas F 60 Fb53
Broglie F 20 Ga36
Bron F 48 Jb47
Broons F 28 Ec38
Brossac F 45 Fc48
Brou F 31 Gb39
Brouage F 44 Fa47
Broué F 31 Gb37
Brousse-le-Château F 63 Ha53

Broussey-Raulecourt F 24 Jc36
Bréhec-en-Plouha F 28
Brouvelieures F 34 Ka38
Brouwershaven NL 11 Hc27
Brouzet-lès-Alès F 64 Ja52
Broye F 42 Jc41
Bruay-la-Buissière F 14 Gd31
Bruay-sur-les-Eaux F 15 Hb31
Bruc-sur-Aff F 28 Ec40
Brue-Auriac F 65 Ka54
Brugge B 15 Hb29
Bruinisse NL 11 Hc27
Brûlon F 30 Fc40
Brumath F 25 Kc36
Brummen NL 13 Jd25
Brunehamel F 23 Hd33
Brunet F 65 Ka53
Bruneval F 20 Fd34
Bruniquel F 62 Gc53
Brunssum NL 17 Jc29
Brusque F 63 Hb53
Brussel B 16 Hd30
Bruyères F 34 Ka38
Bruyères-et-Montberault F 22 Hc34
Bruz F 29 Ed39
Bú F 31 Gb37
Buais F 29 Fb38
Bubry F 27 Ea40
Buc F 31 Gd37
Buchy F 21 Gb34
Bucquoy F 15 Ha32
Bucy-lès-Pierrepont F 22 Hc34
Budel NL 12 Jb28
Bugeat F 46 Gd47
Buggenhout B 15 Hc29
Buglose F 60 Fa54
Buironfosse F 22 Hc33
Buis-les-Baronnies F 57 Jc51
Buitenpost NL 9 Jc22
Büllingen B 17 Jd31
Bully-les-Mines F 15 Ha31
Bunschoten NL 12 Ja25
Burcin F 49 Jc48
Burelles F 22 Hc33
Buren NL 8 Jb21
Buren NL 12 Jb26
Burgh-Haamstede NL 11 Hb27
Burgum NL 8 Jb22
Burie F 45 Fc47
Busigny F 22 Hb33
Bussac-Forêt F 53 Fc49
Bussang F 34 Ka39
Busséol F 47 Hd47
Bussière-Badil F 45 Ga47
Bussières F 22 Hb36
Busson F 33 Jb38
Bussum NL 12 Ja25
Bussy-le-Repos F 32 Hb39
Bütgenbach B 17 Jc31
Buurse NL 13 Jd25
Buxières-les-Mines F 40 Hb44
Buxy F 41 Ja43
Buzançais F 39 Gb43
Buzancy F 23 Ja34
Byans-sur-Doubs F 42 Jd42

C

Cabanac F 52 Fb51
Cabasse F 65 Ka54
Cabourg F 20 Fc35
Cabrerets F 54 Gc51
Cabrières F 63 Hc54
Cadalen F 62 Gd53
Caden F 36 Ec41
Cadenet F 65 Jc53

Cadillac F 53 Fc51
Cadillon F 61 Fc54
Cadis F 62 Gd54
Cadouin F 53 Ga50
Cadzand NL 11 Hb28
Caen F 20 Fc36
Cagnes-sur-Mer F 66 Kc53
Cagnotte F 60 Fa54
Cahors F 54 Gc51
Cahuzac-sur-Vére F 62 Gd53
Cajarc F 54 Gc51
Calacuccia F 72 Ld57
Calais F 14 Gc30
Cala Rossa F 73 Ma59
Calcatoggio F 73 Lc58
Calenzana F 72 Lc56
Calignac F 53 Fd52
Callac F 27 Ea38
Callantsoog NL 8 Hd23
Callas F 66 Kb53
Callelongue F 65 Jc55
Calonne-Ricouart F 14 Gd31
Calvi F 72 Lc56
Calviac F 54 Gd50
Calvinet F 55 Ha50
Calvisson F 64 Ja53
Camarès F 63 Hb53
Camaret-sur-Mer F 26 Db38
Cambo-les-Bains F 60 Ed55
Cambrai F 15 Hb32
Camiers F 14 Gc31
Camors F 27 Ea40
Campagne F 60 Fb53
Campel F 28 Ec40
Campénéac F 28 Ec40
Camperduin F 8 Hd24
Campitello F 72 Ld56
Camps-en-Amiénois F 21 Gc33
Canaples F 21 Gd33
Canari F 72 Ld55
Cancale F 29 Ed37
Canchy F 14 Gc32
Cancon F 53 Ga51
Candé F 37 Fa41
Candes-Saint-Martin F 38 Fd42
Canet F 71 Hb57
Canet F 63 Hc54
Canet-Plage F 71 Hb57
Canillo AND 70 Gc57
Cannes F 66 Kc54
Canteleu F 20 Ga35
Cantobre F 55 Hc52
Cany-Barville F 20 Ga34
Capbreton F 60 Ed54
Capdenac-Gare F 54 Gd51
Cap de Pin F 52 Fa52
Capelle aan de IJssel NL 12 Hd26
Capendu F 63 Ha55
Capestang F 63 Hb55
Cap Ferret F 52 Fa51
Caporalino F 72 Ld57
Cap Pelat F 61 Fc53
Captieux F 52 Fc52
Caraman F 62 Gc54
Carantec F 27 Dd37
Carbonne F 62 Gb55
Carcanières-les-Bains F 70 Gd57
Carcans F 52 Fa49
Carcans-Plage F 52 Fa49
Carcassonne F 63 Ha55
Carcès F 65 Ka54
Cardesse F 60 Fb55
Carennac F 54 Gc50
Carentan F 19 Fa35
Carentoir F 28 Ec40
Cargèse F 73 Lc58
Carhaix-Plouguer F 27 Dd38
Carignan F 23 Jb34
Carlepont F 22 Ha34

Carlux F 54 Gb50
Carmaux F 62 Gd53
Carnac F 36 Ea41
Carnoët F 27 Dd38
Carnon-Plage F 64 Hd54
Carolles F 37 Ed42
Caromb F 65 Jc52
Carpentras F 65 Jc52
Carquefou F 37 Ed42
Carresse F 60 Fa55
Carro F 65 Jc55
Carros F 66 Kc53
Carrouges F 30 Fc38
Carry-le-Rouet F 65 Jc55
Carsac F 54 Gb50
Carteret F 19 Ed35
Cartigny F 22 Ha33
Carvin F 15 Ha31
Casamozza F 72 Ma56
Cassagnas F 64 Hd52
Cassagnes-Bégonhès F 55 Ha52
Cassel F 14 Gd30
Casseneuil F 53 Ga51
Cassis F 65 Jd55
Casson F 37 Ed42
Cassuejouls F 55 Hb50
Castanet-Tolosan F 62 Gc54
Castayrols F 62 Gd53
Castelculier F 53 Ga51
Casteljaloux F 53 Fd52
Castellane F 66 Kb53
Castelmoron-sur-Lot F 53 Ga51
Castelnau-Barbarens F 61 Ga54
Castelnaudary F 62 Gd55
Castelnau-d'Auzan F 61 Fd53
Castelnau-de-Médoc F 52 Fb49
Castelnau-de-Montmirail F 62 Gc53
Castelnau-le-Lez F 64 Hd54
Castelnau-Magnoac F 61 Ga55
Castelnau-Montratier F 54 Gb52
Castelnau-Rivière-Basse F 61 Fc54
Castelnou F 71 Ha57
Castelsarrasin F 62 Gb53
Castéra-Verduzan F 61 Fd53
Castets F 60 Fa53
Castex F 61 Fd55
Castillon-du-Gard F 64 Ja53
Castillon-en-Couserans F 70 Gb56
Castillon-la-Bataille F 53 Fc50
Castillonnès F 53 Ga51
Castres F 62 Gd54
Castres-Gironde F 52 Fb51
Castricum NL 8 Hd24
Castries F 64 Hd54
Cateraggio F 72 Ma57
Catus F 54 Gb51
Caudebec-en-Caux F 20 Ga34
Caudebec-lès-Elbeuf F 21 Gb35
Caudecoste F 53 Ga52
Caudiès-de-Fenouillèdes F 71 Ha57
Caudrot F 53 Fc51
Caudry F 15 Hb32
Caujac F 62 Gc55
Caulnes F 28 Ec39
Caumont F 62 Gb53
Caumont-l'Éventé F 19 Fb36
Caumont-sur-Durance F 64 Jb53
Caunes-Minervois F 63 Ha55

Cauro F 73 Ld58
Caussade F 54 Gc52
Cauterets F 69 Fc56
Cavagnac F 54 Gd51
Cavaillon F 65 Jc53
Cavalaire-sur-Mer F 66 Kb55
Cavalière F 66 Kb55
Caveirac F 64 Ja53
Cavignac F 53 Fc49
Cayeux-sur-Mer F 14 Gb32
Caylus F 54 Gc52
Cayres F 56 Hd50
Cayrols F 54 Gd50
Cazals F 54 Gb51
Cazaubon F 61 Fc53
Cazaux F 52 Fa51
Cazères F 62 Gb55
Cazes-Mondenard F 54 Gb52
Cazouls-lès-Béziers F 63 Hb55
Ceaucé F 29 Fb38
Ceilhes-et-Rocozels F 63 Hb53
Ceintrey F 34 Jd37
Celles B 15 Hb30
Celles B 16 Ja32
Celles-sur-Belle F 45 Fc45
Cellettes F 39 Gb41
Celliers F 49 Ka47
Cénevières F 54 Gc51
Censeau F 42 Jd43
Centuri F 72 Ld55
Cépet F 62 Gc54
Cérans-Foulletourte F 30 Fd40
Cerbère F 71 Hc58
Cercy-la-Tour F 40 Hc43
Cerdon F 39 Gd41
Céré F 39 Gc43
Cérences F 29 Fa37
Céreste F 65 Jd53
Céret F 71 Hb58
Cerfontaine B 16 Hd32
Cérilly F 40 Ha44
Cérilly F 33 Ja40
Cerisiers F 32 Hb39
Cérisy-la-Forêt F 19 Fb36
Cerisy-la-Salle F 19 Fa36
Cerizay F 37 Fd43
Cernay F 35 Kb39
Cernay-la-Ville F 31 Gc37
Cerneux F 32 Hb37
Cernoy-en-Berry F 40 Ha41
Cerny-en-Laonnois F 22 Hc35
Cervières F 58 Kb49
Cervione F 72 Ma57
Cervon F 40 Hc42
Cescau F 60 Fb55
Cessenon F 63 Hb54
Cessières F 22 Hb34
Cestas F 52 Fb50
Ceton F 30 Ga39
Céüse 2000 F 57 Jd51
Ceyzériat F 49 Jc45
Cézens F 55 Hb49
Chaam NL 12 Ja28
Chabanais F 45 Ga47
Chabeuil F 56 Jb49
Chablis F 32 Hc40
Chabrac F 45 Ga46
Chabreloche F 47 Hc46
Chabris F 39 Gc42
Chaffayer F 57 Jd50
Chaffois F 42 Jd43
Chagny F 41 Ja43
Chailland F 29 Fb39
Chaillé-les-Marais F 44 Fa45
Chailley-Turny F 32 Hc39
Chailly-en-Bière F 32 Ha38
Chailly-en-Brie F 32 Hb37
Chailly-sur-Armançon F 41 Ja42

Chaintré F 48 Ja45
Chaintrix F 23 Hd36
Chalabre F 70 Gd56
Chalais F 53 Fd49
Chalamont F 48 Jb46
Châlette-sur-Loing F 32 Ha39
Chalindrey F 33 Jb40
Chalivoy-Milon F 40 Ha43
Challain-la-Potherie F 37 Fa41
Challans F 37 Ed43
Chalmazel F 48 Hd47
Chalmoux F 40 Hc44
Chalonnes-sur-Loire F 37 Fb42
Châlons-en-Champagne F 23 Hd36
Chalon-sur-Saône F 41 Jb43
Chalou-Moulineux F 31 Gd38
Châlus F 46 Gb47
Chalvraines F 33 Jb38
Chamalières-sur-Loire F 56 Hd49
Chamaloc F 57 Jc50
Chambeire F 41 Jb42
Chambellay F 37 Fb41
Chamberet F 46 Gc47
Chambéria F 42 Jc44
Chambéry F 49 Jd47
Chambilly F 48 Hd45
Chamblet F 47 Ha45
Chambley-Bussières F 24 Jc36
Chambly F 21 Gd36
Chambois F 30 Fd37
Chambon-la-Forêt F 31 Gd39
Chambon-sur-Voueize F 47 Ha45
Chambord F 39 Gd41
Chamborigaud F 64 Hd52
Chambost-Allières F 48 Ja46
Chambray F 21 Gb36
Chamdeniers-Saint-Denis F 45 Fc45
Chammes F 30 Fc39
Chamonix-Mont-Blanc F 50 Kb46
Chamouilley F 33 Jb37
Chamoy F 32 Hc39
Champagnac F 47 Ha48
Champagnac-le-Vieux F 47 Hc48
Champagné-les-Marais F 44 Fa45
Champagne-Mouton F 45 Fd46
Champagnole F 42 Jd43
Champaubert F 22 Hc36
Champdieu F 48 Hd47
Champeaux F 29 Fa39
Champeix F 47 Hb47
Champier F 49 Jc48
Champigne F 37 Fb41
Champignelles F 32 Hb40
Champigneul-Champagne F 23 Hd36
Champignol-lez-Mondeville F 33 Ja39
Champigny F 32 Ha37
Champigny-le-Sec F 38 Fd44
Champigny-sur-Veude F 38 Fd43
Champlemy F 40 Hb42
Champlitte F 34 Jc40
Champmotteux F 31 Gd38
Champniers F 45 Fd47
Champrond-en-Gâtine F 31 Gb38
Champs-sur-Yonne F 32 Hc40
Champtoceaux F 37 Fa42
Champvans F 42 Jc41
Chamrousse F 57 Jd49

Chanac F 55 Hc51
Chanceaux F 41 Ja41
Chancelade F 53 Ga49
Chancia F 49 Jc45
Chandai F 30 Ga37
Changé F 29 Fb39
Changé F 30 Fd40
Changy F 48 Hd45
Changy F 33 Ja37
Chaniers F 44 Fb47
Channay-sur-Lathan F 38 Fd41
Chantelle F 47 Hb45
Chanteloup F 37 Fb44
Chantemerle F 58 Kb49
Chantenay-Villedieu F 30 Fc40
Chantepie F 29 Ed39
Chantilly F 21 Gd35
Chantonnay F 37 Fa44
Chaon F 39 Gd41
Chaource F 33 Hd39
Chapaize F 41 Ja44
Chapeau-Rouge F 22 Hc33
Chapeauroux F 56 Hd50
Chapelle-Royale F 31 Gb39
Chappes F 47 Hb46
Charbonnat F 41 Hd43
Charcenne F 42 Jc41
Charenton-du-Cher F 40 Ha44
Charleroi B 16 Hd31
Charleval F 21 Gb35
Charleville-Mézières F 23 Ja33
Charlieu F 48 Hd45
Charly F 22 Hb36
Charmant F 45 Fd48
Charmes F 34 Jd38
Charmes-sur-Rhône F 56 Jb50
Charmoille F 34 Jd40
Charmont-en-Beauce F 31 Gd40
Charmont-sur-Barbuise F 33 Hd38
Charnay-lès-Mâcon F 48 Ja45
Charny F 22 Ha36
Charny F 32 Hb40
Charolles F 41 Hd44
Chârost F 39 Gd43
Charpey F 56 Jb49
Charquemont F 42 Ka41
Charras F 45 Fd48
Charritte-de-Bas F 60 Fa55
Charron F 44 Fa45
Charroux F 45 Fd46
Chars F 21 Gc36
Charsonville F 31 Gc40
Chartres F 31 Gc38
Chasné F 29 Ed39
Chasseneuil-sur-Bonnieure F 45 Fd47
Chassepierre B 23 Jb33
Chasse-sur-Rhône F 48 Jb47
Chassillé F 30 Fc39
Chastanier F 56 Hd50
Chastellux-sur-Cure F 40 Hc41
Chatain F 45 Fd46
Château-Arnoux F 65 Ka52
Châteaubernard F 45 Fc47
Château-Bernard F 57 Jc49
Châteaubourg F 29 Fa39
Châteaubriant F 29 Fa40
Château-Chervix F 46 Gb47
Château-Chinon F 41 Hd42
Château-des-Prés F 42 Jd44

Château d'Olonne F 37 Ed44
Château-du-Loir F 38 Fd41
Châteaudun F 31 Gb39
Châteaufort F 57 Ka51
Château-Garnier F 45 Fd45
Châteaugiron F 29 Ed39
Château-Gontier F 29 Fb40
Château-Landon F 32 Ha39
Château-Larcher F 45 Fd45
Château-la-Vallière F 38 Fd41
Château-l'Evêque F 53 Ga49
Châteaulin F 26 Dc39
Châteaumeillant F 39 Gd44
Châteauneuf-de-Galaure F 48 Jb48
Châteauneuf-de-Randon F 55 Hc50
Châteauneuf-d'Ille-et-Vilaine F 29 Ed38
Châteauneuf-du-Faou F 27 Dd39
Châteauneuf-du-Pape F 64 Jb52
Châteauneuf-en-Auxois F 41 Ja42
Châteauneuf-en-Thymerais F 31 Gb38
Châteauneuf-la-Forêt F 46 Gc47
Châteauneuf-les-Bains F 47 Hb46
Châteauneuf-sur-Charente F 45 Fc48
Châteauneuf-sur-Cher F 39 Gd43
Châteauneuf-sur-Loire F 31 Gd40
Châteauneuf-sur-Sarthe F 37 Fb41
Châteauneuf-Val-de-Bargis F 40 Hb42
Châteauponsac F 46 Gb46
Château-Porcien F 23 Hd34
Château-Queyras F 58 Kb49
Châteauredon F 65 Ka52
Château-Renard F 32 Ha40
Châteaurenard F 64 Jb53
Château-Renault F 38 Ga41
Châteauroux F 39 Gc43
Châteauroux F 58 Kb50
Château-Salins F 24 Jd36
Château-Thierry F 22 Hb36
Châteauvillain F 33 Ja39
Châtel F 50 Ka45
Châtelaillon-Plage F 44 Fa46
Châtelard F 49 Ka47
Châtelaudren F 27 Ea38
Châtel-Censoir F 40 Hc41
Châtel-de-Neuvre F 47 Hb45
Châtel B 16 Hd31
Châtel-Gérard F 41 Hd41
Châtelguyon F 47 Hb46
Châtellerault F 38 Ga44
Châtel-Montagne F 47 Hc46
Châtel-sur-Moselle F 34 Jd38
Châtelus-le-Marcheix F 46 Gc46
Châtelus-Malvaleix F 46 Gd46
Châtenois F 34 Jc38
Châtenoy F 31 Gd40

Châtillon F 40 Hb44
Châtillon F 42 Jc44
Châtillon-Coligny F 32 Ha40
Châtillon-en-Bazois F 40 Hc42
Châtillon-en-Diois F 57 Jc50
Châtillon-en-Vendelais F 29 Fa39
Châtillon-la-Palud F 49 Jc46
Châtillon-sur-Chalaronne F 48 Jb45
Châtillon-sur-Colmont F 29 Fb38
Châtillon-sur-Indre F 39 Gb43
Châtillon-sur-Loire F 40 Ha41
Châtillon-sur-Marne F 22 Hc36
Châtillon-sur-Seine F 33 Ja40
Châtillon-sur-Thouet F 38 Fc44
Chatrans F 42 Jd42
Châtres-sur-Cher F 39 Gc42
Chattancourt F 23 Jb35
Chaudefontaine F 42 Jd41
Chaudes-Aigues F 55 Hb50
Chaudieu F 49 Jd46
Chauffailles F 48 Ja45
Chaulnes F 22 Ha33
Chaumard F 41 Hd42
Chaumergy F 42 Jc43
Chaumes-en-Brie F 32 Ha37
Chaumont F 33 Jb39
Chaumont-en-Vexin F 21 Gc35
Chaumont-Porcien F 23 Hd34
Chaumont-sur-Aire F 23 Jb36
Chaumont-sur-Loire F 39 Gb41
Chaumont-sur-Tharonne F 39 Gc41
Chaunay F 45 Fd46
Chauny F 22 Hb34
Chauray F 45 Fc45
Chaussin F 42 Jc43
Chauvé F 36 Ec42
Chauvigné F 39 Gd44
Chauvigny F 38 Ga44
Chaux-Neuve F 42 Jd43
Chavagnes-en-Paillers F 37 Fa43
Chavanay F 48 Ja48
Chavanges F 33 Ja38
Chazelles-sur-Lyon F 48 Ja47
Chazeuil F 47 Hc45
Chef-Boutonne F 45 Fc46
Chef-du-Pont F 19 Fa35
Cheissaux F 46 Gc47
Chelun F 29 Fa40
Chemazé F 29 Fb40
Chémeré-le-Roi F 30 Fc40
Chémery F 39 Gc42
Chémery-sur-Bar F 23 Ja34
Chemillé F 37 Fb42
Chemillé-sur-Dême F 38 Ga41
Cheminon F 33 Ja37
Chemiré-le-Gaudin F 30 Fc40
Chenay F 45 Fc45
Chenay-le-Châtel F 48 Hd45
Chénelette F 48 Ja45
Chénerailles F 46 Gd46
Chennebrun F 30 Ga37
Chennevières F 31 Gb37
Chenoise F 32 Hb37

Chenonceaux – Deinze

Chenonceaux F 39 Gb42
Chenôve F 41 Jb42
Chepoix F 21 Gd34
Chepy F 23 Hd36
Chera F 73 Ma59
Cherain B 17 Jc32
Cherbonnières F 45 Fc46
Cherbourg-Octeville F 19 Ed34
Chérencé-le-Roussel F 29 Fa37
Chéroy F 32 Ha39
Cherves-Richemont F 45 Fc47
Chesley F 33 Hd39
Chevagnes F 40 Hc44
Chevanceaux F 53 Fc49
Cheverny F 39 Gb41
Chevetogne B 16 Ja32
Chevillon F 32 Hb40
Chevilly F 31 Gc39
Cheviré-le-Rouge F 38 Fc41
Chevreuse F 31 Gd37
Chevroux F 48 Jb45
Cheylade F 55 Ha49
Chezal-Benoit F 39 Gd43
Chézeaux F 34 Jc39
Chézery-Forens F 49 Jd45
Chiché F 38 Fc44
Chichilianne F 57 Jc50
Chièvres B 15 Hc31
Chigné F 38 Fd41
Chilleurs-aux-Bois F 31 Gd39
Chimay B 16 Hd32
Chinon F 38 Fd42
Chirens F 49 Jc48
Chirols F 56 Ja50
Chissey-en-Morvan F 41 Hd42
Chizé F 45 Fc46
Choiseul F 34 Jc39
Choisy-au-Bac F 22 Ha35
Choisy-en-Brie F 32 Hb37
Cholet F 37 Fb43
Chomérac F 56 Jb50
Chorges F 57 Ka50
Chouvigny F 47 Hb46
Choye F 42 Jc41
Chuelles F 32 Ha39
Cieux F 46 Gb46
Ciney B 16 Ja32
Cinq-Mars-la-Pile F 38 Fd42
Cintegabelle F 62 Gc55
Cintrey F 34 Jc40
Ciral F 30 Fc38
Ciré-d'Aunis F 44 Fa46
Cires-lès-Mello F 21 Gd35
Cirey-sur-Vezouze F 34 Ka37
Ciry-le-Noble F 41 Hd44
Citou F 63 Ha55
Civaux F 45 Ga45
Civray F 45 Fd46
Clairac F 53 Fd52
Clairavaux F 46 Gd47
Clairvaux-les-Lacs F 42 Jc44
Clamart F 31 Gd37
Clamecy F 40 Hc41
Claret F 64 Hd53
Claudon F 34 Jd39
Claye-Souilly F 22 Ha36
Clécy F 30 Fc37
Cléder F 26 Dc37
Clefmont F 34 Jc39
Clefs F 38 Fc41
Cléguérec F 27 Ea39
Clelles F 57 Jd50
Clémont F 39 Gd41
Cléon-d'Andran F 56 Jb50
Cléré-les-Pins F 38 Fd41
Clères F 21 Gb34
Clérey F 33 Hd39
Clergoux F 46 Gd48
Clermont F 21 Gd35
Clermont F 49 Jd46

Clermont-Créans F 30 Fc40
Clermont-en-Argonne F 23 Jb35
Clermont-Ferrand F 47 Hb47
Clermont-l'Hérault F 63 Hc54
Clermont-sur-Lauquet F 71 Ha56
Cléron F 42 Jd42
Clerval F 42 Ka41
Clervaux L 17 Jc32
Cléry-Saint-André F 31 Gc40
Clesse F 38 Fc44
Clety F 14 Gd31
Clion F 39 Gb43
Clisson F 37 Fa43
Clomot F 41 Ja42
Cloyes-sur-le-Loir F 31 Gb40
Clugnat F 46 Gd45
Cluis F 39 Gc44
Clumanc F 65 Ka52
Cluny F 41 Ja44
Cluses F 49 Ka45
Coarraze F 69 Fc56
Coclois F 33 Hd38
Coësmes F 29 Fa40
Cœuvres-et-Valsery F 22 Hb35
Coevorden NL 9 Jd23
Coëx F 37 Ed44
Cognac F 45 Fc47
Cognac-la-Forêt F 46 Gb47
Cognin-les-Gorges F 49 Jc48
Cogolin F 66 Kb55
Cohade F 47 Hc48
Cohiniac F 28 Eb38
Coincy F 22 Hb36
Colfontaine B 15 Hc31
Coligny F 49 Jc45
Collinée F 28 Eb38
Collioure F 71 Hb57
Collobrières F 66 Kb55
Collonges F 49 Jd45
Collonges-la-Rouge F 54 Gc49
Colmar F 35 Kb38
Colmars F 58 Kb51
Cologne F 62 Gb54
Colombey-les-Belles F 34 Jc37
Colombey-les-Deux-Églises F 33 Ja38
Colombier F 34 Jd40
Colombier F 42 Ka42
Colonard F 30 Ga38
Colondannes F 46 Gc45
Coly F 54 Gb49
Combeaufontaine F 34 Jc40
Comberouger F 62 Gb53
Comblain-au-Pont B 16 Jb31
Combles F 22 Ha34
Combloux F 49 Ka46
Combourg F 29 Ed38
Combres F 31 Gb38
Combronde F 47 Hb46
Combs-la-Ville F 32 Ha37
Comines F 15 Ha30
Commarin F 41 Ja42
Commensacq F 52 Fb52
Commentry F 47 Ha45
Commequiers F 37 Ed44
Commercy F 34 Jc37
Compiègne F 22 Ha35
Compolibat F 54 Gd51
Comprignac F 46 Gb46
Comps-sur-Artuby F 66 Kb53
Concarneau F 26 Dc40
Concèze F 46 Gb48
Conches-en-Ouche F 20 Ga36
Conchigliu F 72 Ld55

Conchy-les-Pots F 22 Ha34
Concoret F 28 Ec39
Concots F 54 Gc51
Concoules F 56 Hd51
Concressault F 40 Ha41
Condamine-Châtelard, la F 58 Kb51
Condat F 47 Ha48
Condé-en-Brie F 22 Hc36
Condé-Folie F 21 Gc33
Condé sur-Huisne F 30 Ga38
Condé-sur-les-Eaux F 15 Hb31
Condé-sur-Noireau F 29 Fb37
Condé sur-Sarthe F 30 Fd38
Condé-sur-Vesgre F 31 Gc37
Condé sur-Vire F 19 Fa36
Condom F 61 Fd53
Condrieu F 48 Jb48
Conflans-sur-Lanterne F 34 Jd40
Conflans-sur-Seine F 32 Hc38
Confolens F 45 Ga46
Confolent-Port-Dieu F 47 Ha48
Congrier F 29 Fa40
Conlie F 30 Fc39
Connaux F 64 Ja52
Connerré F 30 Fd39
Conquereuil F 37 Ed41
Conques F 55 Ha51
Conques-sur-Orbiel F 63 Ha55
Consenvoye F 23 Jb35
Contamine-Sarzin F 49 Jd46
Contay F 21 Gd33
Contes F 67 Kd53
Conteville F 21 Gc34
Contis-Plage F 52 Fa52
Contres F 39 Gb41
Contrexéville F 34 Jc38
Conty F 21 Gd34
Coo B 17 Jc31
Coole F 33 Hd37
Coray F 27 Dd39
Corbeil-Essonnes F 31 Gd37
Corbeilles F 32 Ha39
Corbeny F 22 Hc34
Corberon F 41 Jb42
Corbie F 21 Gd33
Corbigny F 40 Hc42
Corbon F 20 Fc36
Corcelles-en-Beaujolais F 48 Ja45
Corcelles-Ferrières F 42 Jc42
Corcoué-sur-Logne F 37 Ed43
Corcy F 22 Hb35
Cordéac F 57 Jd49
Cordesse F 41 Hd42
Cordes-sur-Ciel F 62 Gd53
Corlay F 27 Ea38
Cormainville F 31 Gc39
Cormatin F 41 Ja44
Cormeilles F 20 Fd35
Cormery F 38 Ga42
Cormoz F 41 Jb44
Corné F 38 Fc41
Corneuil F 31 Gb37
Cornil F 54 Gc49
Cornimont F 34 Ka39
Cornus F 63 Hb53
Cornusse F 40 Ha43
Corny-sur-Moselle F 24 Jd36
Corps F 57 Jd49
Corps-Nuds F 29 Ed40
Corrano F 73 Ld58
Corre F 34 Jd39
Corrençon-en-Vercors F 57 Jc49

Corrèze F 46 Gc48
Corseul F 28 Ec38
Corsica F 72 Ld57
Corsicana F 72 Ma57
Corte F 72 Ld57
Cosne-Cours-sur-Loire F 40 Ha41
Cosne-d'Allier F 40 Ha44
Cossé-le-Vivien F 29 Fb40
Costaros F 56 Hd50
Coubert F 32 Ha37
Coublanc F 34 Jc40
Coubon F 56 Hd49
Couches F 41 Ja43
Coucy-le-Château-Auffrique F 22 Hb34
Couddes F 39 Gb42
Coudekerque-Branche F 14 Gd30
Coudray F 29 Fb40
Coudrecieux F 30 Ga40
Coudron F 39 Gd43
Coudures F 60 Fb54
Couflens F 70 Gb57
Couhé F 45 Fd45
Couiza F 71 Ha56
Coulaines F 30 Fd39
Coulandon F 40 Hb44
Coulanges-lès-Nevers F 40 Hb43
Coulaures F 46 Gb48
Couleuvre F 40 Hb44
Coullons F 40 Ha41
Coulmier-le-Sec F 33 Ja40
Coulombiers F 45 Fd45
Coulombs F 31 Gc37
Coulomby F 14 Gc31
Coulommiers F 32 Hb37
Coulon F 44 Fb45
Coulonges-Cohan F 22 Hc35
Coulonges-sur-l'Autize F 44 Fb45
Couloutre F 40 Ha41
Coupéville F 23 Ja36
Coupray F 33 Ja39
Couptrain F 30 Fc38
Courban F 33 Ja39
Courcelles F 42 Jd42
Courcelles-sur-Nied F 24 Jd35
Courcelles-sur-Seine F 21 Gb36
Courcemont F 30 Fd39
Courchevel F 50 Kb47
Cour-Cheverny F 39 Gb41
Courcité F 30 Fc38
Courcon F 44 Fb45
Cour-et-Buis F 48 Jb48
Courgains F 30 Fc38
Courgeon F 30 Ga38
Courgivaux F 32 Hb37
Courmont F 22 Hc36
Courniou F 63 Ha54
Cournon-d'Auvergne F 47 Hb47
Courpalay F 32 Ha37
Courpière F 47 Hc47
Coursan F 63 Hb55
Coursegoules F 66 Kc53
Courseulles-sur-Mer F 20 Fc35
Cours-la-Ville F 48 Ja46
Courson-les-Carrières F 40 Hc41
Courtacon F 32 Hb37
Courtalain F 31 Gb39
Courtenay F 32 Ha39
Courtenot F 33 Hd39
Courthézon F 64 Jb52
Courtivron F 41 Jb41
Courtomer F 30 Fd37
Court-Saint-Etienne B 16 Hd30
Courville-sur-Eure F 31 Gb38
Cousolre F 15 Hc32
Coussac-Bonneval F 46 Gb48

Coussegrey F 33 Hd39
Coussey F 34 Jc38
Coustellet F 65 Jc53
Coustouges F 71 Hb58
Coutances F 19 Fa36
Couterne F 30 Fc38
Coutras F 53 Fc49
Couture-d'Argenson F 45 Fc46
Coutures F 38 Fc42
Couvin B 16 Hd32
Couvron-et-Aumencourt F 22 Hb34
Couy F 40 Ha42
Cox F 62 Gb54
Cozes F 44 Fb48
Cozzano F 73 Ld58
Cramant F 22 Hc36
Crançot F 42 Jc43
Craon F 29 Fb40
Craponne-sur-Arzon F 48 Hd48
Cravant F 31 Gc40
Cravant F 32 Hc40
Crécy-Couvé F 31 Gb37
Crécy-en-Ponthieu F 14 Gc32
Crécy-la-Chapelle F 32 Ha37
Crécy-s-Serre F 22 Hc34
Creil F 21 Gd35
Crémieu F 49 Jc47
Créon F 53 Fc50
Crépey F 34 Jc37
Crépy F 22 Hb34
Crépy-en-Valois F 22 Ha35
Crespin B 15 Hc31
Cressanges F 47 Hb45
Cressensac F 54 Gc49
Cressia F 42 Jc44
Cressonsacq F 21 Gd35
Crest F 56 Jb50
Créteil F 31 Gd37
Creully F 19 Fb35
Creutzwald F 24 Ka35
Crevant F 46 Gc45
Crevechamps F 34 Jd37
Crèvecœur-en-Auge F 20 Fd36
Crèvecœur-le-Grand F 21 Gd34
Crévoux F 58 Kb50
Criel-sur-Mer F 21 Gb33
Crillon F 21 Gc34
Criquetot-l'Esneval F 20 Fd34
Cristinacce F 72 Ld57
Crocq F 46 Gd46
Crocy F 30 Fc37
Croissilles F 15 Ha32
Croissy-sur-Selle F 21 Gd34
Cronat F 40 Hc44
Cros-de-Cagnes F 66 Kc53
Crosses F 40 Ha43
Crotenay F 42 Jd43
Crots F 58 Kb50
Crouy F 22 Hb35
Crozant F 46 Gc45
Crozon F 26 Db36
Cruas F 56 Jb50
Cruis F 65 Jd52
Crulai F 30 Ga37
Cruseilles F 49 Jd45
Cruzy F 63 Hb55
Cruzy-le-Châtel F 33 Hd40
Cucq F 14 Gc31
Cucuron F 65 Jc53
Cuers F 65 Ka55
Cugand F 37 Fa43
Cuges-les-Pins F 65 Jd55
Cugnaux F 62 Gb54
Cuijk NL 13 Jc27
Cuillé F 29 Fa40
Cuiseaux F 42 Jc44
Cuisery F 41 Jb44
Culan F 39 Gd44

Culemborg NL 12 Ja26
Culoz F 49 Jd46
Cunault F 38 Fc42
Cunfin F 33 Ja39
Cunlhat F 47 Hc47
Cuon F 38 Fc41
Curçay-sur-Dive F 38 Fc43
Cuse F 42 Ka41
Cusey F 33 Jb40
Cussac F 45 Ga47
Cussac-Fort-Médoc F 52 Fb49
Cussangy F 33 Hd39
Cusset F 47 Hc46
Cussey-les-Forges F 33 Jb40
Cussy-les-Forges F 41 Hd41
Cusy F 49 Jd46
Cuxac-Carbadès F 62 Gd55
Cuxac-d'Aude F 63 Hb55
Cuzorn F 53 Ga51
Cysoing F 15 Hb31

D

Dainville-Bertheléville F 33 Jb38
Dalen NL 9 Jd23
Dalfsen NL 9 Jc24
Dalheim L 24 Jd34
Dalhem B 16 Jb30
Daluis F 58 Kb52
Damas-aux-Bois F 34 Jd38
Damazan F 53 Fd52
Damerey F 41 Jb43
Damery F 22 Hc36
Damgan F 36 Eb41
Dammarie F 31 Gb38
Dammarie-les-Lys F 32 Ha38
Dammartin-en-Goële F 22 Ha36
Damme B 15 Hb29
Dampierre F 33 Hd37
Dampierre F 42 Jc42
Dampierre-en-Bray F 21 Gc34
Dampierre-en-Burly F 32 Ha40
Dampierre-en-Yvelines F 31 Gc37
Dampierre-Saint-Nicolas F 21 Gb33
Dampierre-sur-Boutonne F 45 Fc46
Dampierre-sur-Salon F 42 Jc41
Damprichard F 43 Kb41
Damville F 31 Gb37
Damvillers F 23 Jb35
Damwoude NL 8 Jb22
Dangeau F 31 Gb39
Dangé-Saint-Romain F 38 Ga43
Dangy F 19 Fa36
Dannemarie F 35 Kb40
Danzé F 31 Gb40
Daoulas F 26 Dc38
Darnétal F 21 Gb35
Darney F 34 Jd39
Daumazan-sur-Arize F 70 Gb56
Daumeray F 38 Fc41
Dausse F 53 Ga52
Davéziex F 48 Jb48
Dax F 60 Fa54
Deauville F 20 Fd35
De Bilt NL 12 Ja25
De Blesse NL 8 Jb23
Decazeville F 54 Gd51
Decize F 40 Hc43
De Cocksdorp NL 8 Hd22
Dedemsvaart NL 9 Jc24
De Haan B 15 Ha29
Deinze B 15 Hb30

88

De Koog NL 8 Hd22
De Kooy NL 8 Hd23
Délasse F 19 Ed34
Delden NL 13 Jd25
Delft NL 12 Hd26
Delfzijl NL 9 Jd21
Delle F 35 Kb40
Delme F 24 Jd36
De Lutte NL 13 Jd25
Demandolx F 66 Kb53
Demigny F 41 Jb43
Denain F 15 Hb32
Den Burg NL 8 Hd22
Dendermonde B 15 Hc29
Denekamp NL 9 Jd24
Den Haag NL 11 Hc26
Den Ham NL 9 Jc24
Den Helder NL 8 Hd23
Dennebrœucq F 14 Gd31
Den Oever NL 8 Ja22
De Panne B 14 Gd29
Derval F 37 Ed41
Désaignes F 56 Ja49
Descartes F 38 Ga43
Désertines F 29 Fb38
Dessel B 12 Ja28
Dessel B 16 Ja29
Desvres F 14 Gc31
Dettey F 41 Hd43
Dettwiller F 25 Kb36
Deurne NL 12 Jd28
Deux-Chaises F 47 Hb45
Deventer NL 13 Jc25
Deviat F 45 Fd48
De Wijk NL 9 Jc23
Dhuizon F 39 Gc41
Diarville F 34 Jd38
Didam NL 13 Jc26
Die F 57 Jc50
Diekirch L 24 Jc33
Diélette F 19 Ed34
Diemen NL 12 Ja25
Diémoz F 48 Jb47
Dienne F 55 Ha49
Dienville F 33 Jd38
Diepenbeek B 16 Jb29
Diepenheim NL 13 Jd25
Diepenveen NL 13 Jc25
Dieppe F 21 Gb33
Dieren NL 13 Jc26
Dierrey-Saint-Pierre F 32 Hc38
Diest B 16 Ja29
Dieue F 23 Jb36
Dieulefit F 56 Jb51
Dieulouard F 24 Jd36
Dieupentale F 62 Gb53
Dieuze F 24 Ka36
Diever NL 9 Jc23
Differdange L 24 Jc34
Dignac F 45 Fd48
Digne-les-Bains F 65 Ka52
Digny F 31 Gb38
Digoin F 41 Hd44
Dijon F 41 Jb41
Diksmuide B 15 Ha29
Dilsen B 16 Jc29
Dinan F 28 Ec38
Dinant B 16 Ja32
Dinard F 28 Ec37
Dingé F 29 Ed38
Dinteloord NL 12 Hd27
Dinxperlo NL 13 Jd26
Diors F 39 Gc43
Diou F 40 Hc44
Dippach L 24 Jc34
Dirksland NL 11 Hc27
Dison B 17 Jc30
Dives-sur-Mer F 20 Fc35
Divonne F 42 Jd44
Dixmont F 32 Hb39
Dizy F 22 Hc36
Docelles F 34 Ka38
Doesburg NL 13 Jc26
Doetinchem NL 13 Jc26
Doische B 16 Ja32
Dokkum NL 8 Jb21
Dolancourt F 33 Ja38
Dol-de-Bretagne F 29 Ed38

Dole F 42 Jc42
Dolus-d'Oléron F 44 Fa46
Domaine-de-Méjanes F 64 Ja54
Domats F 32 Hb39
Dombasle-sur-Meurthe F 34 Jd37
Dombergen B 15 Hc30
Dombrot-le-Sec F 34 Jc39
Domburg NL 11 Hb28
Domène F 49 Jd48
Domerat F 47 Ha45
Domèvre-sur-Vezouze F 34 Ka37
Domfront F 29 Fb38
Domino F 44 Ed46
Dommartin-les-Cuiseaux F 42 Jc44
Domme F 54 Gb50
Dompaire F 34 Jd38
Dompierre-du-Chemin F 29 Fa39
Dompierre-sur-Besbre F 40 Hc44
Dompierre-sur-Mer F 44 Fa46
Dompierre-sur-Veyle F 48 Jb46
Domps F 46 Gc47
Domrémy-la-Pucelle F 34 Jc38
Donchery F 23 Ja34
Dongen NL 12 Ja27
Donges F 36 Ec42
Donkerbroek NL 9 Jc22
Donnemarie-Dontilly F 32 Hb38
Dontreix F 47 Ha46
Dontrien F 23 Hd35
Donzac F 53 Ga52
Donzère F 56 Jb51
Donzy F 40 Hb42
Doorn NL 12 Ja26
Dordives F 32 Ha39
Dordrecht NL 12 Hd27
Dore-l'Eglise F 47 Hc48
Dormans F 22 Hc36
Dornas F 56 Ja50
Dornecy F 40 Hb42
Dornes F 40 Hb44
Dortan F 49 Jc45
Dottignies B 15 Hb30
Douai F 15 Ha32
Douarnenez F 26 Dc39
Douchy F 32 Hb40
Douchy-les-Mines F 15 Hb32
Doucier F 42 Jd44
Doudeville F 20 Ga34
Doue F 32 Hb37
Doué-la-Fontaine F 38 Fc42
Doulaincourt-Saucourt F 33 Jb38
Doulevant-le-Château F 33 Ja38
Doullens F 14 Gd32
Dounoux F 34 Jd39
Dour B 15 Hc31
Dourdan F 31 Gd38
Dourgne F 62 Gd54
Douriez F 14 Gc32
Dournazac F 45 Ga47
Doussard F 49 Ka46
Douvaine F 49 Ka45
Douvres-la-Délivrande F 20 Fc35
Douzy F 23 Ja34
Dozulé F 20 Fc36
Drachten NL 8 Jb22
Draguignan F 66 Kb54
Draveil F 31 Gd37
Dreux F 31 Gb37
Driebergen-Rijsenburg NL 12 Ja26
Driesum NL 8 Jb21
Drionville F 14 Gc31
Droisy F 31 Gb37
Dronten NL 8 Jb24
Droué F 31 Gb39

Drulingen F 25 Kb36
Drunen NL 12 Ja27
Druten NL 12 Jb26
Druyes-les-Belles-Fontaine F 40 Hb41
Ducey F 29 Fa38
Duclair F 20 Ga35
Dudelange L 24 Jc34
Duffel B 16 Hd29
Duingt F 49 Ka46
Duiven NL 13 Jc26
Dunes F 61 Ga53
Dunières F 48 Ja48
Dunkerque F 14 Gd29
Dun-le-Palestel F 46 Gc45
Dun-sur-Auron F 40 Ha43
Dun-sur-Meuse F 23 Jb34
Dun-sur-Meuse F 23 Jb35
Durance F 53 Fd52
Duras F 53 Fd51
Durban-Corbières F 71 Hb56
Durbuy B 16 Jb31
Durdat-Larequille F 47 Ha45
Durfort F 64 Hd53
Durfort-Lacapelette F 54 Gb52
Durtal F 38 Fc41
Dury F 21 Gd33
Dussen NL 12 Ja27
Duzy-le-Gros F 22 Hc34
Dwingeloo NL 9 Jc23

E

Eaux-Bonnes F 69 Fc56
Eauze F 61 Fd53
Ebreuil F 47 Hb46
Écaussinnes-Lalaing B 15 Hc31
Echalot F 41 Ja41
Echassières F 47 Hb45
Echiré F 45 Fc45
Echourgnac F 53 Fd49
Echt NL 17 Jc29
Echteld NL 12 Jb26
Echternach L 24 Jd33
Eclaron-Braucourt F 33 Ja37
Ecly F 23 Hd34
Écommoy F 30 Fd40
Écouché F 30 Fc37
Écouflant F 37 Fb41
Écouis F 21 Gb35
Ecoyeux F 44 Fb47
Ecques F 14 Gd31
Écueillé F 39 Gb43
Écury-sur-Coole F 23 Hd36
Edam NL 8 Ja24
Ede NL 12 Jb26
Eeklo B 15 Hb29
Eelde NL 9 Jc22
Eemshaven NL 9 Jd21
Eerbeek NL 13 Jc26
Eernegem B 15 Ha29
Eersel NL 12 Jb28
Egheзée B 16 Ja31
Égletons F 46 Gd48
Égliseneuve-d'Antraigues F 47 Hb48
Egmond aan Zee NL 8 Hd24
Ègreville F 32 Ha39
Éguilles F 65 Jc54
Eguisheim F 35 Kb39
Eguzon F 46 Gc45
Eibergen NL 13 Jd25
Eijsden NL 16 Jb30
Eindhoven NL 12 Jb28
Einville-au-Jaurd F 34 Jd37
Eisden B 16 Jc29
Eke B 15 Hb30
Elbeuf F 20 Ga35
Elburg NL 8 Jb24
Elincourt-Sainte-Marguerite F 22 Ha34

Ellewoutsdijk NL 11 Hc28
Ellezelles B 15 Hc30
Elliant F 27 Dd39
Elne F 71 Hb57
Eloyes F 34 Ka39
el Pas de la Casa AND 70 Gc58
Elsenborn B 17 Jc31
el Serrat AND 70 Gc57
Elspeet NL 12 Jb25
Elst NL 12 Jb26
Elven F 28 Eb40
Emagny F 42 Jc41
Emanville F 20 Ga36
Embrun F 58 Kb50
Emmeloord NL 8 Jb23
Emmen NL 9 Jd23
Emmer-Compascum NL 9 Jd23
Enghien B 15 Hc30
Engis B 16 Jb30
Englancourt F 22 Hc33
Englefontaine F 15 Hc32
Enkhuizen NL 8 Ja24
Ennezat F 47 Hb46
Ens NL 8 Jb24
Enschede NL 13 Jd25
Enter NL 13 Jd25
Entrages F 65 Ka52
Entraigues F 39 Gc43
Entraigues F 57 Jd49
Entrains-sur-Nohain F 40 Hb41
Entrammes F 29 Fb40
Entraunes F 58 Kb50
Entraygues-sur-Truyère F 55 Ha51
Entrecasteaux F 65 Ka54
Entrechaux F 65 Jc52
Entrevaux F 58 Kb52
Entzheim F 35 Kc37
Envermeu F 21 Gb33
Epagny F 22 Hb35
Epagny F 41 Jb41
Epaignes F 20 Fd35
Epaux-Bézu F 22 Hb36
Epe NL 13 Jc25
Éphy F 22 Hb33
Épernay F 22 Hc36
Épernon F 31 Gc38
Epfig F 35 Kb38
Epierre F 49 Ka47
Épinal F 34 Jd38
Epineuil-le-Fleuriel F 40 Ha44
Epiry F 40 Hc42
Epizon F 33 Jb38
Epoisses F 41 Hd41
Epoye F 23 Hd35
Eppe-Sauvage F 16 Hd32
Epuisay F 30 Ga40
Équeurdreville-Hainneville F 19 Ed34
Equihen-Plage F 14 Gb31
Erbajolo F 72 Ma55
Erbalunga F 72 Ma55
Ercheu F 22 Ha34
Erdeven F 36 Ea41
Eréac F 28 Ec39
Erezée B 16 Jb32
Ergué-Gabéric F 26 Dc39
Erm NL 9 Jd23
Ermelo NL 12 Jb25
Ermenonville F 22 Ha36
Ernée F 29 Fb39
Erôme F 56 Jb49
Erp NL 12 Jb27
Erquelinnes B 15 Hc33
Erquy F 28 Eb37
Erstein F 35 Kc37
Ertvelde B 15 Hb30
Ervauville F 32 Ha39
Ervy-le-Châtel F 32 Hc39
Escalles F 14 Gc30
Escanaffles B 15 Hb30
Escatalens F 62 Gb53
Esch-sur-Alzette L 24 Jc34

Esch-sur-Sûre L 24 Jc33
Escos F 60 Fa55
Escot F 68 Fb56
Escouloubre F 70 Gd57
Escource F 52 Fa52
Escrennes F 31 Gd39
Esnandes F 44 Fa45
Esneux B 16 Jb31
Esnouveaux F 33 Jb39
Espalion F 55 Ha51
Esparron F 65 Jd54
Esparron-de-Verdon F 65 Ka53
Espel NL 8 Jb23
Espeluche F 56 Jb51
Espéraza F 70 Gd56
Espezel F 70 Gd57
Espinasses F 57 Ka51
Esplantas F 55 Hc50
Espoey F 61 Fc55
Esprels F 34 Jd40
Essay F 30 Fd38
Essen B 12 Hd28
Essertaux F 21 Gd34
Essertenne F 42 Jc41
Essômes-sur-Marne F 22 Hb36
Essoyes F 33 Ja39
Establet F 57 Jc51
Estagel F 71 Ha57
Estaing F 55 Ha51
Estaires F 15 Ha31
Estang F 61 Fc53
Esteng F 58 Kb51
Esternay F 32 Hc37
Estissac F 32 Hc38
Estrées-Saint-Denis F 22 Ha35
Estrée-Wamin F 14 Gd32
Estry F 29 Fb37
Étain F 24 Jc35
Etais F 33 Ja40
Etalans F 42 Jd42
Etalle B 23 Jb33
Étampes F 31 Gd38
Étang-sur-Arroux F 41 Hd43
Étaples F 14 Gc31
Etauliers F 52 Fb49
Etel F 36 Ea41
Etevaux F 41 Jb41
Ethe B 23 Jb34
Etival F 42 Jd44
Etival-Clairefontaine F 34 Ka38
Étoges F 22 Hc36
Etoile-Rhône F 56 Jb50
Etouy F 21 Gd35
Étréaupont F 22 Hc33
Etréchy F 31 Gd38
Etrembières F 49 Jd45
Étrépagny F 21 Gc35
Étretat F 20 Fd34
Étreux F 22 Hc33
Étreux F 22 Hc33
Étroeungt F 22 Hc33
Etsaut F 68 Fb56
Ettelbruck L 24 Jc33
Etten-Leur NL 12 Hd27
Etusson F 37 Fb43
Etuz F 42 Jd41
Eu F 21 Gb33
Eugénie-les-Bains F 61 Fc54
Eupen B 17 Jc30
Eursinge NL 9 Jc23
Euzet F 64 Ja52
Evaillé F 30 Ga40
Evaux-les-Bains F 47 Ha45
Evergem B 15 Hb29
Évian-les-Bains F 42 Ka44
Evillers F 42 Jd42
Evisa F 72 Lc57
Evran F 28 Ec38
Evrecy F 19 Fb36
Evreux F 21 Gb35
Évrieu F 49 Jc47
Evriguet F 28 Ec39
Évron F 30 Fc39
Évry F 31 Gd37
Excideuil F 46 Gb48

Exloo NL 9 Jd23
Exmes F 30 Fd37
Eygalières F 64 Jb53
Eygluy-Esculin F 57 Jc50
Eyguians F 57 Jd51
Eyguières F 64 Jb53
Eygurande F 47 Ha47
Eygurande-et-Gardedeuil F 53 Fd49
Eymet F 53 Fd51
Eymoutiers F 46 Gc47
Eyrein F 46 Gd48
Eze F 67 Kd53
Ezinge NL 9 Jc21
Ezy-sur-Eure F 31 Gb37

F

Fabas F 61 Ga55
Fabas F 70 Gb56
Fabrègues F 64 Hd54
Fabrezan F 71 Ha56
Fain-lès-Montbard F 41 Hd41
Falaise F 30 Fc37
Falleron F 37 Ed43
Fallon F 42 Ka41
Fameck F 24 Jd35
Fanjeaux F 62 Gd55
Farciennes B 16 Hd31
Faremoutiers F 32 Ha37
Fargues-Saint-Hilaire F 52 Fb50
Fargues-sur-Ourbise F 53 Fd52
Faucogney-et-la-Mer F 34 Ka39
Faugères F 63 Hb54
Fauguerolles F 53 Fd51
Faulquemont F 24 Ka35
Fauquembergues F 14 Gd31
Fauville-en-Caux F 20 Ga34
Faux F 53 Ga50
Faux F 55 Hc51
Faverges F 49 Ka46
Faverney F 34 Jd40
Faverolles F 20 Ga36
Faverolles F 31 Gc37
Favone F 73 Ma59
Fay-aux-Loges F 31 Gd40
Fay-de-Bretagne F 37 Ed41
Fayence F 66 Kb53
Fayet F 63 Hb53
Fayl-Billot F 34 Jc40
Fay-sur-Lignon F 56 Ja49
Fécamp F 20 Fd34
Feignies F 15 Hc32
Feins F 29 Ed38
Feldbach F 35 Kb40
Félines-Minervois F 63 Ha55
Félines-Termenès F 71 Ha56
Felletin F 46 Gd46
Fendeille F 62 Gd55
Fénétrange F 24 Ka36
Feneu F 37 Fb41
Fenioux F 37 Fb44
Fenioux F 44 Fb47
Féole F 37 Fa44
Fère-Champenoise F 32 Hc37
Fère-en-Tardenois F 22 Hb35
Ferney-Voltaire F 49 Jd45
Ferrette F 35 Kb40
Ferreux F 32 Hc38
Ferrières F 63 Ha54
Ferrières-en-Brie F 32 Ha37
Ferrières-en-Gâtinais F 32 Ha39
Ferrières-Saint-Mary F 55 Hb49
Ferrières-sur-Sichon F 47 Hc46

Fervaques – Grues

Fervaques F 20 Fd36
Ferwerd NL 8 Jb21
Fessenheim F 35 Kc39
Feugarolles F 53 Fd52
Feuges F 33 Hd38
Feuquières F 21 Gc34
Feuquières-en-Vimeu F 21 Gc33
Feurs F 48 Hd47
Feytiat F 46 Gb47
Fienvillers F 14 Gd32
Figari F 73 Ld60
Figeac F 54 Gd51
Fijnaart NL 12 Hd27
Filain F 42 Jd41
Fillières F 24 Jc34
Finhan F 62 Gb53
Fins F 22 Ha33
Firminy F 48 Ja48
Fismes F 22 Hc35
Fitou F 71 Hb56
Fixin F 41 Jb42
Flagy F 32 Ha38
Flaine F 50 Kb45
Flammerans F 42 Jc42
Flammerécourt F 33 Jb38
Flassans-sur-Issole F 65 Ka54
Flaugeac F 53 Fd50
Flavigny-sur-Ozerain F 41 Ja41
Flavin F 55 Ha52
Flavy-le Martel F 22 Hb34
Flayat F 47 Ha47
Flayosc F 66 Kb54
Flers F 29 Fb37
Fleurance F 61 Ga53
Fleuré F 45 Ga45
Fleurus B 16 Hd31
Fleurville F 41 Jb44
Fleury F 63 Hb55
Fleury-la-Vallée F 32 Hb40
Fleury-les-Aubrais F 31 Gc40
Fleury-sur-Andelle F 21 Gb35
Fléville F 23 Ja35
Fleys F 32 Hc40
Flines-les-Raches F 15 Hb31
Flirey F 24 Jc36
Flixecourt F 21 Gd33
Flize F 23 Ja34
Flogny-la-Chapelle F 32 Hc39
Florac F 55 Hc51
Florange F 24 Jd35
Florennes B 16 Hd32
Florensac F 63 Hc55
Florenville B 23 Jb33
Flumet F 49 Ka46
Foissiat F 48 Jb45
Foix F 70 Gc56
Folelli F 72 Ma56
Folgensbourg F 35 Kc40
Foncine-le-Bas F 42 Jd44
Foncquevillers F 15 Ha32
Fons F 64 Ja53
Fonsorbes F 62 Gb54
Fontainebleau F 32 Ha38
Fontaine-Chalendray F 45 Fc46
Fontaine-de-Vaucluse F 65 Jc53
Fontaine-Française F 41 Jb41
Fontaine-la-Gaillarde F 32 Hb39
Fontaine-le-Bourg F 21 Gb34
Fontaine-le-Dun F 20 Ga34
Fontaine-les-Grès F 32 Hc38
Fontaines-en-Duesmois F 33 Jd40
Fontaine-sur-Coole F 33 Hd37
Fontain-l'Eveque B 16 Hd31

Fontan F 58 Kd52
Fontanes-du Causse F 54 Gc51
Fontanières F 47 Ha46
Fontenai-les-Louvets F 30 Fc38
Fontenay-le-Comte F 44 Fb45
Fontenay-le-Marmion F 20 Fc36
Fontenay-Trésigny F 32 Ha37
Fontenelle-en-Brie F 22 Hb36
Fontet F 53 Fc51
Fontette F 33 Ja39
Fontevraud-l'Abbaye F 38 Fd42
Font-Romeu F 70 Gd58
Fontvieille F 64 Jb53
Forbach F 24 Ka35
Forcalqueiret F 65 Ka54
Forcalquier F 65 Jd52
Forest-Montiers F 14 Gc32
Forgès F 54 Gc49
Forges-les-Eaux F 21 Gb34
Formerie F 21 Gc34
Formigny F 19 Fb35
Formiguères F 70 Gd57
Fortan F 30 Ga40
Fort-Mahon-Plage F 14 Gb32
Fos F 69 Ga56
Fossemagne F 54 Gb49
Fosses F 21 Gd36
Fosses-la-Ville B 16 Ja31
Fos-sur-Mer F 64 Jb54
Fouesnant F 26 Dc40
Fougeré F 38 Fc41
Fougères F 29 Fa38
Fougères-sur-Bièvre F 39 Gb41
Fougerolles F 34 Jd39
Fougerolles-du-Plessis F 29 Fb38
Fouilloy F 21 Gc34
Foulain F 33 Jb39
Foulayronnes F 53 Ga52
Fouligny F 24 Jd35
Fouquerolles F 21 Gd35
Fouras F 44 Fa46
Fourcamont F 21 Gb33
Fourcès F 61 Fd53
Fourchambault F 40 Hb43
Fourmies F 22 Hc33
Fournaudin F 32 Hc39
Fournels F 55 Hb50
Fournet F 43 Kb42
Fourques F 71 Hb57
Fours F 40 Hc43
Foussais F 37 Fb44
Frahier-et-Châtebier F 34 Ka40
Frais F 35 Kb40
Fraisse-sur-Agout F 63 Hb54
Fraize F 35 Kb40
Francaltreff F 24 Ka36
Francardo F 72 Ld57
Francescas F 61 Fd53
Francorchamps B 17 Jc31
Franeker NL 8 Jb22
Franekeradeel NL 8 Jb22
Frangy F 49 Jd46
Franqueville F 69 Ga56
Frasne F 42 Jd43
Frasnes-les-Buissenal B 15 Hb31
Frayssinet-le-Gélat F 54 Gb51
Frécourt F 34 Jc39
Fréhel F 28 Ec37
Freissinières F 58 Kb50
Fréjairolles F 62 Gd53
Fréjus F 66 Kb54
Frencq F 14 Gc31
Frenelle F 34 Jd38
Frenelles F 21 Gb35
Fresnay-sur-Sarthe F 30 Fd39

Fresne-Léguillon F 21 Gc35
Fresne-Saint-Mamès F 42 Jc41
Fresnes-au-Mont F 23 Jb36
Fresnes-en-Woëvre F 24 Jc35
Fresnes-sur-Apance F 34 Jc39
Fresnes-sur-les-Eaux F 15 Hb31
Fresnoy-en-Bassigny F 34 Jc39
Fresnoy-Folny F 21 Gb33
Fresnoyrand F 22 Hb33
Fresselines F 46 Gc45
Fretigney-et-Velloreille F 42 Jd41
Frétigny F 30 Ga38
Frettes F 34 Jc40
Frévent F 14 Gd32
Freyming-Merlebach F 24 Ka35
Frisange L 24 Jd34
Friville-Escarbotin F 21 Gb33
Frohen-le-Grand F 14 Gd32
Froidchapelle B 16 Hd32
Froissy F 21 Gd34
Fromentel F 30 Fc37
Fromentine F 36 Ec43
Frontenard F 41 Jb43
Frontenay-Rohan-Rohan F 44 Fb45
Frontenex F 49 Ka47
Frontignan F 64 Hd54
Fronton F 62 Gb53
Frossay F 36 Ec42
Frouard F 24 Jd36
Fruges F 14 Gd31
Fuans F 42 Ka42
Fumay F 23 Ja33
Fumel F 54 Gb51
Fussy F 40 Ha42

G

Gaanderen NL 13 Jc26
Gabarret F 61 Fc53
Gabas F 68 Fb56
Gabriac F 55 Hb51
Gacé F 30 Fd37
Gaël F 28 Ec39
Gaillac F 62 Gd53
Gaillefontaine F 21 Gc34
Gaillon F 21 Gb36
Galan F 61 Fd55
Galéria F 72 Lc57
Gallardon F 31 Gc38
Gallargues F 64 Ja53
Gamaches F 21 Gb33
Gambais F 31 Gc37
Gambsheim F 25 Kc36
Gan F 61 Fc55
Ganges F 64 Hd53
Gannat F 47 Hb46
Gannay-sur-Loire F 40 Hc44
Gap F 57 Ka50
Garancières F 31 Gc37
Gardanne F 65 Jd54
Garderen NL 12 Jb25
Gardonne F 53 Fd50
Gardouch F 62 Gc55
Garein F 60 Fb53
Garel F 21 Gb36
Gargilesse-Dampierre F 39 Gc44
Garlin F 61 Fc54
Garnat-sur-Engièvre F 40 Hc44
Garons F 64 Ja53
Gashy F 21 Gc35
Gasselte NL 9 Jd22
Gasselternijveen NL 9 Jd22
Gastes F 52 Fa52
Gastins F 32 Hb37

Gatheme F 29 Fb37
Gaubert F 31 Gc39
Gaurain-Ramecroix B 15 Hb31
Gavarnie F 69 Fc57
Gavray F 29 Fa37
Gâvres F 27 Ea40
Gazeran F 31 Gc37
Geaune F 61 Fc54
Geay F 38 Fc43
Gedinne B 23 Ja33
Gedre F 69 Fc57
Geel B 16 Ja29
Geertruidenberg NL 12 Ja27
Geldermalsen NL 12 Ja26
Geldrop NL 12 Jb28
Geleen NL 17 Jc29
Gelles F 47 Ha47
Gellin F 42 Jd43
Gelucourt F 24 Ka36
Gembloux sur-Orneau B 16 Hd31
Gemert NL 12 Jb28
Gémozac F 44 Fb48
Genappe B 16 Hd31
Genas F 48 Jb47
Gençay F 45 Fd45
Gendrey F 42 Jc42
Gendringen NL 13 Jc26
Gendt NL 13 Jc26
Genemuiden NL 9 Jc24
Générac F 64 Ja53
Geneston F 37 Ed43
Genevrières F 34 Jc40
Génicourt-sur-Meuse F 23 Jb36
Genillé F 39 Gb42
Génis F 46 Gb48
Genk B 16 Jb29
Genlis F 41 Jb42
Gennep NL 13 Jc27
Gennes F 38 Fc42
Génolhac F 56 Hd51
Genouillac F 46 Gd45
Genouillé F 45 Fd46
Gensac F 53 Fd50
Gent B 15 Hb29
Gentioux-Pigerolles F 46 Gd47
Ger F 29 Fb37
Geraardsbergen B 15 Hc30
Gérardmer F 34 Ka39
Géraudot F 33 Hd38
Gerberoy F 21 Gc34
Gerbéviller F 34 Ka37
Gergy F 41 Jb43
Germay F 33 Jb38
Germigny-des-Prés F 31 Gd40
Gerpinnes B 16 Hd31
Gerstheim F 35 Kc37
Gespunsart F 23 Ja33
Gesté F 37 Fa42
Gesties F 70 Gc57
Gèsves B 16 Ja31
Gévezé F 29 Ed39
Gevigney-et-Mercey F 34 Jc40
Gex F 49 Jd45
Ghislenghien B 15 Hc31
Ghisonaccia F 73 Ma58
Ghisoni F 73 Ld58
Giat F 47 Ha47
Gien F 32 Ha40
Giens F 65 Ka55
Gietelo NL 13 Jc25
Gieten NL 9 Jd22
Giethoorn NL 9 Jc23
Giffaumont-Champaubert F 33 Ja37
Gigean F 64 Hd54
Gignac F 63 Hc54
Gigny F 33 Hd40
Gigny F 42 Jc44
Gigors F 57 Ka51
Gigors-et-Luzeron F 56 Jb50
Gilley F 42 Ka42

Gilocourt F 22 Ha35
Gilze NL 12 Ja27
Gimel-les-Cascades F 46 Gc48
Gimont F 61 Ga54
Ginasservis F 65 Jd53
Ginestas F 63 Hb55
Gingelom B 16 Ja30
Girancourt F 34 Jd38
Girecourt-sur-Durbion F 34 Ka38
Girolata F 72 Lc57
Giromagny F 34 Ka40
Gironcourt-sur-Vraine F 34 Jc38
Gironville F 24 Jc36
Gisors F 21 Gc35
Gistel B 15 Ha29
Giverny F 21 Gc36
Givet F 16 Ja32
Givors F 48 Jb47
Givry B 15 Hc31
Givry F 41 Ja43
Givry-en-Argonne F 23 Ja36
Gizeux F 38 Fd42
Glainans F 42 Ka41
Glandieu F 49 Jc47
Glanerbrug NL 13 Jd25
Glanet F 37 Ed41
Glénic F 46 Gc45
Glère F 43 Kb41
Glomel F 27 Ea39
Glos-la-Ferrière F 30 Ga37
Goderville F 20 Fd34
Goes NL 11 Hc28
Goirle NL 12 Ja28
Golfe-Juan F 66 Kc53
Gombergean F 39 Gb41
Gomont F 23 Hd34
Goncelin F 49 Jd48
Goncourt F 34 Jc38
Gondrecourt-le-Château F 34 Jc37
Gondreville F 34 Jc37
Gondrin F 61 Fd53
Gonfaron F 65 Ka54
Gonfreville l'Orcher F 20 Fd35
Gonsans F 42 Jd42
Goor NL 13 Jd25
Gordes F 65 Jc53
Gorey GBJ 18 Ec36
Gorinchem NL 12 Ja26
Gorre F 46 Gb47
Gorredijk NL 9 Jc22
Gorron F 29 Fb38
Gorssel NL 13 Jc25
Gouarec F 27 Ea39
Gouda NL 12 Hd26
Goudargues F 64 Ja52
Gouesnou F 26 Dc36
Goulven F 26 Dc37
Gourdon F 54 Gb50
Gourdon F 66 Kc53
Gourgançon F 32 Hc37
Gourgé F 37 Fc44
Gourin F 27 Dd39
Gournay-en-Bray F 21 Gc35
Gournier F 57 Ka50
Gourville F 45 Fc47
Goussainville F 21 Gd36
Gouvy B 17 Jc32
Gouzeaucourt F 22 Hb33
Gouzon F 46 Gd45
Goven F 29 Ed39
Graauw NL 11 Hc28
Graçay F 39 Gc42
Gragnague F 62 Gc54
Grainville-Langannerie F 20 Fc36
Gramat F 54 Gc50
Gramont F 61 Ga53
Grand F 33 Jb38
Grand-Auverne F 37 Fa41
Grand-Bornand F 49 Ka46
Grandcamp-Maisy F 19 Fa35

Grand-Champ F 28 Eb40
Grandchamps F 32 Hb40
Grand-Couronne F 20 Ga35
Grand Crohot Océan F 52 Fa50
Grandecourt F 34 Jc40
Grandfontaine F 35 Kb37
Grand-Fort-Philippe F 14 Gc30
Grand-Fougeray F 29 Ed40
Grand Halleux B 17 Jc31
Grandpré F 23 Ja35
Grandrieu F 55 Hc50
Grand-Rullecourt F 14 Gd32
Grand-Vabre F 55 Ha51
Grandvelle-et-le-Perrenot F 42 Jd41
Grandvillars F 35 Kb40
Grandvilliers F 21 Gc34
Grane F 56 Jb50
Grange-le-Bocage F 32 Hb38
Granges-sur-Aube F 32 Hc37
Granges-sur-Vologne F 34 Ka38
Grans F 65 Jc54
Granville F 29 Ed37
Grasse F 66 Kc53
Gratens F 62 Gb55
Gratentour F 62 Gc54
Grau-d'Agde F 63 Hc55
Graulhet F 62 Gd54
Graulinster L 24 Jd33
Grave NL 12 Jb27
Gravelines F 14 Gc30
Gravendeel, ,s- NL 12 Hd27
Gravenhage, ,s- NL 11 Hc26
Gravenzande, ,s- NL 11 Hc26
Graveson F 64 Jb53
Gravigny F 21 Gb36
Gray F 42 Jc41
Grenade F 62 Gb54
Grenade-sur-l'Adour F 60 Fb54
Grenant F 34 Jc40
Grenoble F 49 Jd48
Grentzingen F 35 Kb40
Gréolières F 66 Kc53
Gréoux-les-Bains F 65 Jd53
Gresse-en-Vercors F 57 Jc49
Grésy-sur-Isère F 49 Ka47
Grevenmacher L 24 Jd33
Grézels F 54 Gb51
Grez-en-Bouère F 29 Fb40
Grèzes F 54 Gc51
Grignan F 56 Jb50
Grignols F 53 Fc52
Grignols F 53 Ga49
Grijpskerk NL 9 Jc22
Grimaud F 66 Kb54
Grimbergen B 16 Hd30
Grisolles F 62 Gb53
Grobbendonk B 16 Hd29
Groenlo NL 13 Jd25
Groesbeek NL 13 Jc27
Groix F 27 Dd41
Gron F 32 Hb39
Groningen NL 9 Jc22
Grootegast NL 9 Jc22
Grosbliederstroff F 24 Ka35
Grosbous L 24 Jc33
Grosbreuil F 37 Ed44
Grosseto Prugna F 73 Ld58
Grossouvre F 40 Hb43
Grostenquin F 24 Ka36
Grou NL 8 Jb22
Grubbenvorst NL 13 Jc28
Grues F 44 Fa45

Gruffy F 49 Jd46
Gruissan F 71 Hb56
Gruissan-Plage F 71 Hb56
Grury F 41 Hd44
Guagno F 72 Ld57
Gudmont-Villiers F 33 Jb38
Guebwiller F 35 Kb39
Guémar F 35 Kb38
Guémené-Penfao F 37 Ed41
Guémené-sur-Scorff F 27 Ea39
Guengat F 26 Dc39
Guenrout F 36 Ec41
Guer F 28 Ec40
Guérande F 36 Eb42
Guéret F 40 Gc46
Guérigny F 40 Hb42
Gües-d'Oloron F 60 Fb55
Gueugnon F 41 Hd44
Gugney-aux-Aulx F 34 Jd38
Guichen F 29 Ed40
Guignen F 29 Ed40
Guignes F 32 Ha37
Guillaumes F 58 Kb52
Guillestre F 58 Kb50
Guillos F 52 Fa51
Guilvinec F 26 Dc40
Guimiliau F 26 Dc38
Guînes F 14 Gc30
Guingamp F 27 Ea38
Guipavas F 26 Dc38
Guipry F 29 Ed40
Guipy F 40 Hc42
Guiscard F 22 Ha34
Guiscriff F 27 Dd39
Guise F 22 Hc33
Guitalens F 62 Gd54
Guîtres F 53 Fc49
Gujan-Mestras F 52 Fa51
Gurunhuel F 27 Ea38
Guyancourt F 31 Gd37
Gy F 42 Jc41
Gyé-sur-Seine F 33 Hd39

H

Haaksbergen NL 13 Jd25
Haarlem NL 12 Hd25
Habas F 60 Fa54
Habay-la-Neuve B 23 Jb33
Habère-Poche F 49 Ka45
Hadol F 34 Ka39
Haelen NL 13 Jc28
Hagetmau F 60 Fb54
Hagondange F 24 Jd35
Haguenau F 25 Kc36
Haillainville F 34 Ka38
Hainneville, Équeur-dreville- F 19 Ed34
Halen B 16 Ja27
Halle B 16 Hd30
Hallencourt F 21 Gc33
Halsteren NL 11 Hc28
Ham F 22 Ha34
Hambye F 19 Fa36
Hamoir B 16 Jb31
Hamois B 16 Ja31
Hamont B 12 Jb28
Ham-sur-Heure-Nalinnes B 16 Hd32
Hánanbihen F 28 Ec38
Hannut B 16 Ja27
Han-sur-Lesse B 16 Jb32
Han-sur-Nied F 24 Jd36
Hapert NL 12 Jb28
Harcourt F 20 Ga36
Hardelot-Plage F 14 Gb31
Hardenberg NL 9 Jd24
Harderwijk NL 12 Jc24
Harde, t' NL 8 Jb24
Hardinghen F 14 Gc30
Haren NL 9 Jd22
Hargimont B 16 Jb32
Hargnies F 16 Ja32

Harlingen NL 8 Ja22
Harnes F 15 Ha31
Haroué F 34 Jd37
Harskamp NL 12 Jb25
Hartennes F 22 Hb35
Harville F 24 Jc35
Haselbourg F 25 Kb36
Hasparren F 60 Fa55
Hasselt B 16 Jb29
Hasselt NL 9 Jc24
Hastiere-Lavaux B 16 Ja32
Hattem NL 9 Jc24
Hatten F 25 Kc36
Haubourdin F 15 Ha31
Haudainville F 23 Jb35
Haut-Asco F 72 Ld57
Hautefort F 54 Gb49
Hauteluce F 49 Ka46
Hauterives F 48 Jb48
Hauteville-Lompnès F 49 Jc46
Hauteville-Plage F 19 Ed36
Hautmont F 15 Hc32
Hautvillers F 22 Hc36
Havelange B 16 Jb31
Havelte NL 9 Jc24
Havenbuurt NL 8 Ja24
Haversin B 16 Ja32
Hayange F 24 Jc35
Hazebrouck F 14 Gd30
Hèches F 69 Fd56
Hechtel-Eksel B 16 Jb29
Hédé F 29 Ed39
Heel NL 13 Jc28
Heemskerk NL 8 Hd24
Heemstede NL 12 Hd25
Heerde NL 9 Jc24
Heerenberg, s'- NL 13 Jc26
Heerenveen NL 8 Jb23
Heerhugowaard NL 8 Hd24
Heerlen NL 17 Jc29
Heers B 16 Jb30
Heesch NL 12 Jb27
Heeten NL 13 Jc25
Heeze NL 12 Jb28
Hefshuizen NL 9 Jd22
Heiderscheid L 24 Jc33
Heiligerlee NL 9 Jd22
Heilitz-le-Maurupt F 33 Ja37
Heiloo NL 8 Hd24
Heino NL 9 Jc24
Heist-op-den-Berg B 16 Hd29
Helden NL 13 Jc28
Héliopolis F 66 Kb55
Hellendoorn NL 9 Jc24
Hellevoetsluis NL 11 Hc27
Hellimer F 24 Ka36
Helmdange L 24 Jd33
Helmond NL 12 Jb28
Hemiksem B 16 Hd29
Héming F 34 Ka37
Hendaye F 60 Ec55
Hengelo NL 13 Jc26
Hengelo NL 13 Jd25
Hengevelde NL 13 Jd25
Hénin-Beaumont F 15 Ha31
Hennebont F 27 Ea40
Henrichemont F 40 Ha42
Herbault F 39 Gb41
Herbeumont B 23 Jb33
Herbignac F 36 Ec41
Herbisse F 33 Hd37
Herbitzheim F 25 Kb35
Herent B 16 Hd30
Herentals B 16 Ja29
Hérépian F 63 Hb54
Héric F 37 Ed41
Héricourt F 34 Ka42
Hericourt-en-Caux F 20 Ga34
Hérimoncourt F 43 Kb41
Hérisson F 40 Ha44
Herk-de-Stad B 16 Ja29

Herlies F 15 Ha31
Herm F 60 Fa53
Herment F 47 Ha47
Hermes F 21 Gd35
Herpont F 23 Ja36
Herrere F 68 Fb56
Herry F 40 Hb42
Herselt B 16 Ja29
Hertogenbosch, s'- NL 12 Jb27
Herve B 17 Jc30
Hesdin F 14 Gc32
Hesperange L 24 Jd34
Hettange-Grande F 24 Jd34
Heuchin F 14 Gd31
Heumen NL 12 Jb26
Heusden NL 12 Jb27
Heusden-Zolder B 16 Jb29
Hevilliers F 33 Jb37
Heyrieux F 48 Jb47
Hierden NL 12 Jb25
Hiersac F 45 Fc47
Hillegom NL 12 Hd25
Hillion F 28 Eb38
Hilsenheim F 35 Kc38
Hilvarenbeek NL 12 Ja28
Hilversum NL 12 Ja27
Hindeloopen NL 8 Ja23
Hippolytushoef NL 8 Ja23
Hirel F 29 Ed38
Hirsingue F 35 Kb40
Hirson F 22 Hc33
Hirtzfelden F 35 Kc39
Hoegaarden B 16 Ja30
Hoek NL 11 Hc28
Hoek van Holland NL 11 Hc26
Hoenderloo NL 12 Jb25
Hoeselt B 16 Jb30
Hoffen F 25 Kc36
Hogne B 16 Jb32
Hollange B 24 Jc33
Hollenfels L 24 Jc33
Hollum NL 8 Jb21
Holten NL 13 Jc25
Holwerd NL 8 Jb21
Hombourg-Budange F 24 Jd35
Hombourg-Haut F 24 Ka35
Hommerts NL 8 Jb23
Homps F 63 Ha54
Hondelange B 24 Jc34
Hondschoote F 14 Gd30
Honfleur F 20 Fd35
Hoofddorp NL 12 Hd25
Hoofdplaat NL 11 Hb28
Hoogerheide NL 12 Hd28
Hoogersmilde NL 9 Jc23
Hoogeveen NL 9 Jc23
Hoogezand-Sappemeer NL 9 Jd22
Hooge Zwaluwe NL 12 Hd27
Hooghalen NL 9 Jc23
Hoogkarspel NL 8 Ja24
Hoogkerk NL 9 Jc22
Hoogstade B 15 Ha30
Hoogstraten B 12 Hd28
Hoorn NL 8 Ja24
Hôpital-Camfrout F 26 Dc38
Hornoy-le-Bourg F 21 Gc33
Horntje, t' NL 8 Hd23
Horst NL 13 Jc28
Hortes F 34 Jc40
Hoscheid L 17 Jc32
Hospice de France F 69 Ga57
Hossegor F 60 Ed54
Hostens F 52 Fb51
Hotton B 16 Jb32
Houdain F 14 Gd31
Houdan F 31 Gc37
Houdelaincourt F 33 Jb37
Houeillès F 53 Fd52
Houetteville F 21 Gb36

Houffalize B 17 Jc32
Houlgate F 20 Fc35
Hourtin F 52 Fa49
Hourtin-Plage F 52 Fa49
Houssay F 29 Fb40
Houten NL 12 Ja26
Houthalen-Helchteren B 16 Jb29
Houwerzijl NL 9 Jc21
Houyet B 16 Ja32
Huchet F 60 Ed53
Hucqueliers F 14 Gc31
Huelgoat F 27 Dd38
Huillécourt F 34 Jc39
Huissen NL 13 Jc26
Huizen NL 12 Ja25
Hulst NL 11 Hc28
Humes-Jorquenay F 33 Jb39
Hummelo NL 13 Jc26
Hunawihr F 35 Kb38
Hunspach F 25 Kc35
Huparlac F 55 Ha50
Huppy F 21 Gc33
Hurdegaraw NL 8 Jb22
Huriel F 47 Ha45
Huy B 16 Jb31
Hyenville F 19 Fa36
Hyères F 65 Ka55
Hyères-Plage F 65 Ka55
Hyet F 42 Jd41
Hymont F 34 Jd38

I

Ieper B 15 Ha30
Iffendic F 28 Ec39
Igé F 48 Ja45
Igny-Comblizy F 22 Hc36
Iholdy F 60 Fa55
IJmuiden NL 8 Hd24
IJsselmuiden NL 8 Jb24
IJsselstein NL 12 Ja26
IJzendijke NL 11 Hb28
Île de Fédrun F 36 Ec42
Ille-sur-Têt F 71 Ha56
Illiers-Combray F 31 Gb39
Illkirch-Graffenstaden F 35 Kc37
Illois F 21 Gc34
Illzach F 35 Kb39
Imphy F 40 Hb43
Incourt B 16 Ja30
Ingelmunster B 15 Hb30
Ingrandes F 37 Fb42
Ingrandes F 38 Ga44
Ingwiller F 25 Kb36
Inor F 23 Jb34
Insming F 24 Ka36
Irissarry F 60 Fa55
Irvillac F 26 Dc38
Isdes F 39 Gd41
Isigny-le-Buat F 29 Fa38
Isigny-sur-Mer F 19 Fa35
Isles-sur-Suippe F 23 Hd35
Isola F 58 Kc51
Isola 2000 F 58 Kc51
Isigeac F 53 Ga50
Issoire F 47 Hb47
Issoudun F 39 Gd43
Is-sur-Tille F 41 Jb41
Issy-l'Evêque F 41 Hd44
Istres F 64 Jb54
Iville F 20 Ga36
Ivry-la-Bataille F 31 Gb37
Iwuy F 15 Hb32
Izeaux F 49 Jc48
Izegem B 15 Hb30
Izernore F 49 Jc45
Izon F 53 Fc50

J

Jabbeke B 15 Ha29
Jaligny-sur-Besbre F 47 Hc45
Jallais F 37 Fb42

Jâlons F 23 Hd36
Jametz F 23 Jb34
Jamoigne B 23 Jb33
Janaillat F 46 Gc46
Janville F 31 Gc39
Jarcieu F 48 Jb48
Jard-sur-Mer F 44 Ed45
Jargeau F 31 Gd40
Jarnac F 45 Fc47
Jarnages F 46 Gd45
Jarny F 24 Jc35
Jars F 40 Ha41
Jarzé F 38 Fc41
Jauge F 52 Fb51
Jaulnay F 38 Fd43
Jausiers F 58 Kb51
Javerlhac-et-la-Chapelle-Saint-Robert F 45 Ga48
Javron F 30 Fc38
Jeantes F 22 Hc33
Jégun F 61 Fd54
Jemelle B 16 Jb32
Jemeppe-sur-Sambre B 16 Hd31
Jenlain F 15 Hb32
Jenzat F 47 Hb45
Jésonville F 34 Jd39
Jeugny F 33 Hd39
Jeumont F 15 Hc32
Jeurre F 42 Jc44
Jodoigne B 16 Ja30
Joigny F 32 Hb39
Joinville F 33 Jb38
Joncherey F 35 Kb40
Jonchery F 33 Jb39
Jonchery-sur-Vesle F 22 Hc35
Joncy F 41 Ja44
Jonquières F 64 Jb52
Jonvelle F 34 Jc40
Jonzac F 45 Fc48
Jonzier F 49 Jd45
Josnes F 31 Gc40
Josselin F 28 Ec40
Joué-Etiau F 37 Fb42
Joué-lès-Tours F 38 Ga42
Joué-sur-Erdre F 37 Fa41
Jouet-sur-l'Aubois F 40 Hb43
Jougne F 42 Ka43
Jouhet F 45 Ga46
Jouix F 46 Gd48
Jouques F 65 Jd53
Joure NL 8 Jb23
Journy F 14 Gc30
Joux-la-Ville F 40 Hc41
Jouy-le-Châtel F 32 Hb37
Jouy-le-Potier F 31 Gc40
Joyeuse F 56 Ja51
Juan-les-Pins F 66 Kc53
Jublains F 29 Fb39
Jugon-les-Lacs F 28 Ec38
Jugy F 41 Jb44
Juigné-des-Moutiers F 37 Fa41
Juillac F 46 Gb48
Juilly F 22 Ha36
Julianadorp NL 8 Hd23
Jullouville F 29 Ed37
Jumeaux F 47 Hc48
Jumilhac-le-Grand F 46 Gb48
Junglinster L 24 Jd33
Juniville F 23 Hd35
Jupilles F 30 Fd40
Juprelle B 16 Jb30
Jurbise B 15 Hc31
Juré F 48 Hd46
Jurignac F 45 Fc48
Jussac F 55 Ha49
Jussey F 34 Jc40
Jussy-Champagne F 40 Ha43
Jussy-le-Chaudrier F 40 Hb42
Jutigny F 32 Hb38
Juvigné F 29 Fa40
Juvigny-en-Perthois F 33 Jb37

K

Kalmthout B 12 Hd28
Kampen NL 8 Jb24
Kapellen B 12 Hd28
Kaprijke B 15 Hb29
Kaster B 15 Hb30
Kasterlee B 12 Ja28
Katwijk an Zee NL 12 Hd25
Kaysersberg F 35 Kb38
Keerbergen B 16 Hd29
Kelmis B 17 Jc30
Kemmel B 15 Ha30
Kerauzern F 27 Ea37
Kergrist-Moëlou F 27 Ea38
Kérien F 27 Ea38
Kérity F 26 Dc40
Kerkrade NL 17 Jc29
Kernascléden F 27 Ea39
Kessel NL 13 Jc28
Kesteren NL 12 Jb26
Ketelhaven NL 8 Jb24
Kingersheim F 35 Kb39
Kinrooi B 16 Jb29
Klaaswaal NL 12 Hd27
Klosterhaar NL 9 Jd24
Klundert NL 12 Hd27
Knesselare B 15 Hb29
Knokke-Heist B 11 Hb28
Koekelare B 15 Ha29
Kœnigsmacker F 24 Jd34
Koersel B 16 Jb29
Koetschette L 24 Jc33
Kœtzinge F 35 Kc40
Koksijde-Bad B 14 Gd29
Kollum NL 9 Jc21
Kontich B 16 Hd29
Kootwijk NL 12 Jb25
Kortemark B 15 Ha29
Kortenaken B 16 Ja30
Kortessem B 16 Jb30
Kortgene NL 11 Hc28
Kortrijk B 15 Hb30
Koudekerke NL 11 Hb28
Koudum NL 8 Ja23
Kreileroord NL 8 Ja23
Krimpen aan de IJssel NL 12 Hd26
Kruibeke B 16 Hd29
Kruishoutem B 15 Hb30
Kruth F 35 Kb39
Kuinre NL 8 Jb23

L

Laarne B 15 Hc29
la Bade F 55 Ha49
Labalme F 49 Jc45
la Balme-de-Sillingy F 49 Jd46
la Barre-en-Ouche F 20 Ga36
la Barthe-de-Neste F 69 Fd56
la Bassée F 15 Ha31
la Bastide F 66 Kb53
Labastide-Beauvoir F 62 Gc54
Labastide-Clairence F 60 Fa55
Labastide-d'Armagnac F 61 Fc53
la Bastide-de-Lordat F 70 Gc56
la Bastide-des-Jourdans F 65 Jd53
Labastide-Murat F 54 Gc51
la Bastide-Puylaurent F 56 Hd51

Labastide-Rouairoux – la Roque-d'Anthéron

Labastide-Rouairoux F 63 Ha54
Labastide-Saint-Pierre F 62 Gb53
la Bathie F 49 Ka47
la Bâtie-Neuve F 57 Ka50
la Baule F 36 Ec42
la Bazoche-Gouet F 30 Ga39
la Bazoge F 30 Fd39
l'Abbaye F 64 Hc49
Labeaume F 56 Ja51
Labège F 62 Gc54
la Bégude-Blanche F 65 Ka52
Labenne F 60 Ed54
Labenne-Océan F 60 Ed54
la Bérade F 57 Ka49
la Bernerie-en-Retz F 36 Ec43
l'Aber-Wrac'h F 26 Db37
Lablachère F 56 Ja51
la Bocca F 66 Kc54
la Boissière F 20 Fd36
la Bonneville-sur-Iton F 21 Gb36
Laborel F 57 Jd51
la Borne F 40 Ha42
La Bouëxière F 29 Fa39
Labouheyre F 52 Fa52
la Bouille F 20 Ga35
la Bourboule F 47 Ha47
Laboutarie F 62 Gd53
la Boutière F 49 Jd48
l'Abre F 45 Jc42
la Bresse F 34 Ka39
la Bridoire F 49 Jd47
la Brillanne F 65 Jd52
Labrit F 52 Fb52
Labrousse F 46 Gb46
la Broye F 14 Gc32
la Bruffière F 37 Fa43
Labruguière F 62 Gd54
La Bruyère B 16 Ja31
l'Absie F 37 Fb44
la Burbanche F 49 Jc46
la Bussière F 32 Ha40
la Butte F 38 Fc43
la Caillère F 37 Fb44
la Calmet F 44 Aa53
Lacanau F 52 Fa50
Lacanau-Océan F 52 Fa49
la Canourgue F 55 Hb51
la Capelle F 22 Hc33
la Capelle F 46 Hc51
la Capelle-lès-Boulogne F 14 Gc31
Lacapelle-Marival F 54 Gd50
Lacapelle-Viescamp F 54 Gd50
Lacaune F 63 Ha54
la Cavalerie F 63 Hb53
Lacave F 54 Gc50
Lac de Tignes F 50 Kb47
Lacelle F 46 Gc47
la Celle-Dunoise F 46 Gc45
la Celle-en-Morvan F 41 Hd43
la Celle-Saint-Avant F 38 Ga43
la Chaise-Dieu F 47 Hc48
la Chaize F 37 Fa44
la Chaize-Giraud F 37 Ed44
la Chambre F 49 Ka48
la Champenoise F 39 Gc43
Lachamp Raphaël F 56 Ja50
la Chapelaude F 47 Ha45
La Chapelle F 23 Ja33
la Chapelle F 49 Ka47
la-Chapelle-au-Riboul F 30 Fc38
la Chapelle-aux-Chasses F 40 Hc44

Lachapelle-aux-Pots F 21 Gc35
la Chapelle-Bertrand F 38 Fc44
la Chapelle-Bouëxic F 29 Ed40
la Chapelle-d'Angillon F 39 Gd42
la Chapelle-du-Bois F 30 Ga39
la Chapelle-du-Chêne F 29 Fb39
la Chapelle-du-Noyer F 31 Gb39
la Chapelle-en-Valgaudemar F 57 Ka49
la Chapelle-en-Vercors F 57 Jc49
la Chapelle-Faucher F 45 Ga48
La Chapelle-Glain F 37 Fa41
la Chapelle-la-Reine F 32 Ha38
la Chapelle-Laurent F 55 Hb49
la Chapelle-Montreuil F 38 Fd44
la Chapelle-Rainsoui F 29 Fb39
la Chapelle-Saint-André F 40 Hb41
la Chapelle-Saint-Géraud F 54 Gd49
la Chapelle-Saint-Laurent F 37 Fb44
la Chapelle-Saint-Quillain F 42 Jc41
Lachapelle-sous-Rougemont F 35 Kb40
la Chapelle-Vendômoise F 39 Gb41
la Chapelle Verlain F 45 Ga48
la Chapelle-Vicomtesse F 31 Gb40
la Chapelle-Yvon F 20 Fd36
la Chapelotte F 40 Ha42
la Charce F 57 Jc51
la Charité-sur-Loire F 40 Hb42
la Chartre-sur-le-Loir F 30 Ga40
la Châtaigneraie F 37 Fb44
la Châtelaine F 42 Jd43
la Châtre F 39 Gd44
la Châtre-Langlin F 46 Gb45
la Chaudière F 57 Jc50
la Chaume F 37 Ed44
la Chavade F 56 Hd50
la Cheppe F 23 Hd36
La Chèze F 28 Eb39
la Ciotat F 65 Jd55
la Clayette F 48 Ja45
la Clisse F 44 Fd50
la Clusaz F 49 Ka46
la Cluse F 49 Jc46
la Cluse F 57 Jd50
la Cluse-et-Mijoux F 42 Ka43
la Combe F 49 Jc47
la Coquille F 46 Gb48
la Côte-Saint-André F 49 Jc48
la Cotinière F 44 Fa46
la Couarde-sur-Mer F 44 Fa44
la Couronne F 45 Fd47
Lacourt F 70 Gb56
la Courtine F 46 Gd47
Lacq F 60 Fb55
la Crèche F 45 Fd45
Lacroix F 22 Hd35
la Croix-aux-Bois F 23 Ja34
la Croix-Avranchin F 29 Fa38
Lacroix-Barrez F 55 Ha50

La Croixille F 29 Fa39
La Croix-Laurent F 37 Ed41
Lacroix-sur-Meuse F 23 Jb36
La Croix-Valmer F 66 Kb55
la Cure F 42 Jd44
Ladapeyre F 46 Gd45
Ladignac F 46 Gb47
Ladon F 32 Ha39
la Douze F 53 Ga49
la Drée F 41 Ja43
Laduz F 32 Hb40
la Faurie F 57 Jd50
la Favière F 58 Kb51
Feclaz F 49 Jd47
la Fère F 22 Hb34
la Ferière-en-Parthenay F 38 Fc44
la Ferrière F 37 Fa44
la Ferrière F 49 Ka48
la Ferrière-aux-Étangs F 29 Fb37
la-Ferrière-sur-Risle F 20 Ga36
la Ferté F 41 Ja44
la Ferté-Alais F 31 Gd38
la Ferté-Bernard F 30 Ga39
la Ferté-Frênel F 30 Fd37
la Ferté-Gaucher F 32 Hb37
la Ferté-Imbault F 39 Gc42
la Ferté-Loupière F 32 Hb40
La Ferté-Macé F 30 Fc38
la Ferté-Milon F 22 Hb36
La Ferté-Saint-Aubin F 31 Gc40
la Ferté-Saint-Cyr F 39 Gc41
la Ferté-sous-Jouarre F 22 Hb36
Laferté-sur-Amance F 34 Jc40
Laferté-sur-Aube F 33 Ja39
la Ferté-Vidame F 30 Ga38
la Feuillie F 21 Gb35
Laffitte F 62 Gb53
la Flèche F 38 Fc41
la Flotte F 44 Fa46
la Fontaine-Saint-Martin F 30 Fc40
la Force F 53 Fd50
la Forêt-Fouesnant F 26 Dc40
la Forêt-Sainte-Croix F 31 Gd38
la Forêt-sur-Sèyre F 37 Fb44
la Forie F 47 Hc47
la Fouillade F 54 Gd52
la Fourche F 41 Ja44
la Foux-d'Allos F 58 Kb51
Lafrançaise F 54 Gb53
la Freissinouse F 57 Jd50
la Frette F 49 Jc48
La Gacilly F 28 Ec40
la Garde F 55 Hc50
la Garde F 66 Ka55
la Garde-Adhémar F 56 Jb51
la Garde-Freinet F 66 Kb54
la Garde-Guérin F 56 Hd51
la Gaubretière F 37 Fa44
Lage Mierde NL 12 Ja28
Lagnieu F 49 Jc46
Lagny F 22 Ha34
Lagny-sur-Marne F 32 Ha37
la Godivelle F 47 Hb48
la Goutelle F 47 Ha47
la Grand-Combe F 64 Hd52
la Grand-Croix F 48 Ja47
la Grande-Motte F 64 Hd54

la Grande-Motte F 64 Ja54
Lagrasse F 71 Ha56
la Grave F 40 Ha44
la Grave F 57 Ka49
la Gravelle F 30 Fd38
la Grolle F 37 Ed44
la Guerche-de-Bretagne F 29 Fa40
la Guerche-sur-l'Aubois F 40 Hb43
la Guérinière F 36 Ec43
Laguiole F 55 Hb50
Lahamaide B 15 Hc30
Laharie F 60 Fa53
La Haye-du-Puits F 19 Ed35
la Haye-Pesnel F 29 Fa37
la Hérie-la-Viéville F 22 Hc33
la Herlière F 14 Gd32
Laheycourt F 23 Ja36
la Hulpe B 16 Hd30
la Hutte F 30 Fd39
l'Aigle F 30 Ga37
Laigné F 29 Fb40
Laignes F 33 Hd40
l'Aiguillon-sur-Mer F 44 Fa45
Lailly-en-Val F 31 Gc40
Laimont F 23 Ja36
Laissac F 55 Hb51
Laives F 41 Jb44
Laize-la-Ville F 20 Fc36
la Javie F 65 Ka52
la Jonchère-Saint-Maurice F 46 Gc46
Lalacelle F 30 Fc38
Lalandelle F 21 Gc35
la Latette F 42 Jd43
Lalbenque F 54 Gc52
l'Albaron F 64 Ja54
Lalevade-d'Ardèche F 56 Ja50
Lalinde F 53 Ga50
Lalleu F 29 Ed40
Laloeuf F 34 Jd37
la Londe-les-Maures F 65 Ka55
la Loupe F 31 Gb38
Lalouvesc F 56 Ja49
La Louvière B 16 Hd31
l'Alpe-d'Huez F 57 Ka49
Laluque F 60 Fa53
la Maçana AND 70 Gb57
la Machine F 40 Hc43
la Madelaine F 19 Fa35
la Madeleine-Bouvet F 30 Ga38
Lamaids F 47 Ha45
la Main F 42 Ka42
la Malène F 55 Hc52
la Malmaison F 22 Hc34
Lamalou-les-Bains F 63 Hb54
Lamanère F 71 Ha58
Lamarche F 34 Jc40
Lamargelle F 41 Ja41
la Marolle-en-Sologne F 39 Gc41
Lamarque F 52 Fb49
la Martyre F 26 Dc38
Lamastre F 56 Ja49
Lamballe F 28 Eb39
Lambesc F 65 Jc53
La Meilleraye-de-Bretagne F 37 Fa41
l'Amelie-sur-Mer F 44 Fa48
la Membrolle-sur-Longuenée F 37 Fb41
la Merlatière F 37 Fa44
la Milesse F 30 Fd39
Lamnay F 30 Ga39
la Môle F 66 Kb55
la Mongie F 69 Fc56
Lamontgie F 47 Hc49
la Mothe-Achard F 37 Ed44
la Mothe-Saint-Héray F 45 Fc45

La Motte F 28 Eb39
la Motte F 22 Ha35
la Motte F 57 Ka51
Lamotte-Beuvron F 39 Gd41
la Motte-Bourbon F 38 Fc43
la Motte-Chalancon F 57 Jc51
la Motte-d'Aigues F 65 Jd53
la Motte-Saint-Martin F 57 Jd49
Lamotte-Warfusée F 22 Ha33
Lampaul F 26 Da38
Lampaul-Guimiliau F 26 Dc38
Lampaul-Plouarzel F 26 Db38
la Mure F 57 Jd49
Lamure-sur-Azergues F 48 Ja46
Lanaken B 16 Jb29
la Napoule F 66 Kc54
Lanarce F 56 Hd51
Lancin F 49 Jc47
Lançon-Provence F 65 Jc53
Landaul F 27 Ea40
Landaville-la-Haut F 34 Jc38
Landéan F 29 Fa38
Landeleau F 27 Dd39
Landen B 16 Ja30
Landepereuse F 20 Ga36
Landerneau F 26 Dc38
Landerum NL 8 Ja21
Landévant F 27 Ea40
Landévennec F 26 Dc38
Landgraaf NL 17 Jc29
Landiras F 52 Fb51
Landivisiau F 26 Dc38
Landivy F 29 Fa38
Landos F 56 Hd50
Landouzy-la-Ville F 22 Hc33
Landrecies F 15 Hc32
Landres F 24 Jc36
Landudec F 26 Db39
la Neuville-en-Tourne-à-Fuy F 23 Hd35
Langeac F 55 Hc49
Langeais F 38 Fd42
Langedijk NL 8 Hd24
Langemark B 15 Ha30
Langennerie F 38 Ga41
Langey F 31 Gb39
Langogne F 56 Hd50
Langoiran F 53 Fc51
Langon F 53 Fc51
Langonnet F 27 Dd39
Langres F 33 Jb40
Languidic F 27 Ea40
Lanhélin F 29 Ed38
Lanhouaumeau F 26 Dc37
Lanildut F 26 Db38
Lanloup F 27 Ea37
Lanmeur F 27 Dd37
Lannéanou F 27 Dd38
Lannemezan F 69 Fd56
Lanneray F 31 Gb39
Lannilis F 26 Db37
Lannion F 27 Ea37
la Nocle-Maulaix F 40 Hc43
Lanouaille F 46 Gb48
Lans-en-Vercors F 57 Jc49
Lanslebourg-Mont-Cenis F 50 Kb48
Lanslevillard F 50 Kb48
Lanta F 62 Gc54
Lantenay F 41 Ja41
Lanterot F 34 Jd40
Lantosque F 58 Kd52
Lanuéjols F 55 Hc52
Lanvellec F 27 Dd37
Lanvéoc F 26 Db38
Lanvollon F 27 Ea37

Laon F 22 Hc34
Laons F 31 Gb37
la Pacaudière F 48 Hd45
Lapalisse F 47 Hc45
la Palmyre F 44 Fa47
la Palud-sur-Verdon F 65 Ka53
Lapan F 39 Gd43
la Paquelais F 37 Ed42
Laparade F 53 Fd52
la Petite-Pierre F 25 Kb36
Lapeyrade F 61 Fc53
la Peyrade F 64 Hd54
Lapeyrouse F 47 Hb45
la Pezade F 63 Hc53
la Pierre F 57 Jd51
la Pierre-Percée F 40 Hb44
la Plagne F 50 Kb47
la Plaine F 37 Fb43
la Plaine-sur-Mer F 36 Ec42
la Planchette F 49 Ka48
Lapleau F 46 Gd48
Laplume F 53 Ga52
la Porta F 72 Ma56
Lapouyade F 53 Fc49
la Praye F 41 Hd44
la Preste F 71 Ha58
la Primaube F 55 Ha52
la Puye F 38 Ga44
la Quintaine F 63 Ha53
Laragne-Montéglin F 57 Jd51
la Raille F 58 Kb50
l'Arbresle F 48 Ja46
Larceveau F 60 Fa55
Larchant F 32 Ha38
Larche F 54 Gd49
Lardy F 31 Gd38
Laren NL 12 Ja25
Laren NL 13 Jc25
la Réole F 53 Fc51
Largentière F 56 Ja51
l'Argentière-la-Bessée F 58 Kb49
la Rivière-Thibouville F 20 Ga36
Larmor-Plage F 27 Ea40
la Robine F 65 Ka52
la Rochebeaucourt-et-Argentine F 45 Fd49
La-Roche-Bernard F 36 Ec41
la Roche-Chalais F 53 Fc49
la Roche-de Rame F 58 Kb50
la Roche-Derrien F 27 Ea37
la Roche-des-Arnauds F 57 Jd50
La Roche-en-Ardenne B 16 Jb32
la Rochefoucauld F 45 Fd47
la Roche-Guyon F 21 Gc36
la Rochelle F 44 Fa46
Larochemillay F 41 Hd43
la Roche-Morey F 34 Jc40
la Roche-Posay F 38 Ga44
la Rochepot F 41 Ja43
la Roche-sur-Foron F 49 Ka45
la Roche-sur-Yon F 37 Ed44
la Rochette F 49 Ka47
la Rochette F 58 Kc52
Larochette L 24 Jd33
la Roë F 29 Fa40
la Romagne F 37 Fa43
la Romieu F 61 Ga53
la Ronde F 44 Fa45
Laroquebrou F 54 Gd50
Laroquebrussane F 65 Ka54
la Roque-d'Anthéron F 65 Jc53

Laroque-de-Fa F 71 Ha56
Laroque-d'Olmes F 70 Gd56
la Roque-Gageac F 54 Gb50
la Roque-sur-Cèze F 64 Ja52
Laroque-Timbaut F 53 Ga52
la Rosière 1850 F 50 Kb47
Larrazet F 62 Gb53
Larressingle F 61 Fd53
Larroque F 61 Ga55
Larroque F 62 Gc53
Laruns F 68 Fb56
Lasalle F 64 Hd52
la Salle F 34 Ka38
la Salle-de-Vihiers F 37 Fb42
la Salvetat-Peyralès F 54 Gd52
la Salvetat-Saint-Gilles F 62 Gb54
la Salvetat-sur-Agout F 63 Ha54
la Saulce F 57 Ka51
la-Saulsotte F 32 Hb38
la Sauve F 53 Fc50
la Sauvetat-du-Dropt F 53 Fd51
la Selle-sur-le-Bied F 32 Ha39
la Selve F 55 Ha52
la Serre F 46 Gd48
la Seyne-sur-Mer F 65 Ka55
la Source F 31 Gc40
la Souterraine F 46 Gc45
Lassay-les-Châteaux F 29 Fb38
Lasseube F 60 Fb55
Lassigny F 22 Ha34
Lastic F 47 Ha47
la Suze-sur-Sarthe F 30 Fd40
la Tannière F 29 Fa38
la Terrasse-sur Dorlay F 48 Ja48
la Teste F 52 Fa51
Lathus F 45 Ga45
Latillé F 38 Fd44
Latoue F 69 Ga56
la Tour-Blanche F 45 Fd48
la Tour-d'Aigues F 65 Jd53
la Tour-d'Auvergne F 47 Ha48
Latour-de-Carol F 70 Gd58
la Tour-du-Pin F 49 Jc47
la Tour-Fondue F 65 Ka55
la Toussuire F 49 Ka48
la Tranche-sur-Mer F 44 Ed45
la Tremblade F 44 Fa47
Latresne F 52 Fb50
la Trimouille F 46 Gb45
La Trinité-Porhoët F 28 Eb39
Latronquière F 54 Gd50
Lattrop NL 9 Jd24
la Turballe F 36 Eb42
la Turbie F 67 Kd53
Laubert F 55 Hc51
Laubrières F 29 Fa40
Laudun F 64 Jb52
Laugnac F 53 Ga52
Laujuzan F 61 Fd53
Launac F 62 Gb54
Launaguet F 62 Gc54
Launois-sur-Vence F 23 Hd34
Laurenan F 28 Eb39
Laurière F 46 Gc46
Laussac F 55 Ha50
Lautenbach F 35 Kb39
Lauterbourg F 25 Kd35
Lautrec F 62 Gd54
Lauwersoog NL 9 Jc21

Lauzerte F 54 Gb52
Lauzun F 53 Fd51
la Vacherie F 57 Jc49
Laval F 29 Fb39
Laval-Atger F 56 Hd50
Lavaldens F 57 Jd49
la Valette F 57 Jd49
la Valette-du-Var F 65 Ka55
Laval-Roquecézière F 63 Ha53
Lavardac F 53 Fd52
Lavardens F 61 Ga54
Lavardin F 30 Ga40
Lavaré F 30 Ga39
la Varenne F 37 Fa42
Lavaudieu F 47 Hc48
Lavaufranche F 46 Gd45
Lavaur F 62 Gd54
Lavau-sur-Loire F 36 Ec42
Lavelanet F 70 Gd56
Laventie F 15 Ha31
Lavercantière F 54 Gb51
la Verdière F 65 Ka53
la Verrie F 37 Fa43
Laversines F 21 Gd35
Laveyssière F 53 Fd50
la Vieille-Lyre F 30 Ga37
la Ville-aux-Clercs F 31 Gb40
la Villedieu F 45 Fc46
la Villedieu F 46 Gc47
Lavilledieu F 56 Ja51
la Villedieu-du-Clain F 45 Fd45
la Villedieu-en-Fontenette F 34 Jd40
la Villeneuve F 47 Ha46
Lavit-de-Lomagne F 61 Ga53
la Voulte-sur-Rhône F 56 Jb50
Lavoûte-Chilhac F 55 Hc49
Lavoûte-sur-Loire F 56 Hd49
Lavoux F 38 Ga44
la Vrine F 42 Ka42
la Wantzenau F 25 Kc36
Layrac F 53 Ga52
le Bailleul F 30 Fc40
le Barcarés F 71 Hb57
le Barp F 52 Fb51
le Bastit F 54 Gc50
le Béage F 56 Hd50
le Beausset F 65 Jd55
le Bec-Hellouin F 20 Ga35
le Bégude-de-Mazenc F 56 Jb51
le Bessat F 48 Ja48
Lebiez F 14 Gc31
le Biot F 49 Ka45
le Blanc F 39 Gb44
le Bleymard F 56 Hd51
le Bleymard-Mont-Lozère F 56 Hd51
le Bodéo F 28 Eb38
le Bois F 50 Kb47
le Bois-d'Oingt F 48 Ja46
le Boréon F 58 Kc52
le Bosquet-d'Orb F 63 Hb54
le Boulay F 37 Fa41
le Boulou F 71 Hb57
le Bourg F 54 Gd50
le Bourg-d'Oisans F 57 Jd49
le Bourget-du-Lac F 49 Jd47
le Bourgneuf-la-Forêt F 29 Fb39
le Breil-sur-Mérize F 30 Fd40
le Breuil F 31 Gb38
le Breuil F 47 Hc45
le Breuil-en-Auge F 20 Fd35
le Broc F 66 Kc53
le Bugue F 53 Ga50

le Buisson-de-Cadouin F 53 Ga50
le Busseau F 37 Fb44
le Caloy F 61 Fc53
le Camp-du-Castellet F 65 Jd55
le Cap d'Agde F 63 Hc55
le Castellet F 65 Jd55
le Cateau-Cambrésis F 15 Hb32
le Catelet F 22 Hb33
le Caylar F 63 Hc53
le Cendre F 47 Hb47
l'Echalp F 58 Kc50
le Chambon-Feugerolles F 48 Ja48
le Chambon-sur-Lignon F 56 Ja49
le Champ-Saint-Père F 37 Fa44
le Charme F 32 Hb40
le Château-d'Oléron F 44 Fa47
le Châtelet F 39 Gd44
le Châtelet-en-Brie F 32 Ha38
le Châtenet-en-Dognon F 46 Gc46
Léchelle F 32 Hb37
le Chesne F 23 Ja34
le Cheylard F 56 Ja50
le Conquet F 26 Db38
le Corbier F 49 Ka48
le Coteau F 48 Hd46
le Creusot F 41 Ja43
le Croisic F 36 Eb42
Le Crotoy F 14 Gc32
le Désert F 61 Ga53
le Désert F 57 Ka49
Lédignan F 64 Hd53
le Donjon F 47 Hd45
le Dorat F 46 Gb45
le Douhet F 44 Fb47
Leek NL 9 Jc22
Leende NL 12 Jb28
Leerbeek B 15 Hc30
Leerdam NL 12 Jb26
Leersum NL 12 Jb26
le Faou F 26 Dc38
le Fauöet F 27 Dd39
le Ferté-Villeneuil F 31 Gb40
Leffonds F 33 Jb39
le Fleix F 53 Fd50
le Folgoët F 26 Dc37
le-Fond-de-France F 49 Jd48
le Fossat F 62 Gc55
le Fousseret F 62 Gb55
le Frasnois F 42 Jd44
le Frêche F 61 Fc53
le Fret F 26 Db38
le Gault-Perche F 30 Ga39
Legé F 37 Ed43
Lège F 52 Fa50
Léglise B 23 Jb33
le Gouray F 28 Eb38
le Grand-Bourg F 46 Gc46
le Grand- Lucé F 30 Fd40
le Grand-Madieu F 45 Fd46
le Grand-Piquey F 52 Fa50
le Grand-Pressigny F 38 Ga43
Le Grand-Quevilly F 20 Ga35
le Grand-Serre F 48 Ja48
le Grau-du-Roi F 64 Ja54
Léguevin F 62 Gb54
le Gurp F 44 Fa48
Le Havre F 20 Fd35
le Houga F 61 Fc54
le Houlme F 21 Gb35
Le Hourdel F 14 Gb32

Leiden NL 12 Hd25
Leiderdorp NL 12 Hd25
Leignes-sur-Fontaine F 45 Ga45
Leignon B 16 Ja32
Leke B 15 Ha29
Lekkerkerk NL 12 Hd26
le Lac-d'Issarlès F 56 Hd50
le Landreau F 37 Fa42
le Lardin-Saint-Lazere F 54 Gb49
le Lauzet-Ubaye F 57 Ka51
le Lavandou F 66 Kb55
le Liège F 39 Gb42
le Lion-d'Angers F 37 Fb41
le Logis-de-Nans F 65 Jd54
le Loroux F 29 Fa38
le Loroux-Bottereau F 37 Fa42
le Louroux-Béconnais F 37 Fb41
le Luc F 65 Ka54
le Lude F 38 Fd41
le Luthier F 42 Ka42
Lelystad NL 8 Jb24
le Malzieu-Ville F 55 Hc50
Le Mans F 30 Fd40
le Markstein F 35 Kb39
le Mas F 66 Kc53
le Mas-d'Agenais F 53 Fd51
le Mas-d'Azil F 70 Gc56
le Massegros F 55 Hb52
le Mayet-de-Montagne F 47 Hc46
Lembach F 25 Kc35
Lemberg F 25 Kb35
Lembeye F 61 Fc55
Lemele NL 9 Jc24
Lemelerveld NL 9 Jc24
le Mêle-sur-Sarthe F 30 Fd38
le Ménil F 34 Jd39
le Merlerault F 30 Fd37
Le Mesnil-Vigot F 19 Fa36
le Meux F 22 Ha35
Lemmer NL 8 Jb23
le Molay-Littry F 19 Fb35
le Monastier-sur-Gazeille F 56 Hd49
le Monêtier-les-Bains F 58 Kb49
le Mont F 33 Jb40
le Montat F 54 Gc50
le Mont-Dore F 47 Ha47
le Montet F 47 Hb45
le Mouthic F 52 Fa49
Lempdes F 47 Hb47
Lempdes F 47 Hb48
le Muret F 52 Fb51
le Muy F 66 Kb54
Lencloître F 38 Fd44
l'Enclus F 57 Jd49
Lencouacq F 53 Fc52
Le Neubourg F 20 Ga36
Lengronne F 19 Fa36
le Nouvion-en-Thiérache F 22 Hc33
Lens B 15 Hc31
Lens F 15 Ha31
Lent F 48 Jb45
Leoberghe F 14 Gd30
Léognan F 52 Fb50
Léon F 60 Fa53
Leopoldsburg B 16 Jb29
Léouvé F 58 Kc52
le Pailly F 33 Jb40
le Palais F 36 Ea42
le Parcq F 14 Gd31
Lépaud F 47 Ha45
le Pavillon-Sainte-Julie F 32 Hc38
le Péage-de-Roussillon F 48 Jb48
le Pellerin F 37 Ed42
le Perray-en-Yvelines F 31 Gc37
Le Perthus F 71 Hb58

le Pertuis F 56 Hd49
l'Épine F 36 Ec43
l'Épine F 23 Hd36
le Pin-en-Mauges F 37 Fb42
le Pin-la-Garenne F 30 Ga38
le Planay F 50 Kb46
le Planay F 50 Kb48
le Plessis-Belleville F 22 Ha36
le Plessis-Grimoult F 19 Fb36
le Plot F 49 Ka46
le Poët F 57 Jd51
le Poinçonnet F 39 Gc44
le Poiré-sur-Vie F 37 Ed44
le Pompidou F 55 Hc52
le Pont-Béranger F 37 Ed42
le Pont-d'Agris F 45 Fd47
le Pont-de-Beauvoisin F 49 Jd47
le Pont-de-Claix F 57 Jd49
le Pont-de-Montvert F 56 Hd51
le Pontet F 52 Fb49
le Porge F 52 Fa50
le-Porge-Océan F 52 Fa50
le Portel F 14 Gb31
le Pouldu F 27 Dd40
le Pouliguen F 36 Eb42
le Pouzin F 56 Jb50
le Pradet F 65 Ka55
le Puy-en-Velay F 56 Hd49
le Puy-Notre-Dame F 38 Fc42
le Puy-Saint-Reparade F 65 Jc53
le Quesnel F 22 Ha33
le Quesnoy F 15 Hb32
le Quilho F 28 Eb39
le Raincy F 22 Ha36
Le Relecq-Kerhuon F 26 Dc38
le Reposoir F 49 Ka45
le Revest-les-Eaux F 65 Ka55
le Rival F 49 Jc48
Lerm-et-Musset F 53 Fc52
le Roc-Saint-André F 28 Eb40
le Rouget F 54 Gd50
Lérouville F 23 Jb36
le Roux F 58 Kb49
le Rozier-Peyreleau F 55 Hb52
Lerrain F 34 Jd38
le Russey F 42 Ka42
les 4 Routes F 47 Hb47
les Abrets F 49 Jc47
les Aix-d'Angillon F 40 Ha42
le Sambuc F 64 Jb54
les Ancizes-Comps F 47 Ha46
les Andelys F 21 Gb35
les Angles F 70 Gd57
le Sap F 30 Fd37
les Arcs F 50 Kb47
les Arcs F 66 Kb54
les Arques F 54 Gb51
les Aspres F 30 Ga51
les Auberts F 57 Ka50
les Autels-Villevillon F 30 Ga39
le Sauze F 57 Ka51
le Sauze F 58 Kb51
les Baux-de-Provence F 64 Jb53
les Bertins F 40 Hb42
les Bézards F 32 Ha40
Les Bons Villers B 16 Hd31
les-Bordes F 31 Gd40
les Bordes F 32 Hb40
les Bourdelins F 40 Ha43
les Cabannes F 70 Gc57

L'Escaillère B 23 Hd33
les Cammazes F 62 Gd55
Lescar F 60 Fb55
l'Escarène F 58 Kd52
les Cars F 46 Gb47
les Cerqueux F 37 Fb43
les Chaises F 31 Gc37
Les-Champs-de-Losques F 19 Fa36
les Chapieux F 50 Kb46
les Chênes-Secs F 29 Fb39
Lescheraines F 49 Jd47
les-Choux F 32 Ha40
les Claux F 58 Kb50
les Clayes-sous-Bois F 31 Gc37
Lescoff F 26 Da40
Lesconil F 26 Dc40
les Contamines-Montjoie F 50 Kb46
les Échelles F 49 Jd48
les Ecrennes F 32 Ha38
le Sel-de-Bretagne F 29 Ed40
les Epesses F 37 Fb43
Les Epioux B 23 Jb33
les Essarts F 37 Fa44
les Estables F 56 Hd50
les Étangs F 24 Jd35
les Eyzies-de-Tayac F 54 Gb50
les Fabres F 58 Kb50
les Fins F 42 Ka42
les Forges F 33 Hd40
les Genets F 46 Gc45
les Gets F 49 Ka45
les Grandes-Chapelles F 33 Hd38
Les Hautes-Rivierès F 23 Ja33
les Hayons F 21 Gb34
les Herbiers F 37 Fa43
les Hermaux F 55 Hb51
les Hermites F 38 Ga41
les Hôpitaux-Neufs F 42 Ka43
les Iffs F 29 Ed39
les Islettes F 23 Ja35
les Issambres F 66 Kb54
les Lucs-sur-Boulogne F 37 Ed43
les Mages F 64 Ja52
les Maisons Blanches F 45 Fd46
les Mares F 30 Ga37
les Martys F 63 Ha55
les Matelles F 64 Hd53
les Mées F 65 Ka52
les Menuires F 49 Ka48
les Minières F 45 Fd45
Lesmont F 33 Hd38
les Moulins F 48 Hd46
les Moussières F 49 Jd45
les Moutiers F 36 Ec43
Les Mureaux F 21 Gc36
les Nègres F 45 Fd46
Lesneven F 26 Dc37
les Noières F 57 Jd50
le Soler F 71 Hb57
les Ollières-sur-Eyrieux F 56 Ja50
le Somail F 63 Hb55
les Ormes F 38 Ga43
les Orres F 58 Kb50
le Souquet F 60 Fa53
les Ourgneaux F 40 Hc43
Lesparre-Médoc F 44 Fa48
l'Esperou F 55 Hc52
les Pieux F 19 Ed35

les Placeaux – Mareuil-en-Brie

les Placeaux F 32 Hb40
les Planches-en-
Montagne F 42 Jd43
les Ponts-de-Cé F 37
Fb41
les Portes-en-Ré F 44
Ed45
les Pujols F 70 Gc56
Les Quatre-Chemins B
23 Ja33
les Riceys F 33 Hd39
les Rosaires F 28 Eb38
les Rouges-Eaux F 34
Ka38
les Rousses F 42 Jd44
Les Sables-d'Olonne F
37 Ed44
les Saisies F 49 Ka46
les Salles-du-Gardon F
64 Hd52
Lessay F 19 Ed36
les Scaffarels F 58 Kb52
les Sièges F 32 Hc39
Lessines B 15 Hc30
l'Estaque F 65 Jc54
Lestards F 46 Gc48
Lestelle-Bétharram F
69 Fc56
les Ternes F 51 Hd40
Lesterps F 45 Ga46
les Thilliers-en-Vexin F
21 Gc35
les Thons-le-Grand F
34 Jc39
les Thuiles F 58 Kb51
les Touches F 37 Fa41
l'Estréchure F 64 Hd52
les Trois-Moutiers F
38 Fd43
les Ulis F 31 Gd37
les Vanels F 55 Hc52
les Vans F 56 Hd51
les Verchers-sur-Layon F
38 Fc42
les Vignes F 55 Hb52
le Teil F 56 Jb51
le Teilleul F 29 Fb38
le Temple F 52 Fa50
le Temple F 30 Ga40
Le Temple-de-Bretagne F
37 Ed42
le Theil F 19 Fa34
le Theil F 30 Ga39
le Thillot F 34 Ka39
le Tholy F 34 Ka39
le Thor F 64 Jb53
le Thoronet F 65 Ka54
le Thour F 23 Hd34
le Touquet-Paris-Plage F
14 Gb31
Le-Tour-du-Parc F 36
Eb41
le Touvet F 49 Jd48
Le Trait F 20 Ga35
le Transloy F 22 Hb33
Le Tréport F 21 Gb33
le Trivalou F 62 Gd53
Le Trois Epis F 35 Kb38
le Tronquay F 21 Gb35
Leucate-Plage F 71 Hb56
Leuchey F 33 Jb40
Leuglay F 33 Ja40
Leugny F 32 Hb40
Leuven B 16 Hd30
Leuze B 16 Ja31
Leuze-en-Hainaut B 15
Hb31
le Val F 65 Ka54
le Val-André F 28 Eb38
le Val d'Ajol F 34 Ka39
le Vast F 19 Fa34
Levécourt F 34 Jc39
le Verdon-sur-Mer F
44 Fa48
le Vernet F 57 Ka51
Levet F 39 Gd43
le Veudre F 40 Hb44
Levie F 73 Ld59
Levier F 42 Jd42
le Vigan F 63 Hc53

Lévignac F 62 Gb54
Levignac-de-Guyenne F
53 Fd51
Lévignacq F 60 Fa53
Lévignen F 22 Ha35
le Vilhain F 40 Ha44
le Vivier-sur-Mer F 29
Ed38
Levroux F 39 Gc43
le Wast F 14 Gc30
Leyr F 24 Jd36
Lézan F 64 Hd52
Lézan F 64 Hd53
Lézardrieux F 27 Ea37
Lezat F 42 Jd44
Lézat-sur-Lezé F 62 Gb55
Lezay F 45 Fc45
Lézignan-Corbières F
63 Hb55
Lezoux F 47 Hc47
l'Haÿ-les-Roses F 31
Gd37
l'Herbaudière F 36 Ec43
l'Hebergement F 37 Fa43
l'Hermenault F 37 Fb44
l'Hermitage F 29 Ed39
l'Hermitage-Lorge F
28 Eb38
l'Homy-Plage F 60 Ed53
l'Hôpital d'Orion F 60
Fb55
l'Hôpital-Saint-Blaise F
60 Fb55
l'Hospitalet F 70 Gd57
l'Hospitalet F 65 Jd52
Lhuis F 49 Jc47
Lhuître F 33 Hd37
Liancourt F 21 Gd35
Liart F 23 Hd33
Libin B 23 Jb43
Libos F 53 Ga51
Libourne F 53 Fc50
Libramont-Chevigny B
23 Jb33
Lichères-Aigremont F
32 Hc40
Lichtaart B 12 Ja28
Lichtenvoorde NL 13
Jd26
Lichtervelde B 15 Ha29
Licques F 14 Gc30
Liedekerke B 15 Hc30
Liège B 16 Hd29
Lier B 16 Hd29
Liernais F 41 Hd42
Lierneux B 17 Jc32
Liernolles F 47 Hc45
Lierville F 21 Gc36
Lieshout NL 12 Jb27
Liesse-Notre-Dame F
22 Hc34
Liessies F 15 Hc32
Lieurac F 70 Gc56
Lieurey F 20 Fd36
Liévin F 15 Ha31
Liffol-le-Grand F 34 Jc38
Liffré F 29 Ed39
Ligardes F 61 Fd53
Ligardes F 61 Ga53
Lignières F 39 Gd44
Lignières-de-Touraine F
38 Fd42
Lignières-Sonneville F
45 Fc48
Lignol-le-Château F
33 Ja39
Ligny-en-Barrois F 33
Jb37
Ligny-le-Châtel F 32 Hc40
Ligny-le-Ribault F 39
Gc41
Ligueil F 38 Ga43
Ligugé F 45 Fc45
l'Île-Bouchard F 38 Fd43
Lille F 15 Ha31
Lillebonne F 20 Fd35
Lillers F 14 Gd31
Limbourg B 17 Jc30
Limerzel F 36 Ec41
Limes B 23 Jb34

Limoges F 46 Gb47
Limogne-en-Quercy F
54 Gc51
Limoise F 40 Hb44
Limours-en-Hurepoix F
31 Gd37
Limoux F 70 Gd56
Linards F 46 Gc47
Liniez F 39 Gc43
Linxe F 60 Fa53
Lion-sur-Mer F 20 Fc35
Liposthey F 52 Fb52
Liré F 37 Fa42
Lisieux F 20 Fd36
Lisle F 53 Ga49
l'Isle-Adam F 21 Gd36
l'Isle-d'Abeau F 49 Jc47
l'Isle-deNoé F 61 Fd54
l'Isle-en-Dodon F 61 Ga55
l'Isle-Jourdain F 45 Ga55
l'Isle-Jourdain F 62 Gb54
l'Isle-sur-la-Sorgue F
65 Jc53
l'Isle-sur-le-Doubs F
42 Ka41
l'Isle-sur-Serein F 41 Hd41
Lisle-sur-Tarn F 62 Gc53
Lisse NL 12 Hd25
Lissy F 32 Ha37
Lit-et-Mixe F 60 Fa53
Lith NL 12 Jb27
Livarot F 20 Fd36
Livernon F 54 Gc51
Livré-sur-Changeon F
29 Fa39
Livron-sur-Drôme F
56 Jb50
Livry-Louvercy F 23 Hd36
Lizine F 42 Jd42
Lizio F 28 Ed40
Lizy-sur-Ourcq F 22 Ha36
L'Ile-Rousse F 72 Ld56
Lo B 15 Ha30
Loan-Villegruis-Fontaine
F 32 Hb37
Lochem NL 13 Jc25
Loches F 39 Gb42
Loché-sur-Indrois F 39
Gb43
Locmaria F 36 Ea42
Locmariaquer F 36 Ea41
Locminé F 28 Eb40
Locoal-Mendon F 27
Ea40
Locquémeau F 27 Dd37
Locquirec F 27 Dd37
Locronan F 26 Dc39
Loctudy F 26 Dc40
Lodève F 63 Hc53
Loenen NL 13 Jc25
Logron F 31 Gb39
Lohéac F 29 Ed40
Loiré F 37 Fa41
Loire F 22 Hc35
Lokeren B 15 Hc29
Lombez F 61 Ga55
Lombreuil F 32 Ha40
Lombron F 30 Ga39
Lommel B 12 Jb28
Londerzeel B 16 Hd29
Londinières F 21 Gb33
Longchamp F 49 Ka48
Longchaumois F 42 Jd44
Longeau F 33 Jb40
Longecourt-en-Plaine F
41 Jb42
Longeville-sur-Mer F
44 Ed45
Longnes F 21 Gc36
Longny-au-Perche F
30 Ga38
Longpont F 22 Hb35
Longré F 45 Fc46
Longué-Jumelles F 38
Fc42
Longueval-Barbonval F
22 Hc35
Longueville F 32 Hb38
Longueville-sur-Scie F
21 Gb34

Longuyon F 23 Jb34
Longwy F 24 Jc34
Lons-le-Saunier F 42 Jc44
Lonzac F 45 Fc48
Loon op Zand NL 12 Ja27
Loon-Plage F 14 Gd30
Loos F 15 Ha31
Loosdrecht NL 12 Ja25
Loppersum NL 9 Jd21
Loqueffret F 27 Dd38
Lorentzer F 25 Kb36
Lorgues F 66 Kb54
Lorguichon F 20 Fc36
Lorient F 27 Ea40
Loriol-sur-Drôme F 56
Jb50
Lormaison F 21 Gd35
Lormes F 40 Hc42
Lorrez-le-Bocage F 32
Ha39
Lorris F 32 Ha40
l'Ospedale F 73 Ma59
Losse F 53 Fc52
Losser NL 13 Jd25
Lottum NL 13 Jc28
Louans F 38 Ga42
Louargat F 27 Ea38
Loubillé F 45 Fc46
Louchats F 52 Fb51
Loudéac F 28 Eb39
Loudun F 38 Fd43
Loué F 30 Fc40
Lougratte F 53 Ga51
Louhans F 41 Jb44
Loulans F 42 Jd41
Loulay F 44 Fb46
Lourdes F 69 Fc56
Lourmarin F 65 Jc53
Loury F 31 Gd39
Louverné F 29 Fb39
Louvie-Juzon F 69 Fc56
Louviers F 21 Gb36
Louvigné-de-Bais F
29 Fa39
Louvigné-du-Desert F
29 Fa38
Louvois F 23 Hd36
Louvroil F 15 Hc32
Louze F 33 Ja38
Lovagny F 49 Jd46
Loyettes F 49 Jc46
Lozari F 72 Ld56
Lozen F 12 Jb28
Lubersac F 46 Gb48
Luc F 55 Ha52
Luc F 56 Hd50
Luçay-le-Malle F 39 Gb42
Lucenay-le-Duc F 41 Ja41
Luc-en-Diois F 57 Jc50
Lucéram F 58 Kd52
Lucey F 49 Jd46
Luché-Pringé F 38 Fd41
Lucheux F 14 Gd31
Luchy F 21 Gd34
Lucmau F 53 Fc52
Luçon F 44 Fa45
Luc-sur-Mer F 20 Fc35
Lüe F 52 Fa52
Luglon F 60 Fb53
Lugny F 41 Jb44
Luisant F 31 Gb38
Lumbres F 14 Gd31
Lumes F 23 Ja33
Lumio F 72 Lc56
Lummen B 16 Ja29
Lunas F 63 Hc54
Lunel F 64 Jd47
Lunéville F 34 Jd37
Lunteren NL 12 Jb26
Lupersat F 46 Gd46
Lupiac F 61 Fd54
Luplanté F 31 Gb39
Lurcy-Lévis F 40 Hb44
Lure F 34 Ka41
Luri F 72 Ld55
Lurs F 65 Jd52
Lury-sur-Arnon F 39 Gd42
Lusanger F 37 Ed41
Lusignan F 45 Fd45

Lusigny F 40 Hc44
Lusigny-sur-Barse F
33 Hd38
Lus-la-Croix-Haute F
57 Jd50
Lussac F 53 Fc50
Lussac-les-Châteaux F
45 Ga45
Lussac-les-Eglises F
46 Gb45
Lussan F 64 Ja52
Lussat F 46 Gd45
Luthenay-Uxeloup F
40 Hb43
Luxembourg L 24 Jd33
Luxeuil-les-Bains F 34
Jd40
Luxey F 52 Fb52
Luyères F 33 Hd38
Luynes F 38 Ga42
Luzarches F 21 Gd36
Luzech F 54 Gb51
Luz-Saint-Sauveur F
69 Fc57
Luzy F 41 Hd43
Lyoffans F 34 Ka40
Lyon F 48 Jb47
Lyons-la-Forêt F 21 Gb35

M

Maarheeze NL 12 Jb28
Maarn NL 12 Jb26
Maarssen NL 12 Ja25
Maasbracht NL 17 Jc29
Maasbree NL 13 Jc28
Maaseik B 16 Jb29
Maasmechelen B 16 Jb29
Maassluis NL 11 Hc26
Maastricht NL 16 Jb30
Macau F 52 Fb49
Machault F 23 Hd35
Machecoul F 37 Ed43
Macinaggio F 72 Ma55
Maclas F 48 Ja48
Mâcon F 48 Jb45
Macqueville F 45 Fc47
Made NL 12 Hd27
Madières F 63 Hc53
Madiran F 61 Fc54
Maël-Carhaix F 27 Ea38
Maffe B 16 Jb31
Magescq F 60 Fa54
Magnac-Bourg F 46 Gb47
Magnac-Laval F 46 Ga45
Magnant F 33 Hd39
Magnat-l'Etrange F 46
Gd47
Magnières F 34 Ka37
Magny-Cours F 40 Hb43
Magny-en-Vexin F 21
Gc36
Maguelone F 64 Hd54
Maiche F 42 Ka41
Maignelay-Montigny F
21 Gd34
Maillas F 53 Fc52
Maillé F 44 Fb45
Mailley-et-Chazelot F
42 Jd41
Maillezais F 44 Fb45
Mailly-le-Camp F 33 Hd37
Mailly-Maillet F 21 Gd32
Mainbressy F 23 Hd34
Mainsat F 47 Ha46
Maintenay F 14 Gc32
Maintenon F 31 Gc38
Mainvilliers F 31 Gb38
Maisey-le-Duc F 33 Ja40
Maison-Neuve F 56 Ja51
Maison Pieraggi F 73
Ma58
Maison-Rouge F 32 Hb38
Maisons F 71 Ha56
Maisons-Laffitte F 21
Gd36
Maisse F 31 Gd38
Maissin B 23 Jb33
Maizières F 20 Fc36

Maizières-lès-Vic F 24
Ka36
Makkum NL 8 Ja22
Malaincourt F 34 Jc38
Malaucène F 65 Jc52
Malbouzon F 55 Hb50
Malbuisson F 42 Ka43
Maldegem B 15 Hb29
Malesherbes F 31 Gd38
Malestroit F 28 Ec40
Malicorne-sur-Sarthe F
30 Fc40
Malijai F 65 Ka52
Mallemort F 65 Jc53
Malmedy B 17 Jc31
Malo-les-Bains F 14 Gd29
Maltat F 40 Hc44
Maltaverne F 40 Ha42
Mamer L 24 Jd33
Mamers F 30 Fd38
Mametz F 22 Ha33
Mamirolle F 42 Jd42
Manchecourt F 31 Gd39
Manciet F 61 Fd53
Mandelieu-la Napoule F
66 Kc53
Mander NL 9 Jd24
Manderfeld B 17 Jd31
Mandeure F 42 Ka41
Mane F 70 Gb56
Mane F 65 Jd52
Manent-Montaine F 61
Ga55
Manhay B 16 Jb31
Maninghem F 14 Gc31
Manonville F 24 Jc36
Manosque F 65 Jd53
Mansigné F 30 Fd40
Mansle F 45 Fc47
Mantes-la-Jolie F 21 Gc36
Mantes-la-Ville F 21 Gc36
Mantet F 71 Ha58
Manthelan F 38 Ga42
Manzat F 47 Hb46
Manziat F 48 Jb45
Marac F 33 Jb39
Marainviller F 34 Ka37
Marans F 44 Fa45
Maranville F 33 Ja39
Marault F 33 Jb39
Maraye-en-Othe F 32
Hc39
Marboué F 31 Gb39
Marboz F 48 Jb45
Marcé F 38 Fc41
Marcenat F 47 Hb48
Marchais F 22 Hc34
Marche-en-Famenne B
16 Jb32
Marchenoir F 31 Gb40
Marcheprime F 52 Fb50
Marchiennes F 15 Hb31
Marciac F 61 Fd54
Marcigny F 48 Hd45
Marcillac-la-Croisille F
46 Gd48
Marcillac-Vallon F 55 Ha51
Marcillat-en-Combraille F
47 Ha46
Marcilly-sur-Eure F 31
Gb37
Marcilloles F 48 Jb48
Marcilly-en-Gault F 39
Gc41
Marcilly-en-Villette F
31 Gd40
Marcilly-le-Hayer F 32
Hc38
Marcilly-sur-Seine F 32
Hc37
Marck F 14 Gc30
Marckolsheim F 35 Kc38
Marcoing F 15 Hb32
Mardilly F 30 Fd37
Maredret B 16 Jb31
Marennes F 44 Fa47
Mareuil F 45 Fd48
Mareuil-en-Brie F 22 Hc36

94

Mareuil-sur-Arnon F 39 Gd43
Mareuil-sur-Lay F 37 Fa44
Mareuil-sur-Ourcq F 22 Hb36
Margaux F 52 Fb49
Margès F 56 Jb49
Margon F 30 Ga38
Margraten NL 17 Jc30
Marguerittes F 64 Ja53
Margueron F 53 Fd44
Margut F 23 Jb34
Mariembourg B 16 Hd32
Mariënberg NL 9 Jd24
Marignac F 44 Fb48
Marignane F 65 Jc54
Marigné F 29 Fb40
Marigny F 19 Fa36
Marigny-en-Orxois F 22 Hb36
Marigny-le Châtel F 32 Hc38
Marine d'Albo F 72 Ld55
Marine de Sisco F 72 Ma55
Marines F 21 Gc36
Maringues F 47 Hc46
Markelo NL 13 Jd25
Marknesse NL 8 Jb23
Marle F 22 Hc34
Marlenheim F 35 Kb37
Marly F 24 Jd35
Marly-Gomont F 22 Hc33
Marmagne F 41 Ja43
Marmande F 53 Fd51
Marmoutier F 25 Kb36
Marnay F 42 Jc41
Marœuil F 15 Ha32
Maroilles F 15 Hc32
Marolles-les-Braults F 30 Fd39
Maron F 34 Jd37
Marquion F 15 Ha32
Marquise F 14 Gc30
Marrault F 41 Hd41
Marroule F 54 Gd51
Marrum NL 8 Jb21
Marsais F 44 Fb46
Marseillan F 63 Hc55
Marseillan-Plage F 63 Hc55
Marseille F 65 Jc55
Marseille-en-Beauvaisis F 21 Gc34
Mars-la-Tour F 24 Jc35
Marson F 23 Jd34
Marssac-sur-Tarn F 62 Gd53
Marssum NL 8 Jb22
Martainville F 21 Gb35
Martel F 54 Gc50
Martelange B 24 Jc33
Marthon F 45 Fd47
Martignas-sur-Jalle F 52 Fb50
Martigné F 29 Fb39
Martigné-Briand F 38 Fc42
Martigné-Ferchaud F 29 Fa40
Martigny-le-Comte F 41 Ja44
Martigny-les-Bains F 34 Jc39
Martigny-lès-Gerbonvaux F 34 Jc38
Martigues F 65 Jc54
Martizay F 39 Gb44
Martragny F 19 Fb38
Martron F 53 Fc49
Marum NL 8 Jc22
Marvejols F 55 Hc51
Marville F 23 Jb34
Mas-Carbadès F 63 Ha55
Masevaux F 35 Kb40
Mas-Grenier F 62 Gb53
Maslacq F 60 Fb55
Masléon F 46 Gc48
Mas-Neuf-sur-Orb F 63 Hb53

Massagette F 47 Ha47
Massais F 38 Fc43
Massat F 70 Gb56
Massay F 39 Gd42
Masseret F 46 Gc48
Masseube F 61 Ga55
Massiac F 47 Hb48
Massignac F 45 Ga47
Massoult F 33 Ja40
Mas Thibert F 64 Jb54
Matha F 45 Fc47
Mathieu F 20 Fc35
Matignon F 28 Ec38
Matigny F 22 Ha33
Matour F 48 Ja45
Maubeuge F 15 Hc32
Maubourguet F 61 Fd55
Maubuisson F 52 Fa49
Mauguio F 64 Hd54
Maulde F 15 Hb31
Maule F 31 Gc37
Mauléon F 37 Fb43
Mauléon-Barousse F 69 Ga56
Mauléon-Licharre F 60 Fa55
Maulévrier F 37 Fb43
Maumusson F 37 Fa41
Mauperthuis F 32 Ha37
Mauprévoir F 45 Ga46
Maure-de-Bretagne F 28 Ec40
Mauriac F 54 Gd49
Mauron F 28 Ec39
Maurrin F 61 Fc53
Maurs F 54 Gd50
Maury F 71 Ha57
Maussane F 64 Jb54
Mauvezin F 69 Fd56
Mauvezin F 61 Ga54
Mauzé-sur-le-Mignon F 44 Fb46
Maxent F 28 Ec40
Maxey-sur-Meuse F 34 Jc38
Maxey-sur-Vaise F 34 Jc37
May-en-Multien F 22 Ha36
Mayenne F 29 Fb39
Mayet F 30 Fd40
Mayreville F 62 Gd55
Mazamet F 63 Ha54
Mazan-l'Abbaye F 56 Hd50
Mazargan F 23 Hd35
Mazé F 38 Fc41
Mazeley F 34 Jd38
Mazéres F 62 Gc55
Mazerny F 23 Hd34
Mazières-en-Gâtine F 38 Fc44
Mazières-lès-Metz F 24 Jd35
Mazille F 48 Ja45
Mazy B 16 Hd31
Méailles F 58 Kb52
Méaudre F 57 Jc49
Meaulne F 40 Ha44
Meaux F 22 Ha36
Meauzac F 62 Gb53
Mébecq F 39 Gc44
Mechelen B 16 Hd29
Médavy F 30 Fd40
Meddo NL 13 Jd26
Medemblik NL 8 Ja23
Médière F 42 Ka41
Médréac F 28 Ec40
Meerhout B 16 Ja29
Meerkerk NL 12 Ja26
Meerle B 12 Hd28
Meeuwen-Gruitrode B 16 Jb29
Megève F 49 Ka46
Mehun-sur-Yèvre F 39 Gd42
Meijel NL 13 Jc28
Meillant F 40 Ha44
Meillerie F 43 Kb44
Meilleur F 48 Ja45
Meixdevant-Virton B 23 Jb34

Melay F 48 Hd45
Melesse F 29 Ed39
Mélisey F 34 Ka40
Melle F 45 Fc45
Mellionnec F 27 Ea39
Mello F 21 Gd35
Melrand F 27 Ea39
Melun F 32 Ha38
Memer F 54 Gd52
Menaldum NL 8 Jb22
Menat F 47 Hb46
Mende F 55 Hc51
Ménéac F 28 Eb39
Menée F 57 Jc50
Menen B 15 Ha30
Ménerbes F 65 Jc54
Menestreau-en-Villette F 31 Gd40
Menetou-Salon F 40 Ha42
Ménétréol-sur-Sauldre F 39 Gd41
Ménigoute F 45 Fc45
Ménil F 29 Fb40
Ménil-la-Tour F 24 Jc36
Mennetou-sur-Cher F 39 Gc42
Menouille F 42 Jc44
Mens F 57 Jd50
Menton F 67 Kd53
Méounes-les-Montrieux F 65 Ka55
Meppel NL 9 Jc23
Mer F 39 Gc41
Merbes-le-Château B 16 Hd32
Merchtem B 16 Hd29
Mercœur F 54 Gd49
Mercues F 54 Gb51
Mercurey F 41 Ja43
Merdrignac F 28 Ec39
Méribel F 50 Kb47
Méribel F 52 Fb50
Mérignac F 45 Fc47
Mérignac F 45 Fc48
Mérindol F 65 Jc53
Merkem B 15 Ha30
Merlevenez F 27 Ea40
Merlimont F 14 Gc31
Merlimont-Plage F 14 Gb31
Merlines F 47 Ha47
Merry-Sec F 32 Hc40
Mersch L 24 Jc34
Mers-sur-Indre F 39 Gc44
Méru F 21 Gd35
Mervans F 41 Jb43
Mervent F 37 Fb44
Merville F 15 Ha31
Méry-sur-Seine F 32 Hc38
Mésandans F 42 Ka41
Meschers-sur-Gironde F 44 Fa48
Meslan F 27 Dd39
Meslay-du-Maine F 29 Fb40
Meslon F 40 Ha44
Mesnil-Saint-Père F 33 Hd38
Mesnil-Sellières F 33 Hd38
Mesquer F 36 Ec40
Messac F 29 Ed40
Messancy B 24 Jc34
Messanges F 60 Ed53
Messanges-Plage F 60 Ed53
Messeix F 47 Ha47
Messigny-et-Vantoux F 41 Jb41
Mesvres F 41 Hd43
Méthamis F 65 Jc52
Metslawier NL 8 Jb21
Mettet B 16 Hd32
Metz F 24 Jd35
Metzeral F 35 Kb39
Metzervisse F 24 Jd35
Meucon F 28 Eb40
Meulan F 21 Gc36
Meulebeke B 15 Hb30
Meung-sur-Loire F 31 Gc40

Meursault F 41 Ja43
Meuse F 34 Jc39
Meussia F 42 Jc44
Meuzac F 46 Gb48
Meximieux F 48 Jb46
Meymac F 46 Gd48
Meyrargues F 65 Jd53
Meyrueis F 55 Hc52
Meysee F 56 Jb50
Meyssac F 54 Gc49
Meyzieu F 48 Jb47
Mèze F 63 Hc54
Mézeray F 30 Fc40
Mézérial F 49 Jc48
Mézidon-Canon F 20 Fc36
Mézières-en-Brenne F 39 Gb43
Mézières-sur-Issoire F 45 Ga46
Mézilhac F 56 Ja50
Mézilles F 32 Hb40
Mézin F 61 Fd53
Mézos F 52 Fa52
Mézos F 60 Ed53
Mialet F 45 Ga48
Mialet F 64 Hd52
Michery F 32 Hb38
Middelbeers NL 12 Ja28
Middelburg NL 11 Hb28
Middelharnis NL 11 Hc27
Middelkerke B 15 Ha29
Middelstum NL 9 Jc21
Middenbeemster NL 8 Ja24
Middenmeer NL 8 Ja23
Midrevaux F 34 Jc38
Miélan F 61 Ga55
Mierlo NL 12 Jb28
Migennes F 32 Hc39
Migné F 39 Gb44
Mignères F 32 Ha39
Mijanès F 70 Gd57
Mijdrecht NL 12 Ja25
Mijoux F 42 Jd44
Milhars F 54 Gd52
Millancay F 39 Gc41
Millas F 71 Ha57
Millau F 55 Hb52
Millevaches F 46 Gd47
Millingen aan de Rijn NL 13 Jc26
Mill-Sint Hubert NL 12 Jb27
Milly-la-Forêt F 31 Gd38
Milly-le-Meugnon F 38 Fc42
Mimizan F 52 Fa52
Mimizan-Plage F 52 Fa52
Minerve F 63 Ha55
Minot F 33 Ja40
Miomo F 72 Ma55
Mions F 48 Jb47
Mirabeau F 65 Jd53
Mirabel F 65 Jc52
Mirabel F 56 Ja50
Mirabel-aux-Baronnies F 57 Jc51
Miradoux F 61 Ga53
Miramar F 66 Kc54
Miramas F 64 Jb54
Mirambeau F 44 Fb49
Miramont-de-Guyenne F 53 Fd51
Mirande F 61 Fd54
Mirandol-Bourgnounac F 54 Gd52
Miraumont F 15 Ha32
Miré F 29 Fb40
Mirebeau F 38 Fd44
Mirebeau-sur-Bèze F 41 Jb41
Mirebel F 42 Jc43
Mirecourt F 34 Jd38
Mirepoix F 70 Gd56
Mireval F 64 Hd54
Miribel F 48 Jb46
Mirmande F 56 Jb50

Missery F 41 Hd42
Missillac F 36 Ec41
Misy-sur-Yonne F 32 Hb38
Mitry-Mory F 22 Ha36
Mittersheim F 24 Ka36
Modane F 50 Kb48
Modave B 16 Jb31
Moëlan-sur-Mer F 27 Dd40
Moerbeke B 15 Hc30
Moergestel NL 12 Ja27
Mohon F 28 Eb39
Moirans F 49 Jc48
Moirans-en-Montagne F 42 Jc44
Moirax F 53 Ga52
Moircy B 23 Jb33
Moissac F 54 Gb52
Moissac-Bellevue F 65 Ka53
Moissey F 42 Jc42
Moisson F 21 Gc36
Moisy F 31 Gb40
Moita F 72 Ma57
Mol B 16 Ja29
Molas F 61 Ga55
Moliens-Dreuil F 21 Gc33
Molières F 54 Gb52
Moliets-et-Maa F 60 Ed53
Moliets-Plage F 60 Ed53
Molineuf F 39 Gb41
Molinges F 49 Jd45
Molitg-les-Bains F 71 Ha57
Mollans-sur-Ouvèze F 65 Jc52
Mollières F 58 Kc51
Molompize F 55 Hb49
Moloy F 41 Jb41
Molsheim F 35 Kb37
Momignies B 23 Hd33
Momuy F 60 Fb54
Monbahus F 53 Ga51
Moncel-sur-Seille F 24 Jd36
Monclar F 53 Ga51
Monclar-de-Quercy F 62 Gc53
Moncontour F 28 Eb38
Moncontour F 38 Fc43
Moncoutant F 37 Fb44
Mondonville F 62 Gb54
Mondorf-les-Bains L 24 Jd34
Mondoubleau F 30 Ga40
Mondragon F 64 Jb52
Monein F 60 Fb55
Monestier-de-Clermont F 57 Jd49
Monestiés F 54 Gd52
Moneteau F 32 Hc40
Monflanquin F 53 Ga51
Monguillem F 61 Fc53
Mon-Idée F 23 Hd33
Monistrol-d'Allier F 55 Hc49
Monistrol-sur-Loire F 48 Hd48
Monlezun-d'Armagnac F 61 Fc53
Monlong F 61 Ga53
Monnai F 30 Fd37
Monnaie F 38 Ga41
Monnerville F 31 Gd38
Monnickendam NL 8 Ja24
Monpazier F 53 Ga51
Mons B 15 Hc31
Mons F 66 Kb53
Monsegur F 53 Fd51
Monsols F 48 Ja45
Monster NL 11 Hc26
Montady F 63 Hb55
Montagnac F 63 Hc54
Montagnac-d'Auberoche F 54 Gb49
Montagne F 57 Jc49
Montagnol F 63 Hb53
Montagny F 48 Hd46
Montaigu F 37 Fa43

Montaigu-de-Quercy F 54 Gb52
Montaiguët-en-Forez F 47 Hc45
Montaigu-les-Bois F 29 Fa37
Montaigut F 47 Ha45
Montaigut-le-Blanc F 46 Gc46
Montaigut-sur-Save F 62 Gb54
Montainville F 31 Gc39
Montalba-le-Château F 71 Ha57
Montalieu-Vercieu F 49 Jc46
Montalivet-les-Bains F 44 Fa48
Montamy F 19 Fb36
Montaner F 61 Fc55
Montans F 62 Gd53
Montargis F 32 Ha39
Montastruc-la-Coceillère F 62 Gc54
Montauban F 62 Gb53
Montauban-de-Bretagne F 28 Ec39
Montaud F 49 Jc48
Montbard F 41 Hd41
Montbarrey F 42 Jc42
Montbazens F 54 Gd51
Montbazon F 38 Ga42
Montbéliard F 34 Ka40
Montbeugny F 40 Hc44
Montbizot F 30 Fd39
Montbozon F 42 Jd41
Montbrand F 57 Jd50
Montbrison F 48 Hd47
Montbron F 45 Ga47
Montbrun-les-Bains F 65 Jc52
Montceau-les-Mines F 41 Ja44
Montceaux-les-Provins F 32 Hb37
Montcenis F 41 Ja43
Montchanin F 41 Ja43
Montchevrier F 46 Gc45
Montcornet F 22 Hc34
Montcresson F 32 Ha40
Montcuq F 54 Gb52
Montdardier F 63 Hc53
Mont-Dauphin F 58 Kb50
Mont-de-Marsan F 60 Fb53
Montdidier F 21 Gd34
Mont-Dol F 29 Ed38
Montebourg F 19 Fa35
Monte-Carlo MC 67 Kd53
Montech F 62 Gb53
Monte Estremo F 72 Lc57
Montel-de-Gelat F 47 Ha46
Montélimar F 56 Jb51
Montellier F 48 Jb46
Montendre F 53 Fc49
Monteneuf F 28 Ec40
Montereau F 32 Ha38
Montesquieu-Volvestre F 62 Gb55
Montesquieu F 54 Gb52
Montesquiou F 61 Fd54
Montestruc-sur-Gers F 61 Ga54
Monteux F 64 Jb52
Montfaucon F 53 Fd51
Montfaucon-d'Argonne F 23 Jb35
Montfaucon-en-Velay F 56 Ja49
Montferrand-du-Périgord F 53 Ga50
Montferrat F 66 Kb53
Montfleur F 49 Jc45
Montfort NL 12 Ja26
Montfort F 61 Ga53
Montfort NL 17 Jc29
Montfort-en-Chalosse F 60 Fb54

Montfort-l'Amaury – Noyon

Montfort-l'Amaury F 31 Gc37
Montfort-sur-Meu F 29 Ed39
Montfort-sur-Risle F 20 Ga35
Montfranc F 63 Ha53
Montfrin F 64 Jb53
Montfront-le-Gesnois F 30 Fd39
Montgeron F 31 Gd37
Montgerval F 29 Ed39
Montgueux F 32 Hc38
Montguyon F 53 Fc49
Monthermé F 23 Ja33
Monthois F 23 Ja35
Monthureux-sur-Saône F 34 Jd39
Montier-en-Der F 33 Ja38
Montiers-sur-Saulx F 33 Jb37
Montignac F 54 Gb49
Montignac-le-Coq F 45 Fd48
Montignac-sur-Charente F 45 Fd47
Montigny F 40 Ha42
Montigny F 34 Ka37
Montigny-la-Resle F 32 Hc40
Montigny-le-Chartif F 31 Gb39
Montigny-Lencoup F 32 Hb38
Montigny-le-Roi = Val-de-Meuse F 34 Jc39
Montigny-lès-Metz F 24 Jd35
Montigny-sur-Aube F 33 Ja39
Montigny-sur-Loing F 32 Ha38
Montilly F 40 Hb44
Montivilliers F 20 Fd34
Montjay F 57 Jd51
Montjean F 29 Fb40
Montjean F 45 Fd46
Montjean-sur-Loire F 37 Fb42
Montlaur F 71 Ha56
Mont-lès-Lamarche F 34 Jc39
Montlieu-la-Garde F 53 Fc49
Montlivault F 39 Gb41
Mont-Louis F 70 Gd58
Montlouis-sur-Loire F 38 Ga42
Montluçon F 47 Ha45
Montluel F 48 Jb46
Montmarault F 47 Hb45
Montmaur F 57 Jd50
Montmaurin F 61 Ga55
Montmédy F 23 Jb34
Montmelian F 49 Jd47
Montmerle-sur-Saône F 48 Jb46
Montmeyan F 65 Ka53
Montmeyran F 56 Jb50
Montmirail F 30 Gd42
Montmirail F 22 Hb36
Montmirat F 64 Hd53
Montmoreau-Saint-Cybard F 45 Fd48
Montmorency F 21 Gd36
Montmorillon F 45 Ga45
Montmort-Lucy F 22 Hc36
Montmoyen F 33 Ja40
Mont-Notre-Dame F 22 Hb35
Montoir-de-Bretagne F 36 Ec42
Montoire-sur-le-Loir F 30 Ga40
Montoison F 56 Jb50
Montpascal F 49 Ka48
Montpellier F 64 Hd54
Montpezat-de-Quercy F 54 Gc52

Montpezat-sous-Bauzon F 56 Ja50
Montpon-Ménestérol F 53 Fd50
Montpont-en-Bresse F 41 Jb44
Montréal F 61 Fd53
Montréal F 62 Gd55
Montredon-Labessonnie F 63 Ha54
Montréjeau F 69 Ga56
Montrésor F 39 Gb42
Montret F 41 Jb44
Montreuil F 14 Gc31
Montreuil-aux-Lions F 22 Hb36
Montreuil-Bellay F 38 Fc42
Montreuil-l'Argillé F 20 Fd36
Montrevel-en-Bresse F 48 Jb45
Montrichard F 39 Gb42
Montricoux F 62 Gc53
Montrigaud F 48 Jb48
Montrond-le-Château F 42 Jd42
Montrond-les-Bains F 48 Hd47
Monts F 38 Ga42
Mont-Saint-Aignan F 21 Gb35
Mont-Saint-Léger F 34 Jd40
Mont-Saint-Michel F 29 Ed37
Montsalvy F 55 Ha50
Montsapey F 49 Ka47
Montsauche-les-Settons F 41 Hd42
Montsaunes F 70 Gb56
Montségur F 70 Gd56
Montségur-sur-Lauzon F 56 Jb51
Monts-sur-Guesnes F 38 Fd43
Montsûrs F 29 Fb39
Montsurvent F 19 Ed36
Montvert F 54 Gd49
Moraines F 32 Hc37
Morannes F 30 Fc40
Morbier F 42 Jd44
Morcenx F 60 Fa53
Mordelles F 29 Ed39
Morée F 31 Gb40
Morestel F 49 Jc47
Moret-sur-Loing F 32 Ha38
Moreuil F 21 Gd34
Morez F 42 Jd44
Morgat F 26 Db39
Morgny F 21 Gc35
Morhange F 24 Ka36
Morhet B 23 Jb33
Morialmé B 16 Hd32
Moriani-Plage F 72 Ma57
Morienval F 22 Ha35
Morières F 31 Gb39
Morlaàs F 61 Fc55
Morlac F 39 Gd44
Morlaix F 27 Dd37
Morlanne F 60 Fb54
Morley F 33 Jb37
Mormoiron F 65 Jc52
Mormont B 16 Jb31
Mornant F 48 Ja47
Mornas F 64 Jb52
Mornay-Berry F 40 Ha43
Mornay-sur-Allier F 40 Hb43
Morosaglia F 72 Ld56
Morsains F 32 Hb37
Mortagne-au-Perche F 30 Ga38
Mortagne-sur-Gironde F 44 Fb48
Mortagne-sur-Sèvre F 37 Fa43
Mortain F 29 Fb37
Mortaizé F 38 Fd43

Mortcerf F 32 Ha37
Morteau F 42 Ka42
Mortemart F 45 Ga46
Mortemer F 21 Gb34
Mortrée F 30 Fd37
Mortsel B 16 Hd29
Morvillars F 35 Kb40
Morzine F 50 Kb45
Mosculdy F 60 Fa55
Mosles F 19 Fb35
Mosset F 71 Ha57
Mouchamps F 37 Fa44
Mouchan F 61 Fd53
Mouchard F 42 Jc42
Mougins F 66 Kc53
Mougon F 45 Fc45
Mouilleron-en-Pareds F 37 Fb44
Moulay F 29 Fb39
Mouliherne F 38 Fd41
Moulins F 29 Fa40
Moulins F 40 Hb44
Moulins-Engilbert F 40 Hc43
Moulins-la-Marche F 30 Fd37
Moulismes F 45 Ga45
Moulle F 14 Gd30
Moult F 20 Fc36
Mourenx F 60 Fb55
Mourèze F 63 Hc54
Mouriès F 64 Jb53
Mourmelon-le-Grand F 23 Hd35
Mouscron B 15 Hb30
Moussac F 64 Ja53
Moussey F 34 Ka37
Moustéru F 27 Ea38
Moustey F 52 Fb52
Moustiers-Sainte-Marie F 65 Ka53
Moutfort L 24 Jd34
Mouthe F 42 Jd43
Mouthier-Haute-Pierre F 42 Jd42
Moutier-d'Ahun F 46 Gd46
Moûtiers F 49 Ka47
Moutiers-au-Perche F 30 Ga38
Moutiers-les-Mauxfaits F 44 Ed45
Moutiers-sur-le-Lay F 37 Fa44
Moux-en-Morvan F 41 Hd42
Mouy F 21 Gd35
Mouzon F 23 Ja34
Moyaux F 20 Fd36
Moy-de-l'Aisne F 22 Hb34
Moyenvic F 24 Ka36
Moyeuvre F 24 Jc35
Mozac F 47 Hb46
Mugron F 60 Fb54
Muides-sur-Loire F 39 Gc41
Mulhouse F 35 Kb40
Mulsanne F 30 Fd40
Mundolsheim F 35 Kc37
Munster F 24 Ka36
Munster F 35 Kb39
Muntzenheim F 35 Kc38
Murat F 55 Hb49
Murato F 72 Ld56
Murat-sur-Vèbre F 63 Hb54
Mur-de-Barrez F 55 Ha50
Mur-de-Bretagne F 27 Ea39
Mur-de-Sologne F 39 Gc41
Muret F 62 Gb55
Muro F 72 Ld56
Murol F 47 Hb47
Muron F 44 Fb46
Murs F 65 Jc53
Mûrs-Erigné F 37 Fb42
Murviel-lès-Béziers F 63 Hb54
Musselkanaal NL 9 Jd22

Mussidan F 53 Fd49
Mussy-sur-Seine F 33 Ja39
Mutzig F 35 Kb37
Muzillac F 36 Eb41
Myon F 42 Jd42

N

Naaldwijk NL 11 Hc26
Naarden NL 12 Ja25
Nachamps F 44 Fb46
Nagele NL 8 Jb24
Nailloux F 62 Gc55
Nailly F 32 Hb39
Naizin F 28 Eb39
Najac F 54 Gd52
Nalliers F 44 Fa45
Nalzen F 70 Gc56
Nampcel F 22 Hb34
Nampont F 14 Gc32
Namur B 16 Ja31
Nançay F 39 Gd42
Nancras F 44 Fb47
Nancray F 42 Jd41
Nancy F 34 Jd37
Nangis F 32 Hb38
Nans-les-Pins F 65 Jd54
Nans-sous-Sainte-Anne F 42 Jd42
Nant F 63 Hc53
Nanterre F 31 Gd37
Nantes F 37 Ed42
Nanteuil-en-Vallée F 45 Fd46
Nanteuil-la-Forêt F 22 Hc36
Nanteuil-le-Haudouin F 22 Ha36
Nantiat F 46 Gb46
Nanton F 41 Jb44
Nantua F 49 Jc45
Naours F 21 Gd33
Narbonne F 63 Hb55
Narbonne-Plage F 63 Hb55
Narcy F 40 Hb42
Nasbinals F 55 Hb50
Natoye B 16 Ja31
Naucelle F 55 Ha52
Nauviale F 55 Ha51
Navarrenx F 60 Fb55
Navilly F 41 Jb43
Nay F 69 Fc56
Nécy F 30 Fc37
Nederweert NL 12 Jb28
Neede NL 13 Jd25
Neerijnen NL 12 Ja26
Neeroeteren B 16 Jb29
Neerpelt B 12 Jb28
Nègrepelisse F 62 Gc53
Négrondes F 45 Ga48
Nemours F 32 Ha39
Nérac F 53 Fd52
Néré F 45 Fc46
Néris-les-Bains F 47 Ha45
Nérondes F 40 Ha43
Nersac F 45 Fd47
Nes NL 8 Jb21
Nesle F 22 Ha34
Nettancourt F 23 Ja36
Neuchâtel-Hardelot F 14 Gc31
Neuf-Brisach F 35 Kc39
Neufchâteau B 23 Jb33
Neufchâteau F 34 Jc38
Neufchâtel-en-Bray F 21 Gb34
Neufchâtel-en-Saosnois F 30 Fd38
Neufchâtel-sur-Aisne F 22 Hc35
Neuf-Marché F 21 Gc35
Neuillay-les-Bois F 39 Gc44
Neuillé-Pont-Pierre F 38 Ga41
Neuilly-en-Donjon F 48 Hd45

Neuilly-en-Thelle F 21 Gd35
Neuilly-le-Réal F 40 Hc44
Neuilly-Saint-Front F 22 Hb36
Neuilly-sur-Eure F 30 Ga38
Neulise F 48 Hd46
Neulliac F 27 Ea39
Neung-sur-Beuvron F 39 Gc41
Neupré B 16 Jb31
Neussargues-Moissac F 55 Hb49
Neuves-Maisons F 34 Jd37
Neuvic F 53 Fd49
Neuvic F 46 Gd48
Neuvic-Entier F 46 Gc47
Neuville F 54 Gd49
Neuville-aux-Bois F 31 Gd39
Neuville-de-Poitou F 38 Fd44
Neuville-les-Dames F 48 Jb45
Neuville-les-Decize F 40 Hb43
Neuville-sur-Saône F 48 Jb46
Neuvilly-en-Argonne F 23 Ja35
Neuvy-Bouin F 37 Fb44
Neuvy-le-Roi F 38 Ga41
Neuvy-Pailloux F 39 Gc43
Neuvy-Saint-Sépulcre F 39 Gc44
Neuvy-Sautour F 32 Hc39
Neuvy-sur-Barangeon F 39 Gd42
Neuvy-sur-Loire F 40 Ha41
Neuwiller-lès-Saverne F 25 Kb36
Névache F 58 Kb49
Nevele B 15 Hb29
Nevers F 40 Hb43
Nexon F 46 Gb47
Nice F 67 Kd53
Nicey F 33 Hd40
Niederbronn-les-Bains F 25 Kc35
Niedorp NL 8 Hd23
Niel B 16 Hd29
Nieuil F 46 Gd46
Nieuil-l'Espoir F 45 Fd45
Nieul-le-Dolent F 37 Ed44
Nieuw-Amsterdam NL 9 Jd23
Nieuw Bergen NL 13 Jc27
Nieuwegein NL 12 Ja26
Nieuwekerk aan de IJssel NL 12 Hd26
Nieuwendijk NL 12 Ja27
Nieuwe Pekela NL 9 Jd22
Nieuwerkerken B 16 Ja30
Nieuwenschans NL 9 Ka22
Nieuwerkerke B 15 Ha30
Nieuwkoop NL 12 Hd25
Nieuwleusen NL 9 Jc24
Nieuw Milligen NL 12 Jb25
Nieuwolda NL 9 Jd21
Nieuwpoort B 15 Ha29
Nieuwpoort-Bad B 15 Ha29
Nij Beets NL 8 Jb22
Nijkerk NL 12 Jb25
Nijlen B 16 Hd29
Nijmegen NL 12 Jb26
Nijverdal NL 13 Jc25
Nîmes F 64 Ja53
Ninove B 15 Hc30
Niort F 44 Fb45
Nispen NL 12 Hd28
Nissan-lez-Enserune F 63 Hb55
Nistelrode NL 12 Jb27
Nitry F 32 Hc40
Nivelles B 16 Hd31

Nizy-le-Comte F 22 Hc34
Noailhac F 63 Ha54
Noailles F 21 Gd35
Noailly F 48 Hd45
Nocé F 30 Ga38
Nods F 42 Ka42
Noé F 62 Gb55
Nœux-les-Mines F 15 Ha31
Nogaro F 61 Fc54
Nogent F 33 Jb39
Nogent-le-Roi F 31 Gc37
Nogent-le-Rotrou F 30 Ga38
Nogent-sur-Aube F 33 Hd38
Nogent-sur-Marne F 31 Gd37
Nogent-sur-Seine F 32 Hb38
Nogent-sur-Vernisson F 32 Ha40
Nogna F 42 Jc44
Nohant-en-Graçay F 39 Gc42
Nohant-Vic F 39 Gd44
Nohèdes F 71 Ha57
Noidans-le-Ferroux F 34 Jd40
Noirefontaine F 42 Ka41
Noirétable F 47 Hc47
Noirlieu F 78 Fc43
Noirmoutier-en-l'Île F 36 Ec43
Noiseux B 16 Jb32
Nolay F 41 Ja43
Nomeny F 24 Jd36
Nomexy F 34 Jd38
Nonancourt F 31 Gb37
Nonant-le-Pin F 30 Fd37
Nontron F 45 Ga48
Nonvilliers F 31 Gb38
Nonza F 72 Ld55
Noordbeemster NL 8 Ja24
Noordwijk aan Zee NL 12 Hd25
Noordwijkerhout NL 12 Hd25
Nordausques F 14 Gc30
Norg NL 9 Jc22
Norges-la-Ville F 41 Jb41
Normée F 33 Hd37
Noroy-le-Bourg F 34 Jd40
Nort-sur-Erdre F 37 Ed41
Notre-Dame-de-Gravenchon F 20 Ga35
Notre-Dame-de-Monts F 36 Ec43
Notre Dame du Laus F 57 Ka50
Nouaillé-Maupertuis F 45 Fd45
Nouan-le-Fuzellier F 39 Gd41
Nouans-les-Fontaines F 39 Gb42
Nouart F 23 Ja34
Nouvelle F 40 Ha44
Nouvion F 14 Gc32
Nouzonville F 23 Ja33
Novalaise F 49 Jd47
Noves F 64 Jb53
Noville B 17 Jc32
Novion-Porcien F 23 Hd34
Noyant F 38 Fd41
Noyant-de-Touraine F 38 Ga43
Noyant-la-Plaine F 38 Fc42
Noyelles-sur-Mer F 14 Gc32
Noyen-sur-Seine F 32 Hb38
Noyers F 33 Hd40
Noyers F 65 Jd52
Noyers-Saint-Martin F 21 Gd34
Noyon F 22 Ha34

Nozay F 37 Ed41
Nozeroy F 42 Jd43
Nozières F 56 Ja49
Nuars F 40 Hc41
Nueil-les Aubiers F 37 Fb43
Nuenen NL 12 Jb28
Nuisement-sur-Coole F 23 Hd36
Nuits F 33 Hd40
Nuits-Saint-Georges F 41 Jb42
Numansdorp NL 12 Hd27
Nunspeet NL 8 Jb24
Nyons F 57 Jc51

O

Oberhoffen F 25 Kc36
Obernai F 35 Kb37
Obersteigen F 35 Kb37
Obersteinbach F 25 Kc35
Objat F 54 Gd49
Ocana F 73 Ld58
Octeville, Cherbourg F 19 Ed34
Octeville-sur-Mer F 20 Fd34
Octon F 63 Hc54
Odoorn NL 9 Jd23
Odos F 61 Fd55
Oedelem B 15 Hb29
Oeffelt NL 13 Jc27
Oegstgeest NL 12 Hd25
Œuf-en-Ternois F 14 Gd32
Offranville F 20 Ga33
Ogéviller F 34 Ka37
Ohey B 16 Ja31
Oingt F 48 Ja46
Oinville F 21 Gc36
Oiron F 38 Fc43
Oirschot NL 12 Jb27
Oiselay-et-Grachaux F 42 Jd41
Oisemont F 21 Gc33
Oissel F 21 Gb35
Oisterwijk NL 12 Ja27
Olargues F 63 Hd54
Oldeberkoop NL 9 Jc23
Oldeboorn NL 8 Jc23
Oldebroek NL 8 Jb24
Oldekerk NL 9 Jc22
Oldemarkt NL 8 Jb23
Oldenzaal NL 13 Jd25
Olen B 16 Ja29
Oletta F 72 Ld56
Olette F 71 Ha57
Olivet F 31 Gc40
Olliergues F 47 Hc47
Ollioules F 65 Jd55
Olloy-sur-Viroin B 16 Hd32
Olmeto F 73 Ld59
Olmi-Capella F 72 Ld56
Olonne-sur-Mer F 37 Ed44
Olonzac F 63 Ha55
Oloron-Sainte-Marie F 60 Fb55
Olst NL 13 Jc25
Omblèze F 57 Jc49
Ommen NL 9 Jc24
Omont F 23 Ja34
Omonville-la-Rogue F 19 Ed34
Ondres F 60 Ed54
Onesse-et-Laharie F 60 Fa53
Onet-le-Château F 55 Ha51
Onnaing F 15 Hb32
Onoz F 42 Jc44
Onstwedde NL 9 Jd22
Onville F 24 Jc36
Onzain F 39 Gd41
Oostakker B 15 Hc29
Oostburg NL 11 Hb28
Oost-Cappel F 14 Gd30
Oostduinkerke-Bad B 15 Ha29

Oostende B 15 Ha29
Oosterend NL 8 Hd22
Oosterend NL 8 Ja21
Oosterhesselen NL 9 Jd23
Oosterhout NL 12 Ja27
Oosterwolde NL 9 Jc22
Oosterzee NL 8 Jb23
Oosterzele B 15 Hc30
Oosthuizen NL 8 Ja24
Oostkamp B 15 Hb29
Oostkapelle NL 11 Hb28
Oostmalle B 12 Hd28
Oost-Souburg NL 11 Hb28
Oostvleteren B 15 Ha30
Oost-Vlieland NL 8 Ja22
Oostvoorne NL 11 Hc26
Ootmarsum NL 9 Jd24
Opglabeek B 16 Jb29
Ophasselt B 15 Hc30
Ophemert NL 12 Jb26
Opitter B 16 Jb29
Oploo NL 13 Jc27
Oppède-le-Vieux F 65 Jc53
Oradour-Saint-Genest F 46 Gb45
Oradour-sur-Glane F 46 Gb46
Oraison F 65 Ka52
Orange F 64 Jb52
Orbais-l'Abbaye F 22 Hc36
Orbec F 20 Fd36
Orbigny F 39 Gb42
Orchamps F 42 Jc42
Orchies F 15 Hb31
Orcières F 57 Ka50
Orcival F 47 Hb47
Ordan-Larroque F 61 Fd54
Oreye B 16 Jb30
Orgelet F 42 Jc44
Orgères-en-Beauce F 31 Gc39
Orglandes F 19 Fa35
Orgnac-l'Aven F 56 Ja51
Orgnac-sur-Vézère F 46 Gc48
Orgon F 64 Jb53
Origny-en-Thiérache F 22 Hc33
Origny-Sainte-Benoite F 22 Hb33
Orléans F 31 Gc40
Orly F 31 Gd37
Ornans F 42 Jd42
Orpierre F 57 Jd51
Orp-Jauche B 16 Ja30
Orsan F 39 Gd44
Orsans F 42 Ka41
Orsay F 31 Gd37
Orsmaal B 16 Ja30
Orthez F 60 Fb54
Orto F 72 Ld57
Orval F 40 Ha44
Orvault F 37 Ed42
Orvelte NL 9 Jd23
Orville F 41 Jb41
Orvilliers-Saint-Julien F 32 Hc38
Osani F 72 Lc57
Oslon F 41 Jb42
Osmanville F 19 Fa35
Osmery F 40 Ha44
Osne-le-Val F 33 Jb37
Osny F 21 Gc36
Oss NL 12 Jb27
Osses F 60 Fa55
Ostabat F 60 Fa55
Otterlo NL 12 Jb25
Ouanne F 32 Hb40
Ouarville F 31 Gc38
Ouatre-Champs F 23 Ja34
Oucques F 31 Gb40
Oud-Beijerland NL 12 Hd27
Ouddorp NL 11 Hc27

Oudemirdum NL 8 Jb23
Oudenaarde B 15 Hb30
Oudenbosch NL 12 Hd27
Oude Pekela NL 9 Jd22
Oudeschoot NL 8 Jb23
Oude-Tonge NL 11 Hc27
Oudewater NL 12 Ja26
Oud Gastel NL 12 Hd27
Oudleusen NL 9 Jc24
Ouévy-le-Grand B 15 Hc32
Ouffet B 16 Jb31
Ougney F 42 Jc42
Ouistreham F 20 Fc35
Oulches F 39 Gb44
Oulins F 31 Gb37
Oulmes F 44 Fb45
Ouroër F 40 Hb42
Ouroux-en-Morvan F 41 Hd42
Ouroux-sur-Saône F 41 Jb43
Ourville-en-Caux F 20 Ga34
Oust F 70 Gb56
Outarville F 31 Gd39
Outines F 33 Ja37
Ouveillan F 63 Hb55
Ouzouer-le-Marché F 31 Gc40
Ouzouer-sur-Loire F 32 Ha40
Overijse B 16 Hd30
Overloon NL 13 Jc27
Overpelt B 16 Jb29
Ovezande NL 11 Hc28
Oye-et-Pallet F 42 Ka43
Oye-Plage F 14 Gc30
Oyonnax F 49 Jc45
Oyrières F 42 Jc41
Ozoir-la-Ferrière F 32 Ha37

P

Paal B 16 Ja29
Pacé F 29 Ed39
Pacy-sur-Eure F 21 Gb36
Padern F 71 Ha56
Padirac F 54 Gc50
Padulone F 72 Ma57
Pagny-sur-Meuse F 34 Jc37
Pagny-sur-Moselle F 24 Jc36
Pailhès F 70 Gc56
Paimbœuf F 36 Ec42
Paimpol F 27 Ea37
Paimpont F 28 Ec39
Palaiseau F 31 Gd37
Palavas-les-Flots F 64 Hd54
Palinges F 41 Hd44
Pâlis F 32 Hc39
Paliseul B 23 Ja33
Pallegney F 34 Jd38
Pamiers F 70 Gc56
Pampelone F 54 Gd52
Panassac F 61 Ga55
Panazol F 46 Gb47
Pancey F 33 Jb38
Panissières F 48 Ja47
Panjas F 61 Fc53
Paray-le-Monial F 41 Hd44
Parcé-sur-Sarthe F 30 Fc40
Parcey F 42 Jc42
Parennes F 30 Fc39
Parentis-en-Born F 52 Fa52
Parfondeval F 23 Hd33
Pargny F 33 Ja37
Pargues F 33 Hd39
Parigné-l'Evêque F 30 Fd40
Paris F 31 Gd37
Parisot F 54 Gd52
Parois F 23 Jb35

Parroy F 34 Ka37
Parsac F 46 Gd45
Pars-lès-Romilly F 32 Hc38
Parthenay F 38 Fc44
Pas-de-Jeu F 38 Fc43
Pas-en-Artois F 14 Gd32
Passais F 29 Fb38
Patay F 31 Gc39
Pau F 61 Fc55
Pauillac F 52 Fb49
Paulhac-en-Margeride F 55 Hc50
Paulhaguet F 55 Hc49
Paulhan F 63 Hc54
Paulx F 37 Ed43
Pavezin F 48 Ja48
Pavilly F 20 Ga34
Payrac F 54 Gc50
Payzac F 46 Gb48
Péaule F 36 Ec41
Peer B 16 Jb29
Peille F 67 Kd53
Peillon F 67 Kd53
Peipin F 65 Jd52
Peisey-Nancroix F 50 Kb47
Peize NL 9 Jc22
Pelacoy F 54 Gc51
Pellafol F 57 Jd50
Pellegrue F 53 Fd50
Pellevoisin F 39 Gb43
Pélussin F 48 Ja48
Pénestin F 36 Eb41
Penhors F 26 Db39
Penmarc'h F 26 Dc40
Penne F 62 Gc53
Penne-d'Agenais F 53 Ga52
Penol F 48 Jb48
Penta di Casinca F 72 Ma56
Penvins F 36 Eb41
Péone F 58 Kc52
Pepinster B 17 Jc31
Pèra-Casa F 58 Kd52
Péret F 63 Hc54
Périers F 19 Fa36
Pérignac F 44 Fb47
Périgné F 45 Fc46
Périgueux F 53 Ga49
Perlé L 24 Jc33
Pernay F 38 Fd41
Pernes-les-Fontaines F 65 Jc52
Péronnas F 48 Jb45
Péronne F 22 Ha33
Pérouges F 48 Jb46
Perpezac-le-Noir F 46 Gc48
Perpignan F 71 Hb57
Perrecy-les-Forges F 41 Hd44
Perros-Guirec F 27 Ea37
Persac F 45 Ga45
Persan F 21 Gd36
Perthes F 32 Hd40
Perthes F 23 Hd34
Pertuis F 65 Jd53
Péruwelz B 15 Hb31
Pervijze B 15 Ha29
Perwez B 16 Ja31
Pesmes F 42 Jc41
Pessac F 52 Fb50
Pétange L 24 Jc34
Petit-Palais-et-Cornemps F 53 Fc50
Petreto-Bicchisano F 73 Ld59
Peuton F 29 Fb40
Peypin F 65 Jd54
Peyrat-de-Bellac F 46 Gb46
Peyrat-la-Nonière F 46 Gd46
Peyrat-le-Château F 46 Gc47
Peyrefitte-du-Razès F 70 Gc56
Peyrehorade F 60 Fa54
Peyriac-Minervois F 63 Ha55

Peyrieu F 49 Jd47
Peyrolles-en-Provence F 65 Jd53
Peyruis F 65 Jd52
Peyrus F 56 Jb49
Peyrusse-le-Roc F 54 Gd51
Pézenas F 63 Hc54
Pezens F 62 Gd55
Pézilla-la-Rivière F 71 Hb57
Pezou F 31 Gb40
Pézy F 31 Gc38
Pfaffenhoffen F 25 Kc36
Phalsbourg F 25 Kb36
Philippeville B 16 Hd32
Piaam NL 8 Ja22
Piana F 72 Lc57
Pianottoli-Caldarello F 73 Ld60
Piau-Engaly F 69 Fd57
Picarreau F 42 Jc43
Piccovagia F 73 Ma59
Picquigny F 21 Gd33
Piedicroce F 72 Ma57
Pierlas F 58 Kc52
Pierre-Buffière F 46 Gb47
Pierre-de-Bresse F 41 Jb43
Pierrefeu-du-Var F 65 Ka55
Pierrefiche F 56 Hd50
Pierrefitte-Nestales F 69 Fc56
Pierrefitte-sur-Aire F 23 Jb36
Pierrefitte-sur-Sauldre F 39 Gd41
Pierrefonds F 22 Ha35
Pierrefontaine-les-Blamont F 43 Kb41
Pierrefontaine-les-Varans F 42 Ka41
Pierrefontaines F 33 Jb40
Pierrefort F 55 Hb50
Pierrelatte F 56 Jb51
Pierremont F 14 Gd32
Pierremont-sur-Amance F 34 Jc40
Pierre-Perthuis F 40 Hc41
Pierrepont F 22 Hc34
Pierrepont F 24 Jc34
Pierrepont-sur-Avre F 21 Gd34
Pierroton F 52 Fb50
Pieterburen NL 9 Jc21
Pietralba F 72 Ld56
Pietraserena F 72 Ma57
Piffonds F 32 Hb39
Pijnacker NL 12 Hd26
Pilat-Plage F 52 Fa51
Pillon F 23 Jb34
Pillon F 23 Jb35
Pimelles F 33 Hd40
Pinarello F 73 Ma59
Pindères F 53 Fd52
Piney F 33 Hd38
Pino F 72 Ld55
Pinols F 55 Hc49
Pinsot F 49 Jd48
Piolenc F 64 Jb52
Pionsat F 47 Ha46
Pipriac F 28 Ec40
Piriac-sur-Mer F 36 Eb42
Pirou F 19 Ed36
Pisany F 44 Fb47
Pisseloup F 34 Jc40
Pissos F 52 Fb52
Pithiviers F 31 Gd39
Plabennec F 26 Dc38
Plage de Tahiti F 66 Kb55
Plaigne F 62 Gc55
Plaimpied-Givaudins F 40 Ha43
Plaisance F 61 Fd54
Plaisance F 45 Ga45
Plaisance F 62 Gd54
Plaisance-du-Touloset F 62 Gb54
Plaisians F 65 Jc52
Plaisir F 21 Gc37

Plaissan F 63 Hc54
Plancher-les-Mines F 34 Ka40
Planchez F 41 Hd42
Plancoët F 28 Ec38
Plancy-l'Abbaye F 32 Hc37
Plan-d'Aups-Sainte-Baume F 65 Jd54
Plan-de-Baix F 57 Jc50
Plan-de-la-Tour F 66 Kb54
Plan-du-Var F 58 Kc52
Planty F 32 Hc38
Plassac F 44 Fb48
Plateau-d'Assy F 50 Kb46
Plaudren F 28 Ec40
Pleaux F 54 Gd49
Plédéliac F 28 Ec39
Pleine-Fougères F 29 Ed38
Plélan-le-Grand F 28 Ec39
Plélan-le-Petit F 28 Ec38
Plémet F 28 Eb39
Plénée-Jugon F 28 Ec38
Pléneuf-Val-André F 28 Eb38
Plenoy F 34 Jc39
Plérin F 28 Eb38
Pleslin-Trigavou F 28 Ec38
Plessala F 28 Eb39
Plessé F 37 Fd41
Plestin-les-Grèves F 27 Dd37
Pleumartin F 38 Ga44
Pleurs F 32 Hc37
Pleyben F 26 Dc39
Pleyber-Christ F 27 Dd38
Ploemeur F 27 Dd40
Ploërdut F 27 Ea39
Ploërmel F 28 Ec40
Plœuc-sur-Lié F 28 Eb39
Plombières-les-Bains F 34 Ka39
Plomeur F 26 Dc40
Plomion F 22 Hc33
Plomodiern F 26 Dc39
Plonéour-Lanvern F 26 Dc40
Plonévez-Porzay F 26 Dc39
Plouaret F 27 Dd37
Plouarzel F 26 Db38
Plouay F 27 Ea40
Ploubalay F 28 Ec38
Ploudalmézeau F 26 Db37
Plouédern F 27 Dd37
Plouec F 27 Dd37
Plouezoch F 27 Dd37
Plougasnou F 27 Dd37
Plougastel-Daoulas F 26 Dc38
Plougonvelin F 26 Db38
Plougonven F 27 Dd38
Plougonver F 27 Ea38
Plougrescant F 27 Ea37
Plouguenast F 28 Eb39
Plouguerneau F 26 Db37
Plouguernevel F 27 Ea39
Plouha F 28 Eb37
Plouharnel F 36 Ea41
Ploumanach F 27 Dd37
Plounéour-Menez F 27 Dd38
Plounéventer F 26 Dc38
Plounévez-du-Faou F 27 Dd39
Plounévez-Quintin F 27 Ea38
Plourac'h F 27 Dd38
Plouray F 27 Ea39
Plouvorn F 26 Dc37
Plouzané F 26 Db38
Plozévet F 26 Db39
Plumelec F 28 Eb40
Pluméliau F 28 Ea40
Plumieux F 28 Eb39
Pluviers F 45 Ga47

Pluvigner – Romorantin-Lanthenay

Pluvigner F 27 Ea40
Poelkapelle B 15 Ha30
Pogny F 23 Hd36
Poigny-la-Forêt F 31 Gc37
Poillé-sur-Vègre F 30 Fc40
Poilley F 29 Fa38
Poisieux F 39 Gd43
Poisson F 48 Hd45
Poissons F 33 Jb38
Poissy F 21 Gd36
Poisvilliers F 31 Gb38
Poitiers F 38 Fd44
Poix-de-Picardie F 21 Gc34
Poix-Terron F 23 Ja34
Polaincourt-et-Clairfontaine F 34 Jd39
Polignac F 56 Hd49
Poligny F 42 Jc43
Polisy F 33 Hd39
Pomarez F 60 Fb54
Pommeréval F 21 Gb34
Pomoy F 34 Jd40
Pompey F 24 Jd36
Pompierre F 34 Jc38
Pompignan F 64 Hd53
Poncé-sur-le-Loir F 30 Ga40
Poncin F 49 Jc45
Pons F 44 Fb48
Pont-à-Bucy F 22 Hb34
Pont-à-Celles B 16 Hd31
Pontacq F 69 Fc56
Pontailler-sur-Saône F 42 Jc41
Pontaix F 57 Jc50
Pont-à-Marcq F 15 Ha31
Pont-à-Mousson F 24 Jc36
Pontarion F 46 Gc46
Pontarlier F 42 Ka43
Pontaubault F 29 Fa37
Pont-Audemer F 20 Fd35
Pontaumur F 47 Ha46
Pont-Authou F 20 Ga35
Pont-Aven F 27 Dd40
Pontavert F 22 Hc35
Pontcharra F 49 Jd47
Pontcharra-sur-Tudine F 48 Jd46
Pontcharraud F 46 Gd47
Pontchartrain F 21 Gc37
Pontchâteau F 36 Ec41
Pont-Croix F 26 Db39
Pont-d'Ain F 49 Jc46
Pont-d'Aspach F 35 Kb40
Pont-de-Chéruy F 48 Jd47
Pont-de-Dore F 47 Hc47
Pont-de-la-Chaux F 42 Jd44
Pont-de-l'Arche F 21 Gb35
Pont-de-Pany F 41 Ja42
Pont-de-Poitte F 42 Jc44
Pont-de Rhodes F 54 Gc51
Pont-de Roide F 42 Ka41
Pont-de-Salars F 55 Ha52
Pont-des-Plagnettes F 49 Ka45
Pont-de-Vaux F 41 Jb44
Pont-de-Veyle F 48 Jb45
Pont-d'Hérault F 64 Hd53
Pont-d'Héry F 42 Jd43
Pont-d'Ouilly F 30 Fc37
Pont-du-Château F 47 Hb47
Pont-du-Navoy F 42 Jc43
Ponte Castirla F 72 Ld57
Ponte Leccia F 72 Ld56
Pont-en-Royans F 57 Jc49
Ponte Nuovo F 72 Ld56
Pontenx-les-Forges F 52 Fa52
Pont-Évêque F 48 Jb47
Pont-Farcy F 19 Fa36
Pontgibaud F 47 Ha47
Pont-Hamon F 28 Eb39

Ponthibault F 30 Fd40
Ponthierry F 32 Ha38
Pontigny F 20 Fc36
Pontigny F 32 Hc40
Pontijou F 31 Gb40
Pontivy F 27 Ea39
Pont-l'Abbé F 26 Dc40
Pont-l'Abbé F 19 Fa35
Pont-l'Abbé-d'Arnoult F 44 Fb47
Pont-la-Ville F 33 Ja39
Pont-l'Évêque F 20 Fd35
Pontlevoy F 39 Gb42
Pont-Losquet F 27 Ea37
Pontmain F 29 Fa38
Pontoise F 21 Gd36
Pontonx-sur-l'Adour F 60 Fa54
Pontorson F 29 Ed38
Pont-Rémy F 21 Gc33
Pontrieux F 27 Ea37
Pont-Sainte-Maxence F 22 Ha35
Pont-Saint-Esprit F 64 Jb52
Pont Saint-Mamet F 53 Ga50
Pont-Saint-Martin F 37 Ed42
Pont-Saint-Pierre F 21 Gb35
Pont-Saint-Vincent F 34 Jd37
Port-Scorff F 27 Dd40
Port-Scorff F 27 Ea40
Pont-sur-Yonne F 32 Hb38
Pontvallain F 30 Fd40
Poperinge B 15 Ha30
Poppel B 12 Ja28
Pornic F 36 Ec42
Pornichet F 36 Ec42
Porquerolles F 65 Ka55
Portbail F 19 Ed35
Port-Barcarès F 71 Hb57
Port-Blanc F 27 Ea37
Port-Camargue F 64 Ja54
Port-Cros F 66 Kb55
Port-d'Agrès F 54 Gd51
Port d'Atelier-Amance F 34 Jd40
Port-de-Bouc F 64 Jb54
Port de Chiavari F 73 Lc59
Port-de-Miramar F 65 Ka55
Port-des-Barques F 44 Fa46
Port des Callonges F 52 Fb49
Porte-de-Lanne F 60 Fa54
Portel-des-Corbières F 71 Hb56
Port-en-Bessin F 19 Fb35
Port Goulphar F 36 Ea42
Port Grimaud F 66 Ka55
Porticcio F 73 Ld58
Port-Joinville F 36 Ec44
Port-la-Nouvelle F 71 Hb56
Port-Leucate F 71 Hb56
Port-Louis F 27 Ea40
Port-Manec'h F 27 Dd40
Port Maubert F 44 Fb47
Port-Mort F 21 Gb36
Port-Navalo F 36 Ea41
Porto F 72 Lc57
Porto Pollo F 73 Ld59
Porto-Vecchio F 73 Le59
Port pétrolier du Havre-Antifer F 20 Fd34
Port-Sainte-Marie F 53 Fd52
Port-Saint-Louis-du-Rhône F 64 Jb54
Port-Saint-Père F 37 Ed42
Portsall F 26 Db37
Port-sur-Saône F 34 Jd40
Port-Vendres F 71 Hb57
Posesse F 23 Ja36
Postel B 12 Ja28

Posterholt NL 17 Jc29
Pouancé F 29 Fa40
Pouan-les-Vallées F 33 Hd38
Poudenas F 61 Fd53
Pougny F 40 Hb41
Pougues-les-Eaux F 40 Hb42
Pougy F 33 Hd38
Pouillenay F 41 Ja41
Pouillon F 60 Fa54
Pouilly-en-Auxois F 41 Ja42
Pouilly-sous-Charlieu F 48 Hd45
Pouilly-sur-Loire F 40 Hb42
Pouilly-sur-Saône F 41 Jb42
Poujols F 63 Hc53
Poulaines F 39 Gc42
Pouldreuzic F 26 Dc39
Poullaouen F 27 Dd38
Pourlans F 41 Jb43
Pourrain F 32 Hb40
Pourrières F 65 Jd54
Pouyastruc F 61 Fd55
Pouydesseaux F 61 Fc53
Pouy-de-Touges F 62 Gb55
Pouzac F 69 Fd56
Pouzauges F 37 Fb44
Pouzilhac F 64 Jb52
Poyols F 57 Jc50
Pozières F 22 Ha33
Pradelles F 56 Hd50
Pradelles-Carbadès F 63 Ha55
Prades F 71 Ha57
Prads F 58 Kb51
Prahecq F 45 Fc45
Pralognan F 50 Ka47
Pra-Loup F 58 Kb51
Pramouton F 58 Kb51
Praslay F 33 Jd40
Prat F 70 Gb58
Prat-de-Chest F 63 Hb55
Prats-de-Mollo-la-Preste F 71 Ha58
Prats-du-Périgord F 54 Gb51
Prayssac F 54 Gb51
Prayssas F 53 Ga52
Préaux F 21 Gb35
Préchac F 53 Fc52
Précigné F 30 Fc40
Précy-sous-Thil F 41 Hd41
Précy-sur-Oise F 21 Gd35
Pré-en-Pail F 30 Fc38
Préfailles F 36 Ec42
Prefontaines F 32 Ha39
Prélenfrey F 57 Jd49
Prémery F 40 Hb42
Prémont F 22 Hb33
Prendeignes F 54 Gd50
Prénouvellon F 31 Gc40
Presly F 39 Gd42
Pressac F 45 Ga46
Preuilly-sur-Claise F 38 Ga43
Prévenchères F 56 Hd51
Préveranges F 46 Gd45
Prey F 21 Gb36
Primel-Trégastel F 27 Dd37
Prisches F 15 Hc32
Prissac F 39 Gb44
Privas F 56 Ja50
Priziac F 27 Ea39
Propriano F 73 Ld59
Provenchères F 35 Kb38
Provins F 32 Hb38
Prunelli di Fiumorbo F 73 Ma58
Prunete F 72 Ma57
Pruniers-en-Sologne F 39 Gc42
Puget-Théniers F 58 Kc52
Puget-Ville F 65 Ka54
Pugieu F 49 Jc46

Pugnac F 52 Fb49
Puicheric F 63 Ha55
Puiseaux F 31 Gd39
Puissalicon F 63 Hc54
Puisserguier F 63 Hb55
Puivert F 70 Gd56
Pulversheim F 35 Kb39
Purmerend NL 8 Ja24
Pussay F 31 Gc38
Putanges F 30 Fc37
Putte B 16 Hd29
Putte NL 12 Hd28
Puttelange-aux-Lacs F 24 Ka35
Putten NL 12 Jb25
Puycasquier F 61 Gd54
Puydrouard F 44 Fb46
Puy-Guillaume F 47 Hc46
Puylagarde F 54 Gc52
Puylaroque F 54 Gc52
Puylaurens F 62 Gd54
Puy-l'Évêque F 54 Gb51
Puymiclan F 53 Fd51
Puymirol F 53 Ga52
Puyôo F 60 Fa54
Puy-Saint-Martin F 56 Jb50
Puy-Saint-Vincent F 57 Ka49
Pyla-sur-Mer F 52 Fa51
Pyrénées 2000 F 70 Gd58

Q

Quarré-les-Tombes F 41 Hd41
Quartes B 15 Hb31
Quédillac F 28 Ec39
Quelaines F 29 Fb40
Quemigny-Poisot F 41 Ja42
Quend F 14 Gc32
Quers F 34 Ka40
Quessoy F 28 Eb38
Questembert F 36 Eb41
Quettehou F 19 Fa34
Quettetot F 19 Ed35
Queudes F 32 Hc37
Quevauvillers F 21 Gd33
Quevert F 28 Ec40
Quiberon F 36 Ea41
Quiévrain B 15 Hc31
Quillan F 70 Gd56
Quilly F 36 Ec41
Quimper F 26 Dc39
Quimperlé F 27 Dd40
Quinéville F 19 Fa35
Quingey F 42 Jd42
Quinsac F 52 Fb50
Quinson F 65 Ka53
Quint-Fonsegrives F 62 Gc54
Quintin F 28 Eb38
Quissac F 64 Hd53
Quistinic F 27 Ea40
Quittebeuf F 20 Ga36

R

Raalte NL 9 Jc24
Rabastens F 62 Gc53
Rabouillet F 71 Ha57
Rachecourt-sur-Marne F 33 Jb37
Raddon F 34 Ka39
Raeren B 17 Jc30
Ramatuelle F 66 Kb55
Rambervillers F 34 Ka38
Rambouillet F 31 Gc37
Rance B 16 Hd32
Rancon F 46 Gb46
Randan F 47 Hc46
Randanne F 47 Hb47
Randonnai F 30 Ga37
Rânes F 30 Fc37
Rang-du-Fliers F 14 Gc32
Ranrupt F 35 Kb38
Raon-l'Étape F 34 Ka38

Rasteau F 64 Jb52
Raucourt-et-Flaba F 23 Ja34
Raulhac F 55 Ha50
Rauwiller F 25 Kb36
Ravenstein NL 12 Jb26
Ravières F 33 Hd40
Rayol-Canadel-sur-Mer F 66 Kb55
Razimet F 53 Fd52
Réalcamp F 21 Gc33
Réalmont F 62 Gd53
Réalville F 54 Gc52
Réaup F 53 Fd52
Rebais F 32 Hb37
Rebastens-de-Bigorre F 61 Fd55
Rébénacq F 69 Fc56
Rebirechioulet F 61 Ga55
Recey-sur-Ource F 33 Ja40
Recht B 17 Jc31
Recogne B 23 Jb33
Recologne F 42 Jc41
Recoules-Prévinquières F 55 Hb52
Redange-sur-Attert L 24 Jc33
Redessan F 64 Ja53
Redon F 36 Ec41
Reffannes F 37 Be44
Reffuveille F 29 Fa37
Réguiny F 28 Eb40
Reguisheim F 35 Kb39
Reichshoffen F 25 Kc36
Reignac F 52 Fb49
Reignac-sur-Indre F 38 Ga42
Reims F 22 Hc35
Rémalard F 30 Ga38
Remauville F 32 Ha39
Réméréville F 34 Jd37
Remich L 24 Jd34
Rémilly F 40 Hc43
Remiremont F 34 Ka39
Remoncourt F 34 Jd38
Remouchamps B 16 Jb31
Remoulins F 64 Ja53
Remungol F 28 Eb40
Rémuzat F 57 Jc51
Remy F 22 Ha35
Renac F 28 Ec40
Renaison F 48 Hd46
Renazé F 29 Fa40
Renesse NL 11 Hb27
Renève F 42 Jc41
Reningelst B 15 Ha30
Renkum NL 12 Jb26
Rennes F 29 Ed39
Renwez F 23 Hd34
Repel F 34 Jc38
Réquista F 63 Ha53
Ressons-sur-Matz F 22 Ha34
Rétaud F 44 Fb47
Rethel F 23 Hd34
Rethondes F 22 Ha35
Retie B 12 Ja28
Retiers F 29 Fa40
Retournac F 56 Hd49
Reugny F 38 Ga41
Reugny F 47 Ha45
Reuilly F 39 Gd43
Reuland B 17 Jc32
Reusel NL 12 Ja28
Revel F 62 Gd54
Revest-du-Bion F 65 Jd52
Revigny-sur-Ornain F 23 Ja36
Revin F 23 Hd33
Rezé F 37 Ed42
Rheden NL 13 Jc26
Rhenen NL 12 Jb26
Rhinau F 35 Kc38
Rhisnes F 16 Hd31
Ribeauvillé F 35 Kb38
Ribécourt-Dreslincourt F 22 Ha34
Ribemont F 22 Hb33
Ribérac F 53 Fd49

Richebourg F 31 Gc37
Richebourg F 33 Jb39
Richelieu F 38 Fd43
Ridderkerk NL 12 Hd26
Riec-sur-Bélon F 27 Dd40
Rieumes F 62 Gb55
Rieupeyroux F 54 Gd52
Rieussec F 63 Hb55
Rieux F 36 Ec41
Rieux F 62 Gb55
Riez F 65 Ka53
Rignac F 54 Gd51
Rigney F 42 Jd41
Rigny-Ussé F 38 Fd42
Rijen NL 12 Ja27
Rijnwarden NL 13 Jc26
Rijsbergen NL 12 Hd28
Rijswijk NL 11 Hc26
Rilly-la-Montagne F 22 Hc35
Rimaucourt F 33 Jb38
Rinsumageest NL 8 Jb21
Riom F 47 Hb46
Riom-ès-Montagnes F 47 Ha48
Rion-des-Landes F 60 Fa53
Riotord F 48 Ja48
Rioux F 44 Fb47
Rioz F 42 Jd41
Rips NL 12 Jb27
Riquewihr F 35 Kb38
Riscle F 61 Fc54
Risoul 1850 F 58 Kb50
Riva-Bella F 20 Fc35
Rive-de-Gier F 48 Ja47
Rives F 49 Jc48
Rivesaltes F 71 Hb57
Rixensart B 16 Hd30
Roaillan F 53 Fc51
Roanne F 48 Hd46
Robertville B 17 Jc31
Rocamadour F 54 Gc50
Rochechouart F 45 Ga47
Rochecolombe F 56 Ja51
Rochefort B 16 Jb32
Rochefort F 44 Fa46
Rochefort-en-Terre F 28 Ec40
Rochefort-Montagne F 47 Ha47
Rochegude F 64 Jb52
Rochehaut B 23 Ja33
Rochemaure F 56 Ja51
Rocheservière F 37 Ed43
Rochetaillée F 57 Jd49
Rochetaillée-sur-Saône F 48 Jb46
Rockanje NL 11 Hc26
Rocroi F 23 Hd33
Roden NL 9 Jc22
Rodez F 55 Ha51
Roermond NL 13 Jc28
Roeselare B 15 Ha30
Roffiac F 55 Hb49
Roggel NL 13 Jc28
Rogliano F 72 Ld55
Rognes F 65 Jd53
Rogny-les-Sept-Écluses F 32 Ha40
Rohan F 28 Eb39
Rohrbach-lès-Bitche F 25 Kb35
Roisel F 22 Ha33
Roissy F 32 Ha37
Roizy F 23 Hd34
Rolampont F 33 Jb39
Rolde NL 9 Jd22
Rom F 45 Fd45
Romans-sur-Isère F 56 Jb49
Rombas F 24 Jd35
Romenay F 41 Jb44
Romeny-sur-Marne F 22 Hb36
Romilly-sur-Seine F 32 Hc38
Romorantin-Lanthenay F 39 Gc42

Ronce-les-Bains F 44 Fa47
Ronchamp F 34 Ka40
Ronquières B 16 Hd31
Ronse B 15 Hb30
Roodeschool NL 9 Jd21
Roosendaal NL 12 Hd28
Roppe F 35 Kb40
Roquebillière F 58 Kd52
Roquebrun F 63 Hb54
Roquebrune-sur-Argens F 66 Kb54
Roquecourbe F 62 Gd54
Roquefort F 61 Fc53
Roquefort-sur-Soulzon F 63 Hb53
Roquesteron F 58 Kc52
Rosans F 57 Jc51
Roscanvel F 26 Db38
Roscoff F 26 Dc37
Rosheim F 35 Kb37
Rosières F 56 Ja51
Rosières-aux-Salines F 34 Jd37
Rosières-en-Blois F 34 Jc37
Rosières-en-Santerre F 22 Ha33
Rosmalen NL 12 Jb27
Rosnay F 39 Gd44
Rosnay-l'Hôpital F 33 Ja38
Rosoy F 32 Hb39
Rosporden F 27 Dd39
Rossignol F 53 Ga49
Rossum NL 9 Jd24
Rostrenen F 27 Ea39
Rostudel F 26 Db39
Rotterdam NL 12 Hd26
Rottum NL 8 Jb23
Rouaine F 58 Kb52
Roubaix F 15 Hb31
Roudouallec F 27 Dd39
Rouen F 21 Gb35
Rouffach F 35 Kb39
Rouge F 29 Ed40
Rougemont F 42 Jd41
Rouillac F 45 Fc47
Rouillé F 45 Fd45
Roujan F 63 Hc54
Roulans F 42 Jd41
Roullet-Saint-Estèphe F 45 Fd48
Roumazières-Loubert F 45 Ga47
Roupy F 22 Hb33
Roussac F 46 Gb46
Rousset-les-Vignes F 57 Jc51
Roussillon F 48 Jb48
Roussillon F 65 Jc53
Rouvray F 41 Hd41
Rouvres-sur-Aube F 33 Jb40
Rouvroy-sur-Audry F 23 Hd33
Rouy F 40 Hc43
Rovon F 49 Jc48
Roya F 58 Kc51
Royan F 44 Fa47
Royat F 47 Hb47
Roybon F 49 Jc48
Roye F 22 Ha34
Royère-de-Vienne F 46 Gc47
Rozay-en-Brie F 32 Ha37
Rozelieures F 34 Jd37
Rozier-Côtes-d'Aurec F 48 Hd48
Rozoy-sur-Serre F 23 Hd34
Rucphen NL 12 Hd28
Rue F 14 Gc32
Ruelle-sur-Touvre F 45 Fd47
Ruffec F 45 Fd46
Ruffieu F 49 Jd46
Ruffieux F 49 Jd46
Rugles F 30 Ga37
Ruinen NL 9 Jc23

Rully F 22 Ha35
Rumes B 15 Hb31
Rumigny F 23 Hd33
Rumilly F 49 Jd46
Rumilly-lès-Vaudes F 33 Hd39
Rumont F 23 Jb36
Ruoms F 56 Ja51
Rupt-sur-Moselle F 34 Ka39
Rustrel F 65 Jd53
Rutten NL 8 Jb23
Ruurlo NL 13 Jd25
Ruynes-en-Margeride F 55 Hb49
Rye F 42 Jc43

S

Saales F 35 Kb38
Sabarat F 70 Gc56
Sables-d'Or-les-Pins F 28 Ec37
Sablé-sur-Sarthe F 30 Fc40
Sabres F 52 Fb52
Saclas F 31 Gd38
Sacquenay F 41 Jb41
Saeul L 24 Jc33
Saffré F 37 Ed41
Sagone F 73 Lc58
Sahune F 57 Jc51
Saignes F 47 Ha48
Saignon F 65 Jc53
Saillagouse F 70 Gd58
Saillans F 57 Jc50
Sains-en-Amiénois F 21 Gd33
Sains-Richaumont F 22 Hc33
Saint-Affrique F 63 Hb53
Saint-Agil F 30 Ga39
Saint-Agnan F 41 Hd44
Saint-Agrève F 56 Ja49
Saint-Aignan F 39 Gb42
Saint-Aignan F 42 Jd41
Saint-Aignan-le-Jaillard F 31 Gd40
Saint-Aignan-sur-Roë F 29 Fa40
Saint-Aigulin F 53 Fc49
Saint-Alban F 28 Eb38
Saint-Alban-sur-Limagnole F 55 Hc50
Saint-Allouestre F 28 Eb40
Saint-Amand-de-Coly F 54 Gb49
Saint-Amand-en-Puisaye F 40 Hb41
Saint-Amandin F 47 Ha48
Saint-Amand-les-Eaux F 15 Hb31
Saint-Amand-Longpré F 39 Gb41
Saint-Amand-Montrond F 40 Ha44
Saint-Amands B 15 Hc29
Saint-Amand-sur-Fion F 33 Ja37
Saint-Amans F 55 Hc50
Saint-Amans-de-Mounis F 63 Hb54
Saint-Amans-des-Cots F 55 Ha50
Saint-Amans-Soult F 63 Ha54
Saint-Ambroix F 64 Ja52
Saint-Amé F 34 Ka39
Saint-Amour F 42 Jc44
Saint-Andiol F 64 Jb53
Saint-André-de-Corcy F 48 Jb46
Saint-André-de-Cubzac F 52 Fb50

Saint-André-de-l'Eure F 31 Gb37
Saint-André-de-Sangonis F 63 Hc54
Saint-André-de-Valborgne F 64 Hd52
Saint-André-les-Alpes F 58 Kb52
Saint-Angeau F 45 Fd47
Saint-Angel F 46 Gd48
Saint-Anne GBA 18 Ec34
Saint-Anthème F 48 Hd47
Saint-Antoine F 73 Ma58
Saint-Antoine l'Abbaye F 49 Jc48
Saint-Antoine-sur-l'Isle F 53 Fd49
Saint-Antonin-Noble-Val F 54 Gc52
Saint-Antonius B 12 Hd28
Saint-Août F 39 Gd44
Saint-Apollinaire F 41 Jb41
Saint-Apollinaire F 57 Ka50
Saint-Arcons-d'Allier F 55 Hc49
Saint-Arnoult-des-Bois F 31 Gb38
Saint-Astier F 53 Ga49
Saint-Auban F 65 Ka52
Saint-Auban F 66 Kb53
Saint-Auban d'Aubigné F 29 Ed39
Saint-Auban-des-Châteaux F 29 Ed40
Saint-Aubin-des-Coudrais F 30 Ga39
Saint-Aubin-du-Cormier F 29 Fa39
Saint-Aubin-lès-Elbeuf F 20 Ga35
Saint-Aubin-sur-Aire F 33 Jb37
Saint-Aubin-sur-Loire F 40 Hc44
Saint-Aubin-sur-Mer F 20 Fc35
Saint-Augustin F 46 Gc48
Saint-Augustin-des-Bois F 37 Fb41
Saint-Aulaye F 53 Fd49
Saint-Avit F 47 Ha46
Saint-Avit-de-Tardes F 46 Gd46
Saint-Avold F 24 Ka35
Saint-Aygulf F 66 Kb54
Saint-Barthélemy F 27 Ea40
Saint-Barthélemy-d'Anjou F 37 Fb41
Saint-Barthélemy-le-Plain F 56 Jb49
Saint-Baudille-et-Pipet F 57 Jd50
Saint-Bauzille-de-Montmel F 64 Hd53
Saint-Bauzille-de-Putois F 64 Hd53
Saint-Beat F 69 Ga56
Saint-Beauzély F 55 Hb52
Saint-Beauzire F 47 Hb48
Saint-Benin-d'Azy F 40 Hb43
Saint-Benoît F 49 Jc47
Saint-Benoît-des-Ondes F 29 Ed37
Saint-Benoît-du-Sault F 46 Gb45
Saint-Benoît-en-Woëvre F 24 Jc36
Saint-Benoît-sur-Loire F 31 Gd40
Saint-Bernard F 49 Jd48
Saint-Berthevin F 29 Fb39
Saint-Bertrand-de-Comminges F 69 Ga56

Saint-Blaise-la-Roche F 35 Kb37
Saint-Blimont F 14 Gc32
Saint-Blin F 33 Jb38
Saint-Bonnet F 57 Ka50
Saint-Bonnet-de-Joux F 41 Ja44
Saint-Bonnet-le-Château F 48 Hd48
Saint-Bonnet-le-Froid F 56 Ja49
Saint-Brelade GBJ 18 Ec36
Saint-Brévin-les-Pins F 36 Ec42
Saint-Brice-Courcelles F 22 Hc35
Saint-Brice-en-Cógles F 29 Fa38
Saint-Brieuc F 28 Eb38
Saint-Bris-le-Vineux F 32 Hc40
Saint-Brisson F 41 Hd42
Saint-Calais F 30 Ga40
Saint-Caprais F 39 Gd43
Saint-Capraise-de-Lalinde F 53 Ga50
Saint-Cast-le-Guildo F 28 Ec37
Saint-Cénéri-le-Gérei F 30 Fc38
Saint-Céré F 54 Gd50
Saint-Cernin F 55 Ha49
Saint-Cernin-de-l'Herm F 54 Gb51
Saint-Chamant F 54 Gd49
Saint-Chamas F 65 Jc54
Saint-Chamond F 48 Ja48
Saint-Chaptes F 64 Ja53
Saint-Chély-d'Apcher F 55 Hc50
Saint-Chély-d'Aubrac F 55 Hb51
Saint-Chéron F 31 Gd38
Saint-Chinian F 63 Hb55
Saint-Christol F 65 Jd52
Saint-Christol-lès-Alès F 64 Hd52
Saint-Christoly-Médoc F 44 Fb48
Saint-Christophe-de-Double F 53 Fc49
Saint-Christophe-du-Ligneron F 37 Ed43
Saint-Christophe-en-Brionnais F 48 Hd45
Saint-Christophe-en-Oisans F 57 Ka49
Saint-Ciers-Champagne F 45 Fc48
Saint-Ciers-du-Taillon F 52 Fb49
Saint-Cirgues-de-Jordanne F 55 Ha49
Saint-Cirgues-en-Montagne F 56 Ja50
Saint-Cirq-Lapopie F 54 Gc51
Saint-Clair-sur-Epte F 21 Gc36
Saint-Clar F 61 Ga53
Saint-Clar-de-Rivière F 62 Gb55
Saint-Claude F 42 Jd44
Saint-Claud-sur-le-Son F 45 Fd47
Saint-Clément F 46 Gc48
Saint-Clement F 32 Hb39
Saint-Clément-des-Baleines F 44 Ed45
Saint-Clément-sur-Durance F 58 Kb50
Saint-Clet F 27 Ea37
Saint-Cloud F 33 Jb38
Saint-Colombier F 36 Eb41
Saint-Côme-d'Olt F 55 Hb51
Saint-Cosme-en-Vairais F 30 Fd39

Saint-Crepin F 21 Gd35
Saint-Cyprien F 54 Gb50
Saint-Cyprien F 71 Hb57
Saint-Cyprien F 48 Hd47
Saint-Cyprien-Plage F 71 Hb57
Saint-Cyr-en-Val F 31 Gc40
Saint-Cyr-les-Colons F 32 Hc40
Saint-Dalmas-de-Tende F 58 Kd52
Saint-Dalmas-le-Selvage F 58 Kb51
Saint-Denis F 21 Gd36
Saint-Denis-de-Gastines F 29 Fb38
Saint-Denis-de-l'Hotel F 31 Gd40
Saint-Denis-de-Pile F 53 Fc50
Saint-Denis-d'Oléron F 44 Ed46
Saint-Denis-d'Orques F 30 Fc39
Saint-Denoual F 28 Ec38
Saint-Désiré F 40 Ha44
Saint-Didier-en-Velay F 48 Ja48
Saint-Dié-des-Vosges F 34 Ka38
Saint-Dier-d'Auvergne F 47 Hc47
Saint-Disdier F 57 Jd50
Saint-Dizier F 33 Ja37
Saint-Dizier-Leyrenne F 46 Gc46
Saint-Dolay F 36 Ec41
Saint-Domineuc F 29 Ed38
Saint-Donat-sur-l'Herbasse F 56 Jb49
Saint-Doulchard F 39 Gd42
Saint-Dyé-sur-Loire F 39 Gc41
Sainte-Anne-d'Auray F 27 Ea40
Sainte-Bazeille F 53 Fd51
Sainte-Cécile-d'Andorge F 64 Hd52
Sainte-Cécile-les-Vignes F 64 Jb53
Sainte-Colombe F 20 Ga36
Sainte-Colombe F 40 Hb42
Sainte-Croix F 57 Jc50
Sainte-Croix-de-Verdon F 65 Ka53
Sainte-Croix-du-Mont F 53 Fc51
Sainte-Croix-en-Plaine F 35 Kb39
Sainte-Croix-Volvestre F 70 Gb56
Sainte-Engrace F 68 Fb56
Sainte-Enimie F 55 Hc51
Sainte-Eulalie F 56 Ha50
Sainte-Eulalie-d'Olt F 55 Hb51
Sainte-Eulalie-en-Royans F 57 Jc50
Sainte-Féréole F 54 Gc49
Sainte-Feyre F 46 Gc46
Sainte-Fortunade F 54 Gc49
Sainte-Foy de Morlaàs F 61 Fc55
Sainte-Foy-la-Grande F 53 Fd50
Sainte-Foy-l'Argentière F 48 Ja47
Sainte-Foy-Tarentaise F 50 Kb47
Sainte-Gauburge-Sainte-Colombe F 30 Fd37
Sainte-Geneviève-des-Bois F 31 Gd37
Sainte-Geneviève-des-Bois F 32 Ha40
Sainte-Geneviève-sur-Argence F 55 Ha50

Saint-Egrève F 49 Jd48
Sainte-Hélène F 52 Fb50
Sainte-Hermine F 37 Fa44
Sainte-Jalle F 57 Jc51
Sainte-Livrade-sur-Lot F 53 Ga52
Saint-Elix-Theux F 61 Fd55
Saint-Eloy-les-Mines F 47 Ha45
Sainte-Lucie-de-Porto-Vecchio F 73 Ma59
Sainte-Lucie-de-Tallano F 73 Ld59
Sainte-Marie F 55 Hb50
Sainte-Marie-aux-Mines F 35 Kb38
Sainte-Marie-de-Campan F 69 Fd56
Sainte-Marie-de-Ré F 44 Fa46
Sainte-Marie-du-Ménez-Hom F 26 Dc39
Sainte-Marie-du-Mont F 19 Fa35
Sainte-Maure-de-Touraine F 38 Ga43
Sainte-Maxime F 66 Kb54
Sainte-Menehould F 23 Ja36
Sainte-Mère F 61 Ga53
Sainte-Mère-Église F 19 Fa35
Saint-Emiland F 41 Ja43
Saint-Émilion F 53 Fc50
Sainte-Montaine F 39 Gd41
Sainteny F 19 Fa35
Sainte-Odile F 35 Kb37
Saint-Epain F 38 Ga42
Sainte-Pazanne F 37 Ed42
Saint-Erme-Outre-et-Ramecourt F 22 Hc34
Saintes F 44 Fb47
Sainte-Sabine F 41 Ja42
Sainte-Savine F 33 Hd38
Sainte-Scolasse-sur-Sarthe F 30 Fd38
Sainte-Sévère-sur-Indre F 39 Gd44
Sainte-Sigolene F 48 Ja48
Saintes-Maries-de-la-Mer F 64 Ja54
Saint-Esteban F 60 Fa55
Saint-Estèphe F 52 Fb49
Saint-Estève F 71 Hb57
Saint-Estève F 65 Jc52
Saint-Suzanne F 30 Fc39
Saint-Thorette F 39 Gd42
Saint-Etienne F 48 Ja48
Saint-Etienne-de-Baïgorry F 60 Ed55
Saint-Etienne-de-Cuines F 49 Ka48
Saint-Etienne-de-Fursac F 46 Gc46
Saint-Etienne-de-Montluc F 37 Ed42
Saint-Etienne-de-Saint-Geoirs F 49 Jc48
Saint-Etienne-des-Sorts F 64 Jb52
Saint-Etienne-de-Tinée F 58 Kc51
Saint-Etienne-du-Bois F 49 Jc45
Saint-Etienne-du-Rouvray F 21 Gb35
Saint-Etienne-en-Dévoluy F 57 Jd50
Saint-Etienne-Estréchoux F 63 Hb54
Saint-Etienne-les-Orgues F 65 Jd52
Sainte-Vertu F 32 Hc40
Saint-Evroult-Notre-Dame-du-Bois F 30 Fd37
Saint-Fargeau F 40 Hb41

Saint-Félicien F 56 Ja49
Saint-Félix F 44 Fb46
Saint-Félix-de-Reillac F 53 Ga49
Saint-Félix-de-Sorgues F 63 Hb53
Saint-Félix-de-Villadeix F 53 Ga50
Saint-Félix-Lauragais F 62 Gd55
Saint-Ferme F 53 Fd51
Saint-Firmin F 57 Ka50
Saint-Florent-des-Bois F 37 Fa44
Saint-Florentin F 32 Hc39
Saint-Florent-le-Vieil F 37 Fa42
Saint-Florent-sur-Cher F 39 Gd43
Saint-Flour F 55 Hb49
Saint-Flovier F 39 Gb43
Saint-Folquin F 14 Gd30
Saint-Fort-sur-Gironde F 44 Fb48
Saint-Fort-sur-le-Né F 45 Fc48
Saint-Fraigne F 45 Fc46
Saint-Fraimbault F 29 Fb38
Saint-Front-sur-Lémance F 54 Gb51
Saint-Fulgent F 37 Fa43
Saint-Galmier F 48 Ja47
Saint-Gatien-des-Bois F 20 Fd35
Saint-Gaudens F 69 Ga56
Saint-Gaultier F 39 Gb44
Saint-Gély-du-Fesc F 64 Hd54
Saint-Genest-Malifaux F 48 Ja48
Saint-Geneviève F 21 Gd35
Saint-Gengoux-le-National F 41 Ja44
Saint-Geniès-de-Saintonge F 44 Fb48
Saint-Geniès-des-Mourgues F 64 Hd54
Saint-Geniez-d'Olt F 55 Hb51
Saint-Génis-des-Fontaines F 71 Hb57
Saint-Genis-Laval F 48 Jb47
Saint-Genis-Pouilly F 49 Jd45
Saint-Genix-sur-Guiers F 49 Jc47
Saint-George-Motel F 31 Gb37
Saint-Georges-d'Aurac F 55 Hc49
Saint-Georges-de-Commiers F 57 Jd49
Saint-Georges-de-Didonne F 44 Fa47
Saint-Georges-de-Noisne F 45 Fc45
Saint-Georges-d'Oléron F 44 Fa46
Saint-Georges-en-Couzan F 48 Hd47
Saint-Georges-les-Baillargeux F 38 Fd44
Saint-Georges-les-Landes F 46 Gb45
Saint-Georges-sur-la-Prée F 39 Gc42
Saint-Georges-sur-Loire F 37 Fb42
Saint-Georges-sur-Meuse B 16 Jb31
Saint-Gérand F 28 Eb39
Saint-Gérand-le-Puy F 47 Hc45
Saint-Germain F 38 Ga44
Saint-Germain-Chassenay F 40 Hc43

Saint-Germain-de-Calberte F 64 Hd52
Saint-Germain-de-Confolens F 45 Ga46
Saint-Germain-de-Coulamer F 30 Fc39
Saint-Germain-de-la-Coudre F 30 Ga39
Saint-Germain-de-la-Rivière F 53 Fc50
Saint-Germain-des-Fossés F 47 Hc45
Saint-Germain-de-Tallevende F 29 Fb37
Saint-Germain-du-Bois F 41 Jb43
Saint-Germain-du-Plain F 41 Jb43
Saint-Germain-du-Puy F 40 Ha42
Saint-Germain-en-Laye F 31 Gd37
Saint-Germain-Laval F 48 Hd46
Saint-Germain-Lavolps F 46 Gd47
Saint-Germain-Lembron F 47 Hb48
Saint-Germain-les-Arlay F 42 Jc43
Saint-Germain-les-Belles F 46 Gc47
Saint-Germain-l'Herm F 47 Hc48
Saint-Germer-de-Fly F 21 Gc35
Saint-Gervais-d'Auvergne F 47 Ha46
Saint-Gervais-de-Vic F 30 Ga40
Saint-Gervais-la-Forêt F 39 Gb41
Saint-Gervais-les-Bains F 50 Kb46
Saint-Gervais-les-Trois-Clochers F 38 Fd43
Saint-Gervais-sur-Mare F 63 Hb54
Saint-Géry F 53 Fd50
Saint-Géry F 54 Gc51
Saint-Gildas-de-Rhuys F 36 Eb41
Saint-Gildas-des-Bois F 36 Ec41
Saint-Gilles F 29 Ed39
Saint-Gilles F 19 Fa36
Saint-Gilles F 38 Fd42
Saint-Gilles F 64 Ja54
Saint-Gilles-Croix-de-Vie F 36 Ec44
Saint-Gilles-Pligeaux F 27 Ea38
Saint-Gillis-Waas B 15 Hc29
Saint-Gingolph F 43 Kb44
Saint-Girons F 70 Gb56
Saint-Girons-en-Marensin F 60 Fa53
Saint-Girons-Plage F 60 Ed53
Saint-Gobain F 22 Hb34
Saint-Gondon F 32 Ha40
Saint-Gondran F 29 Ed39
Saint-Gonnery F 28 Eb39
Saint-Gravé F 28 Ec40
Saint-Guénolé F 26 Dc40
Saint-Guilhem-le-Désert F 63 Hc53
Saint-Guillaume F 57 Jc49
Saint-Haon-le-Châtel F 48 Hd46
Saint-Helier GBJ 18 Ec36
Saint-Hilaire F 71 Ha56
Saint-Hilaire-Bonneval F 46 Gb47
Saint-Hilaire-de-Riez F 36 Ec44
Saint-Hilaire-des-Loges F 44 Fb45

Saint-Hilaire-de-Villefranche F 44 Fb47
Saint-Hilaire-du-Harcouët F 29 Fa38
Saint-Hilaire-du-Rosier F 57 Jc49
Saint-Hilaire-Foissac F 46 Gd48
Saint-Hilaire-Fontaine F 40 Hc43
Saint-Hilaire-la-Pallud F 44 Fb45
Saint-Hilaire-le-Château F 46 Gc46
Saint-Hilaire-le-Grand F 23 Hd35
Saint-Hilaire-Petitville F 19 Fa35
Saint-Hippolyte F 42 Ka41
Saint-Hippolyte F 35 Kb38
Saint-Hippolyte-du-Fort F 64 Hd53
Saint-Honoré-les-Bains F 40 Hc43
Saint-Hubert B 16 Jb32
Saint-Hubert F 30 Fd40
Saint-Inglevert F 14 Gc30
Saint-Ismier F 49 Jd48
Saint-Jacut-de-la-Mer F 28 Ec38
Saint-Jacut-du-Mené F 28 Eb39
Saint-James F 29 Fa38
Saint-Jean F 57 Ka51
Saint-Jean-Brévelay F 28 Eb40
Saint-Jean-d'Angely F 44 Fb46
Saint-Jean-d'Angle F 44 Fa47
Saint-Jean-d'Ardières F 48 Ja45
Saint-Jean-d'Avelanne F 49 Jd47
Saint-Jean-de-Barrou F 71 Hb56
Saint-Jean-de-Belleville F 49 Ka47
Saint-Jean-de-Blaignac F 53 Fc50
Saint-Jean-de-Bonneval F 33 Hd39
Saint-Jean-de-Bournay F 48 Jb47
Saint-Jean-de-Côle F 45 Ga48
Saint-Jean-de-Daye F 19 Fa35
Saint-Jean-de-Durfort F 65 Jc52
Saint-Jean-de-Gonville F 49 Jd45
Saint-Jean-de-Losne F 41 Jb42
Saint-Jean-de-Luz F 60 Ed55
Saint-Jean-de-Maruéjols F 64 Ja52
Saint-Jean-de-Maurienne F 49 Ka48
Saint-Jean-de-Monts F 36 Ec43
Saint-Jean-de-Niost F 49 Jc46
Saint-Jean-de-Sauves F 38 Fd43
Saint-Jean-des-Baisants F 19 Fb36
Saint-Jean-de-Sixt F 49 Ka46
Saint-Jean-de-Verges F 70 Gc56
Saint-Jean-d'Illac F 52 Fb50
Saint-Jean-du-Bruel F 63 Hc53
Saint-Jean-du-Doigt F 27 Dd37

Saint-Jean-du-Gard F 64 Hd52
Saint-Jean-en-Royans F 57 Jc49
Saint-Jean-la-Rivière F 58 Kc52
Saint-Jean-le-Blanc F 31 Gc40
Saint-Jean-Pied-de-Port F 68 Fa56
Saint-Jean-Poutge F 61 Fd54
Saint-Jean-Saint-Maurice-sur-Loire F 48 Hd46
Saint-Jean-sur-Reyssouze F 41 Jb44
Saint-Jeoire F 49 Ka46
Saint-Jeure-d'Ay F 56 Jb49
Saint-Joachim F 36 Ec42
Saint-John GBJ 18 Ec35
Saint-Jory F 62 Gb54
Saint-Jouin F 20 Fd44
Saint-Jouin-de-Marnes F 38 Fc43
Saint-Juan F 42 Ka41
Saint-Juéry F 62 Gd53
Saint-Julia F 62 Gd54
Saint-Julien F 42 Jc44
Saint-Julien F 57 Ka50
Saint-Julien Beychevelle F 52 Fb49
Saint-Julien-Chapteuil F 56 Hd49
Saint-Julien-de-Jonzy F 48 Hd45
Saint-Julien-de-Vouvantes F 37 Fa41
Saint-Julien-du-Sault F 32 Hb39
Saint-Julien-en-Born F 60 Fa53
Saint-Julien-en-Genevois F 49 Jd45
Saint-Julien-en-Quint F 57 Jc50
Saint-Julien-l'Ars F 38 Ga44
Saint-Julien-le-Faucon F 20 Fd36
Saint-Julien-Molins-Molette F 48 Ja48
Saint-Julien-près-Bort F 47 Ha48
Saint-Julien-sur-Cher F 39 Gc42
Saint-Junien F 45 Ga47
Saint-Junien-la-Bregère F 46 Gc46
Saint-Junien-la-Bregère F 46 Gc47
Saint-Just F 40 Ha43
Saint-Just-en-Chaussée F 21 Gd34
Saint-Just-en-Chevalet F 48 Hd46
Saint-Just-Ibarre F 60 Fa55
Saint-Justin F 61 Fc53
Saint-Just-Malmont F 48 Ja48
Saint-Just-Saint-Rambert F 48 Ja48
Saint-Juvin F 23 Ja35
Saint-Lambert-du-Lattay F 37 Fb42
Saint-Lary-Soulan F 69 Fd57
Saint-Launeuc F 28 Ec39
Saint-Laurent F 46 Gd46
Saint-Laurent F 58 Kb51
Saint-Laurent-d'Aigouze F 64 Ja54
Saint-Laurent-d'Andenay F 41 Ja43
Saint-Laurent-de-Chamousset F 48 Ja47
Saint-Laurent-de-la-Cabrerisse F 71 Ha56

Saint-Laurent-de-la-Plaine F 37 Fb42
Saint-Laurent-de-la-Salanque F 71 Hb57
Saint-Laurent-des-Autels F 37 Fa42
Saint-Laurent-de-Trèves F 55 Hc52
Saint-Laurent-du-Pont F 49 Jd48
Saint-Laurent-en-Caux F 20 Ga34
Saint-Laurent-en-Gâtines F 38 Ga41
Saint-Laurent-en-Grandvaux F 42 Jd44
Saint-Laurent-et-Benon F 52 Fb49
Saint-Laurent-la-Vernède F 64 Ja52
Saint-Laurent-Nouan F 31 Gc40
Saint-Laurent-sur-Gorre F 46 Gb47
Saint-Laurent-sur-Sèvre F 37 Fb43
Saint-Léger B 23 Jb34
Saint-Léger-des-Vignes F 40 Hc43
Saint-Léger-en-Yvelines F 31 Gc37
Saint-Léger-sous-Beuvray F 41 Hd43
Saint-Léger-sous-Cholet F 37 Fb43
Saint-Léger-sur-Dheune F 41 Ja43
Saint-Léon F 62 Gc55
Saint-Léonard-de-Noblat F 46 Gc47
Saint-Léonard-en-Beauce F 31 Gb40
Saint-Léon-sur-Vézère F 54 Gb49
Saint-Leu-d'Esserent F 21 Gd35
Saint-Lizier F 70 Gb56
Saint-Lô F 19 Fa36
Saint-Longis F 30 Fd38
Saint-Loubès F 52 Fb50
Saint-Loup-de-la-Salle F 41 Jb43
Saint-Loup-de-Naud F 32 Hb38
Saint-Loup-Lamairé F 38 Fc44
Saint-Loup-sur-Semouse F 34 Jd39
Saint-Lunaire F 28 Ec37
Saint-Lyé F 31 Gc39
Saint-Lyphard F 36 Ec42
Saint-Lys F 62 Gb54
Saint-Macaire-en-Mauges F 37 Fa42
Saint-Maclou F 20 Fd35
Saint-Magne F 52 Fb51
Saint-Maime F 65 Jd53
Saint-Maixent-l'École F 45 Fc45
Saint-Malo F 28 Ec37
Saint-Mamert-du-Gard F 64 Ja53
Saint-Mandrier-sur-Mer F 65 Ka55
Saint-Marc F 36 Ec42
Saint-Marceau F 30 Fd39
Saint-Marcel-de-Careiret F 64 Ja52
Saint-Marcel-lès-Valence F 56 Jb49
Saint-Marcellin F 49 Jc48
Saint-Mard-de-Réno F 30 Ga38
Saint-Mards-en-Othe F 32 Hc39
Saint-Mars-d'Outilie F 30 Fd40
Saint-Mars-la-Jaille F 37 Fa41

Saint-Martial-et-Saint-Aubin F 54 Gb50
Saint-Martial-sur-Isop F 45 Ga46
Saint-Martin F 28 Ec40
Saint-Martin F 19 Fb36
Saint-Martin F 35 Kb38
Saint-Martin-d'Ardeche F 56 Ja51
Saint-Martin-d'Auxigny F 39 Gd42
Saint-Martin-de-Boscherville F 20 Ga35
Saint-Martin-de-Bréhal F 29 Ed37
Saint-Martin-de-Crau F 64 Jb54
Saint-Martin-de-la-Lieue F 20 Fd36
Saint-Martin-de-Landelles F 29 Fa38
Saint-Martin-de-la-Place F 38 Fc42
Saint-Martin-de-Londres F 64 Hd53
Saint-Martin-d'Entraunes F 58 Kb52
Saint-Martin-de-Queyrières F 58 Kb49
Saint-Martin-de-Ré F 44 Fa45
Saint-Martin-de-Salencey F 41 Ja44
Saint-Martin-des-Besaces F 19 Fb36
Saint-Martin-de-Seignanx F 60 Ed54
Saint-Martin-des-Puits F 71 Ha56
Saint-Martin-d'Estréaux F 47 Hc45
Saint-Martin-de-Valmas F 56 Ja49
Saint-Martin-d'Oney F 60 Fb53
Saint-Martin-du-Fouilloux F 38 Fc44
Saint-Martin-en-Bresse F 41 Jb43
Saint-Martin-en-Campagne F 21 Gb33
Saint-Martin-en-Haut F 48 Ja47
Saint-Martin-en-Vercors F 57 Jc49
Saint-Martin-la-Méanne F 54 Gd49
Saint-Martin-la-Plaine F 48 Ja47
Saint-Martin-l'Ars F 45 Ga45
Saint-Martin-le-Supérieur F 56 Ja50
Saint-Martin-Osmonville F 21 Gb34
Saint-Martin-sur-Armançon F 33 Hd40
Saint-Martin-sur-Ouanne F 32 Hb40
Saint-Martin-Valmeroux F 55 Ha49
Saint-Martin-Vésubie F 58 Kc52
Saint-Martory F 70 Gb56
Saint-Mathieu F 45 Ga47
Saint-Mathieu-de-Tréviers F 64 Hd53
Saint-Mathurin-sur-Loire F 38 Fc42
Saint-Matré F 54 Gb51
Saint-Maudan F 28 Eb39
Saint-Maugan F 28 Ec39
Saint-Maulvis F 21 Gc33
Saint-Maur F 21 Gc34
Saint-Maur F 31 Gd37
Saint-Maurice F 63 Hb53
Saint-Maurice-de-Cazevieille F 64 Ja52
Saint-Maurice-des-Lions F 45 Ga46

Saint-Maurice-en-Trieves F 57 Jd50
Saint-Maurice-lès-Charencey F 30 Ga37
Saint-Maurice-lès-Châteauneuf F 48 Hd45
Saint-Maurice-sous-les-Côtes F 24 Jc36
Saint-Maurice-sur-Aveyron F 32 Ha40
Saint-Maurice-sur-Eygues F 56 Jb51
Saint-Maurice-sur-Moselle F 34 Ka39
Saint-Maximin-la-Sainte-Baume F 65 Jd54
Saint-Méard-de-Gurçon F 53 Fd50
Saint-Médard F 54 Gb51
Saint-Médard-de-Guizières F 53 Fc49
Saint-Médard-en-Jalles F 52 Fb50
Saint-Méen-le-Grand F 28 Ec39
Saint-Meloir-des-Ondes F 29 Ed38
Saint-Menges F 23 Ja33
Saint-Menoux F 40 Hb44
Saint-Michel F 23 Hd33
Saint-Michel-de-Castelnau F 53 Fc52
Saint-Michel-de-Double F 53 Fd49
Saint-Michel-de-Lanès F 62 Gc55
Saint-Michel-en-Greve F 27 Dd37
Saint-Michel-en-l'Herm F 44 Fa45
Saint-Michel-les-Portes F 57 Jd49
Saint-Michel-l'Observatoire F 65 Jd53
Saint-Michel-Mont-Mercure F 37 Fb43
Saint-Mihiel F 23 Jb36
Saint-Mitre-les-Remparts F 65 Jc54
Saint-Morillon F 52 Fb51
Saint-Nabord F 34 Ka39
Saint-Nazaire F 36 Ec42
Saint-Nazaire-en-Royans F 57 Jc49
Saint-Nazaire-le-Désert F 57 Jc51
Saint-Nectaire F 47 Hb47
Saint-Nicolas-de-la-Grave F 62 Gb53
Saint-Nicolas-de-Port F 34 Jd37
Saint-Nicolas-des-Eaux F 27 Ea40
Saint-Nicolas-du-Pélem F 27 Ea38
Saint-Nizier-du-Moucherotte F 49 Jd48
Saint-Omer F 14 Gd30
Saint-Omer-en-Chaussée F 21 Gc34
Saint-Ouen F 31 Gb40
Saint-Ouen F 33 Hd37
Saint-Ouen-lès-Parey F 34 Jc38
Saint-Pair-sur-Mer F 29 Ed37
Saint-Palais F 60 Fa55
Saint-Palais-sur-Mer F 44 Fa47
Saint-Pal-de-Senouire F 47 Hc48
Saint-Pantaléon F 54 Gb52
Saint-Papoul F 62 Gd55
Saint-Pardoux-la Riviere F 45 Gd48
Saint-Parres-lès-Vaudes F 33 Hd39
Saint-Paterne-Racan F 38 Fd41

Saint-Paul F 66 Kc53
Saint-Paul-Cap-de-Joux F 62 Gd54
Saint-Paul-de-Fenouillet F 71 Ha57
Saint-Paul-de-Varax F 48 Jb45
Saint-Paul-et-Valmalle F 64 Hd54
Saint-Paulien F 56 Hd49
Saint-Paul-le-Jeune F 56 Hd51
Saint-Paul-le-Jeune F 56 Ja51
Saint-Paul-lès-Dax F 60 Fa54
Saint-Paul-lès-Durance F 65 Jd53
Saint-Paul-sur-Ubaye F 58 Kb50
Saint-Paul-Trois-Châteaux F 56 Jb51
Saint-Pée-sur-Nivelle F 60 Ed55
Saint-Péran F 28 Ec39
Saint-Péravy-la-Colombe F 31 Gc40
Saint-Péray F 56 Ja51
Saint-Père F 40 Hc41
Saint-Père-en-Retz F 36 Ec42
Saint-Peter-Port GBG 18 Eb35
Saint-Péver F 27 Ea38
Saint-Philbert-de-Grand-Lieu F 37 Ed43
Saint-Piat F 31 Gc38
Saint-Pierre F 63 Hb53
Saint-Pierre-à-Champ F 38 Fc43
Saint-Pierre-d'Albigny F 49 Ka47
Saint-Pierre-de Bétirac F 63 Ha53
Saint-Pierre-de-Chartreuse F 49 Jd48
Saint-Pierre-de-Chignac F 53 Ga49
Saint-Pierre-de-la-Fage F 63 Hc53
Saint-Pierre-de-Maille F 38 Ga44
Saint-Pierre-d'Entremont F 29 Fb37
Saint-Pierre-d'Entremont F 49 Jd48
Saint-Pierre-de-Plesguen F 29 Ed38
Saint-Pierre-de-Quiberon F 36 Ea41
Saint-Pierre-des-Nids F 30 Fc38
Saint-Pierre-d'Oléron F 44 Fa46
Saint-Pierre-du-Bû F 30 Fc37
Saint-Pierre-du-Chemin F 37 Fb44
Saint-Pierre-du-Mont F 19 Fa35
Saint-Pierre-Église F 19 Fa34
Saint-Pierre-la-Bourlhonne F 47 Hc47
Saint-Pierre-la-Cour F 29 Fa39
Saint-Pierre-le-Moûtier F 40 Hb43
Saint-Pierre-Montlimart F 37 Fa42
Saint-Pierre-sur-Dives F 20 Fc36
Saint-Pierre-sur-Mer F 63 Hc55
Saint-Pierre-sur-Orthe F 30 Fc39
Saint-Pierre-Toirac F 54 Gd51
Saint-Pierreville F 56 Ja50
Saint-Plaisir F 40 Hb44

Saint-Pois F 29 Fa37
Saint-Pol-de-Léon F 26 Dc37
Saint-Polgues F 48 Hd46
Saint-Pol-sur-Mer F 14 Gd29
Saint-Pol-sur-Ternoise F 14 Gd32
Saint-Pompain F 44 Fb45
Saint-Pons-de-Thomières F 63 Hb54
Saint-Porchaire F 44 Fb47
Saint-Porquier F 62 Gb53
Saint-Pouange F 33 Hd39
Saint-Pourçain-sur-Sioule F 47 Hb45
Saint-Prest F 31 Gb38
Saint-Priest F 48 Jb47
Saint-Priest-en-Jarez F 48 Ja48
Saint-Priest-Laprunge F 47 Hc46
Saint-Priest-Taurion F 46 Gb46
Saint-Privat F 54 Gd49
Saint-Privat-d'Allier F 55 Hc49
Saint-Privat-des-Vieux F 64 Hd52
Saint-Prouant F 37 Fa44
Saint-Puy F 61 Fd53
Saint-Quai F 27 Ea37
Saint-Quay-Portrieux F 28 Eb37
Saint-Quentin F 22 Hb33
Saint-Quentin-des-Isles F 20 Ga36
Saint-Quentin-les-Anges F 29 Fb40
Saint-Quentin-sur-Isère F 49 Jc48
Saint-Quirin F 35 Kb37
Saint-Rabier F 54 Gb49
Saint-Rambert-d'Albon F 48 Jd48
Saint-Raphaël F 66 Kb54
Saint-Remèze F 56 Ja51
Saint-Remy-Blanzy F 22 Hb35
Saint-Rémy-de-Provence F 64 Jb53
Saint-Rémy-des-Landes F 19 Ed35
Saint-Remy-du-Plain F 29 Ed38
Saint-Rémy-en-Bouzemont F 33 Ja37
Saint-Rémy-sur-Durolle F 47 Hc46
Saint-Renan F 26 Db38
Saint-Révérien F 40 Hc42
Saint-Riquier F 14 Gc32
Saint-Rivoal F 26 Dc38
Saint-Robert F 54 Gb49
Saint-Romain-de-Colbosc F 20 Fd34
Saint-Romain-de-Colbosc F 20 Fd35
Saint-Romain-le-Puy F 48 Hd47
Saint-Romain-sur-Cher F 39 Gb42
Saint-Roman F 57 Jc50
Saint-Romans F 57 Jc49
Saint-Rome-de-Cornon F 63 Hb53
Saint-Saëns F 21 Gb34
Saint-Sampson GBG 18 Ec35
Saint-Samson-la-Poterie F 21 Gc34
Saint-Satur F 40 Ha42
Saint-Saturnin F 39 Gd44
Saint-Saturnin F 47 Hb47
Saint-Saturnin F 64 Jb53
Saint-Saturnin-d'Apt F 65 Jc53
Saint-Saturnin-de-Lenne F 55 Hb51
Saint-Saulge F 40 Hc42

Saint-Saury F 54 Gd50
Saint-Sauvant F 44 Fb47
Saint-Sauves-d'Auvergne F 47 Ha47
Saint-Sauveur F 26 Dc38
Saint-Sauveur F 36 Ec44
Saint-Sauveur-d'Aunis F 44 Fb46
Saint-Sauveur-de-Montagut F 56 Ja50
Saint-Sauveur-de-Peyre F 55 Hc50
Saint-Sauveur-en-Puisaye F 40 Hb41
Saint-Sauveur-le-Vicomte F 19 Ed35
Saint-Sauveur-sur-Tinée F 58 Kc52
Saint-Savin F 52 Fb49
Saint-Savin F 38 Ga44
Saint-Savinien F 44 Fb47
Saint-Sébastien F 57 Jd49
Saint-Seine-l'Abbaye F 41 Ja41
Saint-Seine-l'Eglise F 42 Jc41
Saint-Senier-sous-Avranches F 29 Fa37
Saint-Sernin-sur-Rance F 63 Ha53
Saint-Servan F 28 Ec37
Saint-Sever F 60 Fb54
Saint-Sever-Calvados F 29 Fa37
Saint-Séverin F 45 Fd48
Saint-Sorlin-d'Arves F 49 Ka48
Saint-Sorlin-en-Valloire F 48 Jb48
Saint-Sornin-Leulac F 46 Gb45
Saint-Soupplets F 22 Ha36
Saint-Sulpice F 62 Gd54
Saint-Sulpice-les-Champs F 46 Gd46
Saint-Sulpice-les-Feuilles F 46 Gb45
Saint-Sulpice-sur-Lezé F 62 Gb55
Saint-Sylvestre F 56 Jb49
Saint-Sylvestre-sur-Lot F 53 Ga51
Saint-Symphorien F 52 Fb51
Saint-Symphorien F 48 Hd46
Saint-Symphorien-de-Mahun F 56 Ja49
Saint-Symphorien-sur-Coise F 48 Ja47
Saint-Thégonnec F 27 Dd38
Saint-Thibault F 33 Ja41
Saint-Thibéry F 63 Hc55
Saint-Thiébault F 34 Jc38
Saint-Thurin F 48 Hd49
Saint-Trinit F 65 Jc52
Saint-Trivier-de-Courtes F 41 Jb44
Saint-Trivier-sur-Mignans F 48 Jb46
Saint-Trojan-les-Bains F 44 Fa47
Saint-Tropez F 66 Kb54
Saint-Tugen F 26 Db39
Saint-Usuge F 41 Jb44
Saint-Vaast-la-Hougue F 19 Fa34
Saint-Valérien F 41 Ja44
Saint-Vallier F 48 Jd48
Saint-Vallier F 56 Jb49
Saint-Vallier-de-Thiey F 66 Kc53
Saint-Varent F 38 Fc43
Saint-Vaury F 46 Gc45

Saint-Venant F 14 Gd31
Saint-Véran F 55 Hc52
Saint-Véran F 58 Kb50
Saint-Victor F 53 Ga52
Saint-Victor F 47 Ha45
Saint-Victor F 64 Jd52
Saint-Victor-sur-Loire F 48 Ja48
Saint-Vigor-le-Grand F 19 Fb35
Saint-Vincent F 65 Jd52
Saint-Vincent-de-Connezac F 53 Fd49
Saint-Vincent-de-Tyrosse F 60 Fa54
Saint-Vincent-les-Forts F 57 Ka51
Saint-Vincent-sur-Jard F 44 Ed45
Saint-Vit F 42 Jc42
Saint-Vivien-de-Medoc F 44 Fa48
Saint-Voir F 47 Hc45
Saint-Vulbas F 49 Jc46
Saint-Xandre F 44 Fa45
Saint-Yaguen F 60 Fb53
Saint-Yan F 48 Hd45
Saint-Ybars F 62 Gc55
Saint-Yorre F 47 Hc46
Saint-Yrieix-la-Perche F 46 Gb48
Saint-Yrieix-le-Déjalat F 46 Gd48
Saint-Yzans-de-Médoc F 44 Fb48
Sainville F 31 Gc38
Saissac F 62 Gd55
Salbris F 39 Gd41
Salernes F 65 Ka54
Salers F 55 Ha49
Salice F 73 Ld58
Salies-de-Béarn F 60 Fa55
Salignac F 53 Fc49
Salignac-Eyvignes F 54 Gb50
Saligny-sur-Roudon F 40 Hc44
Salin-de-Giraud F 64 Jb54
Salindres F 64 Ja52
Salins-les-Bains F 42 Jd43
Salives F 33 Jb40
Sallanches F 49 Ka46
Salles F 52 Fa51
Salles-Curan F 55 Hb52
Salmiech F 55 Ha52
Salon F 32 Hc37
Salon-de-Provence F 65 Jc54
Salornay-sur-Guye F 41 Ja44
Salses-le-Château F 71 Hb56
Salvagnac F 62 Gc53
Salviac F 54 Gb51
Samadet F 60 Fb54
Samatan F 61 Ga54
Sambin F 39 Gb41
Samer F 14 Gc31
Samoëns F 50 Kb45
Samois-sur-Seine F 32 Ha38
Sanary-sur-Mer F 65 Jd55
Sancergues F 40 Ha42
Sancerre F 40 Ha42
Sancey-le-Grand F 42 Ka41
Sancheville F 31 Gc39
Sancoins F 40 Ha43
Sancy F 22 Ha36
Sandillon F 31 Gd40
Sanem L 24 Jc34
Sangatte F 14 Gc30
Sanguinet F 52 Fa51
Sankt Vith B 17 Jc31
San Martino di Lota F 72 Ma55

San-Nicolao F 72 Ma57
Sansac-de-Marmiesse F 55 Ha50
Sansais F 44 Fb45
Santa-Maria-Siché F 73 Ld58
Sant'Antonino F 72 Ld56
Santa Severa F 72 Ma55
Santenay F 39 Gb41
Santenay F 41 Ja43
Santilly F 31 Gc39
Sant Julià de Lòria AND
Santo-Pietro-di-Tenda F 72 Ld56
Santpoort NL 8 Hd24
Santranges F 40 Ha41
Sanvensa F 54 Gd52
Sanvigne F 33 Hd40
Sanxay F 45 Fc45
Saorge F 58 Kd52
Saou F 56 Jb50
Saramon F 61 Ga54
Sarcelles F 21 Gd36
Sare F 60 Ed55
Sargé-sur-Braye F 30 Ga40
Sari-d'Orcino F 73 Ld58
Sarlat-la-Canéda F 54 Gb50
Sarliac-sur-l'Isle F 53 Ga49
Sarralbe F 24 Ka35
Sarrance F 68 Fb56
Sarras F 56 Jb49
Sarrebourg F 25 Kb36
Sarreguemines F 24 Ka35
Sarre-Union F 25 Kb36
Sarrey F 33 Jb39
Sarrians F 64 Jb52
Sarron F 61 Fc54
Sarry F 33 Hd40
Sartène F 73 Ld59
Sartilly F 29 Fa37
Sart-Saint-Laurent B 16 Ja31
Sarzeau F 36 Eb41
Sassenage F 49 Jd48
Sassenay F 41 Ja41
Sassenheim NL 12 Hd25
Sassetot-le Mauconduit F 20 Fd34
Sas van Gent NL 15 Hc29
Satillieu F 56 Ja49
Saucats F 52 Fb51
Sauclières F 63 Hc53
Saudron F 33 Jb38
Saugues F 55 Hc49
Saujon F 44 Fa47
Saulieu F 41 Hd42
Saulnot F 34 Ka40
Sault F 65 Jc52
Sault-de-Navailles F 60 Fb54
Saulx F 34 Jd40
Saulxerotte F 34 Jc37
Saulxures-sur-Moselotte F 34 Ka39
Saulzais-le-Potier F 40 Ha44
Saulzoir F 15 Hb32
Saumeray F 31 Gb39
Saumos F 52 Fa50
Saumur F 38 Fc42
Saurat F 70 Gc56
Sausset-les-Pins F 65 Jc55
Saussy F 41 Jb41
Sauvagnat F 47 Ha47
Sauve F 64 Hd53
Sauveterre-de-Béarn F 60 Fa55
Sauveterre-de-Guyenne F 53 Fc51
Sauveterre-de-Rouergue F 55 Ha52
Sauveterre-la-Lémance F 54 Gb51
Sauveur-Lendelin F 19 Fa36

101

Sauxillanges F 47 Hc47
Sauzet F 54 Gb51
Sauzet F 64 Ja53
Sauzet F 56 Jb50
Sauzé-Vaussais F 45 Fd46
Sauzon F 36 Ea42
Savenay F 36 Ec42
Saverdun F 62 Gc55
Saverne F 25 Kb36
Savignac F 54 Gd52
Savignac-les-Eglises F 53 Ga49
Savigné F 45 Fd46
Savigné-l'Evêque F 30 Fd39
Savigny F 34 Jc40
Savigny-en-Revermont F 42 Jc44
Savigny-lès-Beaune F 41 Ja42
Savigny-sur-Braye F 30 Ga40
Savines-le-Lac F 57 Ka50
Savournon F 57 Jd51
Scaër F 27 Dd39
Sceaux F 31 Gd37
Sceaux-sur-Huisne F 30 Ga39
Scey-sur-Saône-et-Saint-Albin F 34 Jd34
Schagen NL 8 Hd23
Schagenbrug NL 8 Hd23
Schaijk NL 12 Jb27
Scharendijke NL 11 Hc27
Scheemda NL 9 Jd22
Scheibenhard F 25 Kd35
Schellinghout NL 8 Ja24
Schengen L 24 Jd34
Scherpenheuvel B 16 Ja29
Scherpenisse NL 11 Hc27
Scherpenzeel NL 12 Jb26
Scheveningen NL 11 Hc26
Schiedam NL 12 Hd26
Schiermonnikoog NL 9 Jc21
Schijndel NL 12 Jb27
Schirmeck F 35 Kb37
Schoenberg B 17 Jd31
Schoondijke NL 11 Hb28
Schoonebeek NL 9 Jd23
Schoonhoven NL 12 Ja26
Schoonloo NL 9 Jd23
Schoonoord NL 9 Jd23
Schoorl NL 8 Hd24
Schuddebeurs NL 11 Hc27
Sciez F 42 Ka44
Scionzier F 49 Ka45
Scoury F 39 Gd44
Sébazac-Concurès F 55 Ha51
Seboncourt F 22 Hb33
Séchault F 23 Ja35
Séchilienne F 57 Jd49
Seclin F 15 Ha31
Secondigny F 37 Fb44
Sedan F 23 Ja44
Séderon F 65 Jd52
Seebach F 25 Kc35
Sées F 30 Fd38
Seez F 50 Kb47
Segonzac F 45 Fc47
Segré F 37 Fb41
Ségrie F 30 Fd39
Ségry F 39 Gd43
Ségur F 55 Hb52
Séguret F 64 Jc52
Ségur-le-Château F 46 Gb48
Ségur-les-Villas F 55 Ha49
Seiches-sur-le-Loir F 38 Fc41
Seignelay F 32 Hc40
Seignosse F 60 Ed54
Seignosse-le-Penon F 60 Ed54

Seilh F 62 Gb54
Seilhac F 46 Gc48
Seillans F 66 Kb53
Seilles B 16 Ja31
Seissan F 61 Ga54
Seix F 70 Gb56
Sélestat F 35 Kb38
Sèlieres F 42 Jc43
Selles F 34 Jd39
Selles-Saint-Denis F 39 Gc41
Selles-sur-Cher F 39 Gc42
Selongey F 41 Jb41
Sélonnet F 57 Ka51
Seltz F 25 Kd36
Sembadel-Gare F 47 Hc48
Semblançay F 38 Ga41
Semur-en-Auxois F 41 Hd41
Semur-en-Brionnais F 48 Hd45
Senaide F 34 Jc39
Sénaillac-Lauzès F 54 Gc51
Senan F 32 Hb40
Senarpont F 21 Gc33
Sénas F 65 Jc53
Séné F 36 Eb41
Seneffe B 16 Hd31
Sengouagnet F 69 Ga56
Senlis F 22 Ha35
Sennecey-le-Grand F 41 Jb44
Senneley F 39 Gd41
Senon F 24 Jc35
Senonches F 31 Gb38
Senones F 34 Ka38
Senonnes F 29 Fa40
Sens F 32 Hb39
Seppois F 35 Kb40
Septeuil F 31 Gc37
Septfonds F 54 Gc52
Septfonds F 32 Hb40
Sept-Forges F 29 Fb38
Sept-Saulx F 23 Hd35
Seraincourt F 23 Hd34
Seraing B 16 Jb32
Seraucourt-le-Grand F 22 Hb33
Séreilhac F 46 Gb47
Sérent F 28 Eb40
Sergines F 32 Hb38
Sérignan F 63 Hc55
Sérignan-du-Comtat F 64 Jb52
Sérignan-Plage F 63 Hc55
Sermaises F 31 Gd38
Sermaize-les-Bains F 33 Ja37
Sermamagny F 34 Ka40
Sermano F 72 Ld57
Serqueux F 34 Jc39
Serquigny F 20 Ga36
Serragia F 73 Ld59
Serraval F 49 Ka46
Serres F 57 Jd51
Serrières F 48 Jd48
Serrières-de-Briord F 49 Jc46
Servance F 34 Ka39
Serverette F 55 Hc50
Servian F 63 Hc54
Serviers-et-Labaume F 64 Ja52
Sery F 23 Hd34
Sessenheim F 25 Kc36
Sète F 64 Hd55
Seuilly F 38 Fd42
Seurre F 41 Jb43
Sevenum NL 13 Jc28
Sévérac-le-Château F 55 Hb52
Sévignacq F 61 Fc55
Sévigny-Waleppe F 22 Hc34
Sèvrier F 49 Jd46
Seyches F 53 Fd51

Seyne F 57 Ka51
Seyssel F 49 Jd46
Seysses F 62 Gb54
Sézanne F 32 Hc37
,s-Gravendeel NL 12 Hd27
,s-Gravenhage NL 11 Hc26
,s-Gravenzande NL 11 Hc26
,s-Heerenberg NL 13 Jc26
,s-Hertogenbosch NL 12 Jb27
Siddeburen NL 9 Jd21
Sierck-les-Bains F 24 Jd34
Sierentz F 35 Kc40
Sigean F 71 Hb56
Sigloy F 31 Gd40
Signes F 65 Jd55
Signy-l'Abbaye F 23 Hd34
Signy-le-Petit F 23 Hd33
Sigogne F 45 Fc47
Sigonce F 65 Jd52
Silenrieux B 16 Hd32
Silfiac F 27 Ea39
Sillans-la-Cascade F 65 Ka54
Sillé-le-Guillaume F 30 Fc39
Sillery F 23 Hd35
Simandre F 41 Jb44
Simiane-la-Rotonde F 65 Jd52
Simorre F 61 Ga54
Simpelveld NL 17 Jc30
Sin-le-Noble F 15 Ha32
Sint Annaparochie NL 8 Jb22
Sint Jacobiparochie NL 8 Jb22
Sint Martensbrug NL 8 Hd23
Sint Michielsgestel NL 12 Jb27
Sint Nicolaasga NL 8 Jb23
Sint-Niklaas B 15 Hc29
Sint Oedenrode NL 12 Jb27
Sint Philipsland NL 11 Hc27
Sint-Truiden B 16 Ja30
Sion F 34 Jd38
Sion-les-Mines F 29 Ed40
Siorac-en-Périgord F 54 Gb50
Sisco F 72 Ma55
Sissonne F 22 Hc34
Sisteron F 65 Jd52
Sittard NL 17 Jc29
Sivry-Rance B 16 Hd32
Six-Fours-les-Plages F 65 Jd55
Sixt F 50 Kb45
Sixt-sur-Aff F 28 Ec40
Sizun F 26 Dc38
Slagharen NL 9 Jc24
Sleen NL 9 Jd23
Sliedrecht NL 12 Hd27
Slochteren NL 9 Jd22
Sloten NL 8 Jb23
Sluis NL 11 Hb28
Sluiskil NL 11 Hc28
Smalinger-Land NL 8 Jb22
Smilde NL 9 Jc23
Sneek NL 8 Jb22
Sochaux F 34 Ka40
Soest NL 12 Ja25
Soignies B 15 Hc31
Soings-en-Sologne F 39 Gc41

Solgne F 24 Jd36
Solignac F 46 Gb47
Soligny-lès-Étangs F 32 Hb38
Sollacaro F 73 Ld59
Solliès-Pont F 65 Ka55
Solomiac F 61 Ga53
Solre-le-Château F 15 Hc32
Solutré-Pouilly F 48 Ja45
Somain F 15 Hb32
Sombernon F 41 Ja42
Sombreffe B 16 Hd31
Someren NL 12 Jb28
Sommauthe F 23 Ja34
Sommecaise F 32 Hb40
Somme-Leuze B 16 Jb31
Sommepy-Tahure F 23 Hd35
Sommery F 21 Gb34
Sommesous F 33 Hd37
Somme-Tourbe F 23 Ja35
Sommevoire F 33 Ja38
Sommières F 64 Ja53
Sommières-du-Clain F 45 Fd45
Sompuis F 33 Hd37
Somsois F 33 Hd37
Sonchamp F 31 Gc38
Son en Breugel NL 12 Jb27
Songeons F 21 Gc34
Songy F 33 Hd37
Sons-de-Bretagne F 29 Ed38
Sorbiers F 57 Jd51
Sore F 52 Fb52
Sorede F 71 Hb57
Sorges F 45 Ga48
Sorgues-l'Ouvèze F 64 Jb52
Sorigny F 38 Ga42
Sornac F 46 Gd47
Sos F 61 Fd53
Sospel F 58 Kd52
Sost F 69 Ga56
Sotta F 73 Ma59
Sotteville-lès-Rouen F 21 Gb35
Soual F 62 Gd54
Souancé-au-Perche F 30 Ga39
Soubise F 44 Fb46
Soucy F 32 Hb39
Soudan F 29 Fa40
Soudan F 45 Fc45
Soudé F 33 Hd37
Soues F 61 Fd55
Souesmes F 39 Gd41
Soufflenheim F 25 Kc36
Sougy F 31 Gd40
Souillac F 54 Gc50
Souilly F 23 Jb36
Soulac-sur-Mer F 44 Fa48
Soulaines-Dhuys F 33 Ja38
Soulgé-sur-Ouette F 29 Fb39
Soulignonne F 44 Fb47
Soullans F 36 Ec43
Soulle F 44 Fa46
Soultz-Haut-Rhin F 35 Kb39
Soultz-sous-Forêts F 25 Kc36
Soumoulou F 61 Fc55
Souppes-sur-Loing F 32 Ha39
Souprosse F 60 Fb54
Sourdeval F 29 Fb37
Sourdon F 21 Gd34
Souria F 71 Ha57
Sours F 31 Gc38
Soursac F 46 Gc48
Sousceyrac F 54 Gd50
Sous-Parsat F 46 Gd46
Soussac F 53 Fc50
Soustons F 60 Ed54
Souvigné F 38 Fd41
Souvigny F 40 Hb44

Soveria F 72 Ld57
Soye F 42 Ka41
Spa B 17 Jc31
Spanbroek NL 8 Ja24
Speuld NL 12 Jb25
Spijkenisse NL 11 Hc26
Spincourt F 24 Jc35
Spontin B 16 Ja31
Spontour F 54 Gd49
Sprang-Capelle NL 12 Ja27
Sprimont B 16 Jb32
Staden B 15 Ha30
Stadskanaal NL 9 Jd22
Stainville F 33 Jb37
Staphorst NL 9 Jc24
Stavelot B 17 Jc31
Stavenisse NL 11 Hc27
Stavoren NL 8 Ja23
Stede Broec NL 8 Ja24
Steenbergen NL 12 Hd27
Steenderen NL 13 Jc26
Steenvoorde F 14 Gd30
Steenwijk NL 9 Jc23
Steinfort L 24 Jc33
Stekene B 15 Hc29
Stellendam NL 11 Hc27
Stenay F 23 Jb34
Stiring-Wendel F 24 Ka35
Stival F 27 Ea39
Stompetoren NL 8 Hd24
Stonne F 23 Ja34
Stoumont B 17 Jc31
Straimont B 23 Jb33
Stramproy NL 12 Jb28
Strasbourg F 35 Kc37
Strijen NL 12 Hd27
Sturzelbronn F 25 Kb35
Suare F 72 Lc56
Sublaines F 39 Gb42
Sucé-sur-Erdre F 37 Ed42
Sucy-en-Brie F 32 Ha37
Suèvres F 39 Gb41
Sugères F 47 Hc47
Suippes F 23 Hd35
Sully F 41 Jb43
Sully-la-Chapelle F 31 Gd40
Sully-sur-Loire F 31 Gd40
Sundhouse F 35 Kc38
Super-Besse F 47 Hb48
Superdévoluy F 57 Jd50
Super-Sauze F 58 Kb51
Surdoux F 46 Gc47
Surfonds F 30 Fd40
Surgères F 44 Fb46
Surhuisterveen NL 9 Jc22
Surin F 45 Fd46
Surtainville F 19 Ed35
Sury-ès-Bois F 40 Ha41
Sury-le-Comtal F 48 Hd47
Surzur F 36 Eb41
Susteren NL 17 Jc29
Suze-la-Rousse F 56 Jb51
Suzette F 65 Jc52
Swalmen NL 13 Jc28
Swifterbant NL 8 Jb24
Syam F 42 Jd43
Sylvanès F 63 Hb53
Sylvéréal F 64 Ja54

T

Tagnon F 23 Hd34
Tagsdorf F 35 Kb40
Taillebois F 20 Fc37
Taingy F 40 Hb41
Tain-l'Hermitage F 56 Jb49
Taizé F 38 Fc43
Taizé F 41 Ja44
Taizon F 38 Fc43
Talairan F 71 Ha56
Talais F 44 Fa48
Talasani F 72 Ma56
Talcy F 31 Gb40
Tallard F 57 Ka51
Taller F 60 Fa53
Talloires F 49 Ka46

Talmas F 21 Gd33
Talmay F 42 Jc41
Talmontiers F 21 Gc35
Talmont-Saint-Hilaire F 44 Ed45
Talmont-sur-Gironde F 44 Fb48
Tamines B 16 Hd31
Tamnay-en-Bazois F 40 Hc42
Tannies F 54 Gb50
Taninges F 49 Ka45
Tanlay F 33 Hd40
Tannay F 40 Hc41
Tannay F 23 Ja34
Tantonville F 34 Jd37
Tanus F 55 Ha52
Tarare F 48 Ja46
Tarascon F 64 Jb53
Tarascon-sur-Ariège F 70 Gc57
Tarassac F 63 Hb54
Tarbes F 61 Fd55
Tarcenay F 42 Jd42
Tardets-Sorholus F 68 Fa56
Targon F 53 Fc50
Tarnac F 46 Gd47
Tartas F 60 Fb53
Tartigny F 21 Gd34
Tartonne F 65 Ka52
Tassenières F 42 Jc43
Taulé F 27 Dd37
Taulignan F 56 Jb51
Taussat F 52 Fa50
Tautavel F 71 Hb57
Tauves F 47 Ha47
Tavaux F 42 Jc42
Tavaux-et-Pontséricourt F 22 Hc34
Tavel F 64 Jb52
Tavernes F 65 Ka54
Taverny F 21 Gd36
Tegelen NL 13 Jc28
Teillay F 29 Ed40
Teillet F 63 Ha53
Teillet-Argenty F 47 Ha45
Tellancourt F 23 Jb34
Temse B 15 Hc29
Tenay F 49 Jc46
Ten Boer NL 9 Jd22
Tence F 56 Ja49
Tencin F 49 Jd48
Tende F 58 Kd52
Tenneville B 16 Jb32
Tennie F 30 Fc39
Ter Apel NL 9 Jd23
Tergnier F 22 Hb34
Ter Hole NL 11 Hc28
Termes-d'Armagnac F 61 Fc54
Termignon F 50 Kb48
Terminiers F 31 Gc39
Termunten NL 9 Jd21
Terneuzen NL 11 Hc28
Terrasson-Lavilledieu F 54 Gb49
Tervuren B 16 Hd30
Terwolde NL 13 Jc25
Tessenderlo B 16 Ja29
Tesson F 44 Fb47
Tessy-sur-Vire F 19 Fa36
Thann F 35 Kb39
Thannenkirch F 35 Kb38
Thaon F 20 Fc35
Thaon-les-Vosges F 34 Jd38
t' Harde NL 8 Jb24
Tharon-Plage F 36 Ec42
Thaumiers F 40 Ha43
Theillay F 39 Gd42
Theix F 36 Eb41
Thénezay F 38 Fc44
Thénissey F 41 Ja41
Thenon F 54 Gb49
Thérouanne F 14 Gd31
Theux B 17 Jc31
Thevet-Saint-Julien F 39 Gd44
Theys F 49 Jd48

Thèze F 61 Fc55
Thèze F 57 Jd51
Thiaucourt-Regniéville F 24 Jc36
Thiberville F 20 Fd36
Thibie F 23 Hd36
Thiéblemont-Farémont F 33 Ja37
Thiel-sur-Acolin F 40 Hc44
Thiers F 47 Hc46
Thiery F 58 Kc52
Thines F 56 Hd51
Thionville F 24 Jd34
Thiron F 30 Ga38
Thivars F 31 Gb38
Thiviers F 45 Ga48
Thizay F 39 Gc43
Thizy F 48 Ja46
Thoard F 65 Ka52
Thoirette F 49 Jc45
Thoissey F 48 Jb45
Thollon-les-Mémises F 43 Kb44
Thommen B 17 Jc32
Thonelle F 23 Jb34
Thônes F 49 Ka46
Thonon-les-Bains F 42 Ka44
Thorame-Basse F 58 Kb52
Thorame-Haute F 58 Kb52
Thorembais-les-Béguines B 16 Ja30
Thorenc F 66 Kb53
Thorens-Glières F 49 Ka46
Thorigné-sur-Dué F 30 Ga39
Thorigny-sur-Oreuse F 32 Hb38
Thorn NL 17 Jc29
,t Horntje NL 8 Hd23
Thors F 45 Fc47
Thors F 33 Jb34
Thouarcé F 37 Fb42
Thouars F 38 Fc43
Thourie F 29 Ed40
Thourotte F 22 Ha34
Thourotte F 22 Ha35
Thueyts F 56 Ja50
Thuilley-aux-Groseilles F 34 Jc37
Thuin B 16 Hd32
Thuir F 71 Hb57
Thumeries F 15 Ha31
Thuré F 38 Fd43
Thurey F 41 Jb43
Thury F 41 Ja42
Thury-Harcourt F 20 Fc36
Tibarrelé F 63 Ha53
Tiel NL 12 Jb26
Tielt B 15 Hb29
Tielt B 16 Ja30
Tienen B 16 Ja30
Tiercé F 38 Fc41
Tiffauges F 37 Fa43
Tignécourt F 34 Jc39
Tignes F 50 Kb47
Tigy F 31 Gd40
Tilburg NL 12 Ja27
Til-Châtel F 41 Jb41
Tillac F 61 Fc54
Tillay-le-Péneux F 31 Gc39
Tillières-sur-Avre F 31 Gb37
Tilly F 46 Gb45
Tilly-sur-Seulles F 19 Fb36
Tinchebray F 29 Fb37
Tinlot B 16 Jb31
Tinténiac F 29 Ed38
Tintigny B 23 Jb34
Tiranges F 48 Hd48
Tiuccia F 73 Lc58
Tizzano F 73 Ld59
Tocane-Saint-Apre F 53 Ga49

Tombebœuf F 53 Fd51
Tongeren B 16 Jb30
Tonnay-Boutonne F 44 Fb46
Tonnay-Charente F 44 Fb46
Tonneins F 53 Fd52
Tonnerre F 33 Hd40
Torcé-en Vallée F 30 Fd39
Torcy F 32 Ha37
Torcy F 41 Ja43
Torcy-le-Grand F 21 Gb34
Torfou F 37 Fa43
Torgny B 23 Jb34
Torhout B 15 Ha29
Torigni-sur-Vire F 19 Fb36
Torre F 73 Ma59
Tosse F 60 Ed54
Tôtes F 21 Gb34
Toucy F 32 Hb40
Toudon F 58 Kc53
Touët-sur-Var F 58 Kc52
Touillon F 33 Ja40
Toul F 34 Jc37
Toulon F 65 Ka55
Toulon-sur-Arroux F 41 Hd44
Toulouse F 62 Gc54
Toulx Sainte-Croix F 46 Gd45
Tourcoing F 15 Ha30
Tourlaville F 19 Ed34
Tournai B 15 Hb31
Tournan-en-Brie F 32 Ha37
Tournay F 69 Fd56
Tournecoupe F 61 Ga53
Tournefeuille F 62 Gb54
Tournefort F 58 Kc52
Tournehem-sur-la-Hem F 14 Gc30
Tournon-d'Agenais F 54 Gb51
Tournon-Saint-Martin F 38 Ga44
Tournon-sur-Rhône F 56 Ja49
Tournus F 41 Jb44
Tourny F 21 Gc36
Tourouvre F 30 Ga38
Tours F 38 Ga42
Tours-en-Vimeu F 21 Gc33
Tourteron F 23 Ja34
Tourtoirac F 54 Gb49
Tourtour F 65 Ka53
Tourves F 65 Ka54
Tourville-sur-Sienne F 19 Ed36
Toury F 31 Gc39
Toutencourt F 21 Gd33
Touvois F 37 Ed43
Touzac F 54 Gb51
Trainel F 32 Hb38
Trainou F 31 Gd40
Tramayes F 48 Jb45
Trampot F 33 Jb38
Trancault F 32 Hc38
Trannes F 33 Jb38
Trans F 29 Ed38
Transinne B 16 Jb32
Trappes F 31 Gc37
Traves F 34 Jd40
Travo F 73 Ma58
Tréban F 47 Hb45
Trèbes F 63 Ha55
Trebeurden F 27 Dd37
Tréboul F 26 Dc39
Trédion F 28 Eb40
Tréfeuntec F 26 Dc39
Treffieux F 37 Ed41
Treffort-Cuisat F 49 Jc45
Trégastel-Plage F 27 Dd37
Trégomeur F 28 Eb38
Trégourez F 27 Dd39
Tréguier F 27 Ea37
Trégunc F 27 Dd40
Treignac F 46 Gc48
Treignat F 46 Gd45
Treignes B 16 Ja32

Treigny F 40 Hb41
Treillières F 37 Ed42
Trélazé F 38 Fc41
Trélaze F 38 Fc41
Trélissac F 53 Ga49
Trélon F 15 Hc32
Tremblay F 29 Ed38
Tremblois-lès-Rocroi F 23 Hd33
Tremelo B 16 Hd29
Trémentines F 37 Fb42
Tréminis F 57 Jd50
Trensacq F 52 Fb52
Tréogan F 27 Dd39
Tréon F 31 Gb37
Trept F 49 Jc47
Tresson F 30 Ga40
Treteau F 47 Hc45
Trets F 65 Jd54
Tréveray F 33 Jb37
Trévières F 19 Fb35
Trévignon F 27 Dd40
Trézelles F 47 Hc45
Triaize F 44 Fa46
Triaucourt-en-Argonne F 23 Ja36
Tricot F 22 Ha34
Trie-Château F 21 Gc35
Trie-sur-Baïse F 61 Fd55
Trigance F 66 Kb53
Trignac F 36 Ec42
Triguères F 32 Hb40
Trinay F 31 Gc39
Trinity GBJ 18 Ec35
Trizac F 47 Ha48
Troarn F 20 Fc36
Trois Ponts B 17 Jc31
Troisvierges L 17 Jc32
Trôo F 30 Ga40
Trooz B 16 Jb31
Trouans F 33 Hd37
Trouville-sur-Mer F 20 Fd35
Troyes F 33 Hd38
Trun F 30 Fd37
Tubbergen NL 9 Jd24
Tubize B 16 Hd30
Tuchan F 71 Ha56
Tudeils F 54 Gc49
Tuffé F 30 Ga39
Tulette F 56 Jb51
Tulle F 54 Gc49
Tullins F 49 Jc48
Turckheim F 35 Kb39
Turenne F 54 Gc49
Turnhout B 12 Ja28
Twello NL 13 Jc25
t' Zandt NL 9 Jd21
Tzummarum NL 8 Jb22

U

Ubbergen NL 13 Jc26
Uchacq-et-Parentis F 60 Fb53
Uchizy F 41 Jb44
Uckange F 24 Jd35
Uden NL 12 Jb27
Udenhout NL 12 Ja27
Ugine F 49 Ka46
Uitgeest NL 8 Hd24
Uithoorn NL 12 Hd25
Uithuizen NL 9 Jd21
Ulft NL 13 Jc26
Ulrum NL 9 Jc21
Ulvenhout NL 12 Hd27
Unac F 70 Gc57
Ur F 70 Gd58
Urbeis F 35 Kb38
Urbise F 48 Hd45
Urçay F 40 Ha44
Urcel F 22 Hb34
Urdos F 68 Fb56
Uriage-les-Bains F 49 Jd48
Urk NL 8 Jb24
Urt F 60 Fa54
Useldange L 24 Jc33
Ussat F 70 Gc57

Usseau F 44 Fb46
Ussel F 46 Gd48
Ussel F 55 Hb49
Usson-du-Poitou F 45 Ga45
Usson-en-Forez F 48 Hd48
Usson-les-Bains F 70 Gd57
Ussy F 20 Fc36
Ustaritz F 60 Ed55
Utrecht NL 12 Ja26
Uzel F 28 Eb39
Uzemain F 34 Jd39
Uzerche F 46 Gc48
Uzès F 64 Ja52
Uzeste F 53 Fc51

V

Vaals NL 17 Jc30
Vaas F 38 Fd41
Vaassen NL 13 Jc25
Vabre F 63 Ha54
Vabres-l'Abbaye F 63 Hb53
Vacherauville F 23 Jb35
Vacqueyras F 64 Jb52
Vacquiers F 62 Gc53
Vagney F 34 Ka39
Vahl-Ebersing F 24 Ka35
Vaiges F 29 Fb39
Vaillant F 33 Jb40
Vailly F 49 Ka45
Vailly-sur-Aisne F 22 Hb35
Vailly-sur-Sauldre F 40 Ha41
Vaison-la-Romaine F 65 Jc52
Vaite F 34 Jc40
Valady F 55 Ha51
Valay F 42 Jc41
Valberg F 58 Kc52
Valbonne F 66 Kc53
Valcivières F 48 Hd47
Valdahon F 42 Ka42
Valdebeix F 47 Hb48
Val-de-Meuse F 34 Jc39
Val-de-Reuil F 21 Gb35
Valderiès F 62 Gd53
Val-de-Saâne F 20 Ga34
Val d'Isère F 50 Kb47
Valdivienne F 38 Ga44
Val-d'Izé F 29 Fa39
Valdrôme F 57 Jd51
Valençay F 39 Gc42
Valence F 45 Fd47
Valence F 53 Ga52
Valence F 36 Jb49
Valence-d'Albigeois F 63 Ha53
Valence-en-Brie F 32 Ha38
Valence-sur-Baïse F 61 Fd53
Valenciennes F 15 Hb32
Valensole F 65 Ka53
Valeyrac F 44 Fb48
Valflaunès F 64 Hd53
Valfréjus F 50 Kb48
Valgorge F 56 Hd51
Valhuon F 14 Gd31
Valin F 53 Fc49
Valkenburg aan de Geul NL 17 Jc30
Valkenswaard NL 12 Jb28
Vallauris-Golfe-Juan F 66 Kc53
Valleiry F 49 Jd45
Valleraugue F 55 Hc52
Vallery F 32 Hb39
Vallet F 37 Fa42
Vallières F 46 Gd46
Vallières F 49 Jd46
Valloire F 49 Jd48
Vallon-Pont-d'Arc F 56 Ja51
Vallon-sur-Gée F 30 Fc40
Vallouise F 57 Ka49

Valmanya F 71 Ha57
Valmigère F 71 Ha56
Valmont F 20 Fd34
Valmorel F 49 Ka47
Valognes F 19 Fa35
Valras-Plage F 63 Hc55
Valréas F 56 Jb51
Valsemé F 20 Fd36
Valsenestre F 57 Ka49
Valserres F 57 Ka51
Vals-les-Bains F 56 Ja50
Valsonne F 48 Ja46
Val-Thorens F 50 Kb48
Vanault-les-Dames F 23 Ja36
Vancé F 30 Ga40
Vandenesse F 40 Hc43
Vanlay F 33 Hd39
Vannes F 36 Eb41
Vannes-sur-Cosson F 31 Gd40
Vanzay F 45 Fd45
Vaour F 62 Gc53
Varacieux F 49 Jc48
Varades F 37 Fa42
Varages F 65 Ka54
Varaire F 54 Gc52
Varaize F 45 Fc46
Varen F 54 Gd52
Varengeville-sur-Mer F 20 Ga33
Varennes-Changy F 32 Ha40
Varennes-en-Argonne F 23 Ja35
Varennes-le-Grand F 41 Jb43
Varennes-Saint-Sauveur F 41 Jb44
Varennes-sur-Allier F 47 Hc45
Varennes-sur-Usson F 47 Hc48
Varetz F 54 Gc49
Varilhes F 70 Gc56
Varize F 31 Gc39
Varrains F 38 Fc42
Varreddes F 22 Ha36
Vars F 58 Kb50
Varsseveld NL 13 Jc26
Varzy F 40 Hd42
Vascœuil F 21 Gb35
Vasles F 38 Fc44
Vassieux-en-Vercors F 57 Jc49
Vassy F 29 Fb37
Vassy F 41 Hd41
Vatan F 39 Gc43
Vatry F 33 Hd37
Vauchamps F 22 Hc36
Vauchassis F 32 Hc39
Vauclaix F 40 Hc42
Vaucouleurs F 34 Jc37
Vaudeurs F 32 Hc39
Vaudoy-en-Brie F 32 Hb37
Vaudrey F 42 Jc42
Vaujany F 49 Jd48
Vaulx-Vraucourt F 15 Ha32
Vaupoisson F 33 Hd38
Vausseroux F 38 Fc44
Vautorte F 29 Fb39
Vauvenargues F 65 Jd54
Vauvert F 64 Ja54
Vauvillers F 34 Jd39
Vaux-s-Sûre B 23 Jb33
Vaux-sur-Aubigny F 33 Jb40
Vavincourt F 23 Jb36
Vay F 37 Ed41
Vayrac F 54 Gc50
Veauges F 40 Ha42
Vedrines-Saint-Loup F 55 Hb49
Veendam NL 9 Jd22
Veenendaal NL 12 Jb26
Veenwouden NL 8 Jb22
Veere NL 11 Hb28

Veghel NL 12 Jb27
Veillac F 47 Ha48
Velaines F 33 Jb37
Veldhoek NL 13 Jc26
Veldhoven NL 12 Jb28
Vélines F 53 Fd50
Velisfaux F 42 Jd41
Velle-le-Châtel F 34 Jd40
Velles F 39 Gc44
Vellescot F 35 Kb40
Vellevans F 42 Ka41
Velsen NL 8 Hd24
Venaco F 72 Ld57
Venarey-les-Laumes F 41 Ja41
Venarsal F 54 Gc49
Venasque F 65 Jc52
Vence F 66 Kc53
Vendays-Montalivet F 44 Fa48
Vendegies-sur-Ecaillon F 15 Hb32
Vendenheim F 25 Kc36
Vendeuil F 22 Hb34
Vendeuvre F 20 Fc36
Vendeuvre-sur-Barse F 33 Hd38
Vendine F 62 Gc54
Vendœuvres F 39 Gb44
Vendôme F 31 Gb40
Vendranges F 48 Hd46
Vendrennes F 37 Fa43
Venhuizen NL 8 Ja24
Vénissieux F 48 Jb47
Venlo NL 13 Jc28
Venray NL 13 Jc27
Vensac F 44 Fa48
Ventabren F 65 Jc54
Ventelay F 22 Hc35
Ventiseri F 73 Ma58
Ver F 29 Fa37
Verberie F 22 Ha35
Vercel-Villedieu-le Camp F 42 Ka42
Vercheny F 57 Jc50
Verdaches F 57 Ka51
Verdes F 31 Gb40
Verdille F 45 Fc47
Verdonnet F 33 Hd40
Verdun F 23 Jb35
Verdun-sur-Garonne F 62 Gb53
Verdun-sur-le-Doubs F 41 Jb43
Véreaux F 40 Ha43
Verfeil F 62 Gc54
Verfeil F 54 Gd52
Vergt F 53 Ga49
Vérignon F 65 Ka53
Vérigny F 31 Gb38
Vermand F 22 Hb34
Vermenton F 32 Hc40
Vernantes F 38 Fd42
Vern-d'Anjou F 37 Fb41
Vernet F 62 Gc55
Vernet-les-Bains F 71 Ha57
Verneuil F 22 Hc36
Verneuil-en-Bourbonnais F 47 Hb45
Verneuil-sur-Avre F 30 Ga37
Verneuil-sur-Indre F 39 Gb43
Vernoil F 38 Fd42
Vernon F 45 Fd45
Vernon F 21 Gb36
Vernou-en-Sologne F 39 Gc41
Vernouillet F 31 Gb37
Vernou-sur-Brenne F 38 Ga41
Vernoux-en-Vivarais F 56 Ja50
Vern-sur-Seiche F 29 Ed39
Véron F 32 Hb39
Verrières F 45 Ga45
Versailles F 31 Gd37

Versols-et-Lapeyre F 63 Hb53
Verteillac F 45 Fd48
Verteuil-sur-Charente F 45 Fd46
Vertolaye F 47 Hc47
Vertou F 37 Ed42
Vert-Saint-Denis F 32 Ha38
Vertus F 22 Hc36
Verviers B 17 Jc31
Vervins F 22 Hc33
Vescovato F 72 Ma56
Vesdun F 40 Ha44
Vesoul F 34 Jd40
Vetheuil F 21 Gc36
Veules-les-Roses F 20 Ga33
Veulettes-sur-Mer F 20 Ga33
Veurne B 15 Ha29
Veynes F 57 Jd50
Veyrier F 49 Ka46
Vézelay F 40 Hc41
Vézelise F 34 Jd37
Vézelois F 35 Kb40
Vezels-Roussy F 55 Ha50
Vézénobres F 64 Ja52
Vezins F 37 Fb42
Vézins-de-Lévézou F 55 Hb52
Vezzani F 72 Ld57
Viabon F 31 Gc39
Vianden L 24 Jd33
Viane F 63 Ha54
Vianen NL 12 Ja26
Viarmes F 21 Gd36
Vias F 63 Hc55
Vibraye F 30 Ga39
Vicdessos F 70 Gc57
Vic-en-Bigorre F 61 Fd55
Vic-Fezensac F 61 Fd54
Vicherey F 34 Jc38
Vichy F 47 Hc46
Vic-le-Comte F 47 Hb47
Vic-le-Fesq F 64 Hd53
Vico F 72 Lc57
Vicq-Exemplet F 39 Gd44
Vic-sur-Aisne F 22 Hb35
Vic-sur-Cère F 55 Ha49
Vic-sur-Seille F 24 Jd36
Vidauban F 66 Kb54
Vidouze F 61 Fc55
Vieille-Brioude F 47 Hc48
Vieille-Soubiran F 61 Fc53
Vieillespesse F 55 Hd49
Vieillevigne F 37 Ed43
Vielle F 60 Fa53
Vielleségure F 60 Fb55
Vielmur-sur-Agout F 62 Gd54
Vielsalm B 17 Jc31
Viels-Maisons F 22 Hb36
Vienne F 48 Jb47
Vienne-en-Val F 31 Gd40
Vienne-le-Château F 23 Ja35
Viens F 65 Jd53
Vierhouten NL 12 Jb25
Vierlingsbeek NL 13 Jc27
Vierville-sur-Mer F 19 Fb35
Vierzon F 39 Gd42
Vieux-Boucau-les-Bains F 60 Ed53
Vieux-Fume F 20 Fc36
Vif F 57 Jd49
Vignacourt F 21 Gd33
Vignes-la-Côte F 33 Jb38
Vigneulles-Hattonchâtel F 24 Jc36
Vignory F 33 Jb38
Vigny F 21 Gc36
Vihiers F 37 Fb42
Villabon F 40 Ha42
Villagrains F 52 Fb51
Villaines-en-Duesmois F 33 Ja40
Villaines-la-Juhel F 30 Fc38
Villamblard F 53 Ga49
Villandraut F 53 Fc51

Villandry F 38 Ga42
Villard-de-Lans F 57 Jc49
Villard Saint-Christophe F 57 Jd49
Villars F 45 Ga48
Villars F 31 Gc39
Villars-en-Azois F 33 Ja39
Villars-les-Dombes F 48 Jb46
Villars-Santenoge F 33 Jb40
Villé F 35 Kb38
Villebaudon F 19 Fa36
Villebois-Lavalette F 45 Fd48
Villebrumier F 62 Gc53
Villecerf F 32 Ha38
Villecomtal F 55 Ha51
Villeconin F 31 Gd38
Villecroze F 65 Ka54
Villedaigne F 63 Hb55
Villedieu F 33 Hd40
Villedieu-les-Poêles F 29 Fa37
Villedieu-sur-Indre F 39 Gc43
Villedômain F 39 Gb43
Villefagnan F 45 Fd46
Villefloure F 71 Ha56
Villefontaine F 48 Jb47
Villefort F 56 Hd51
Villefranche-d'Albigeois F 63 Ha53
Villefranche-d'Allier F 47 Ha45
Villefranche-de-Conflent F 71 Ha57
Villefranche-de-Lauragais F 62 Gc55
Villefranche-de-Lonchat F 53 Fd50
Villefranche-de-Panat F 55 Ha52
Villefranche-de-Rouergue F 54 Gb51
Villefranche-du-Périgord F 54 Gb51
Villefranche-sur-Cher F 39 Gc42
Villefranche-sur-Mer F 67 Kd53
Villefranche-sur-Saône F 48 Ja46
Villegailhenc F 63 Ha55
Villegenon F 40 Ha41
Ville-la-Grand F 49 Ka45
Villemaur-sur-Vanne F 32 Hc38
Villemer F 32 Ha38
Villemeux-sur-Eure F 31 Gb37
Villemorien F 33 Hd39
Villemur-sur-Tarn F 62 Gc53
Villenauxe-la-Grande F 32 Hc37
Villeneuve F 54 Gd51
Villeneuve F 48 Jb46
Villeneuve F 48 Jb54
Villeneuve-au-Chemin F 32 Hc39
Villeneuve-d'Ascq F 15 Hb31
Villeneuve-de-Berg F 56 Ja51
Villeneuve-de-Marsan F 61 Fc53
Villeneuve-en-Montagne F 41 Ja43
Villeneuve-la-Comtesse F 44 Fb46
Villeneuve-la-Guyard F 32 Hb38
Villeneuve-l'Archevêque F 32 Hc39
Villeneuve-lès-Avignon F 64 Jb53
Villeneuve-les-Bordes F 32 Hb38

Villeneuve-sur-Allier F 40 Hb44
Villeneuve-sur-Lot F 53 Ga51
Villeneuve-sur-Yonne F 32 Hb39
Villentrois F 39 Gb42
Villeréal F 53 Ga51
Villerest F 48 Hd46
Villeromain F 31 Gb40
Villers-Bocage F 19 Fb36
Villers-Bocage F 21 Gd33
Villers Bretonneux F 21 Gd33
Villers-Carbonnel F 22 Ha33
Villers-Cotterêts F 22 Hb35
Villers-en-Argonne F 23 Ja36
Villersexel F 34 Ka40
Villers-Farlay F 42 Jc42
Villers-le-Gambon B 16 Hd32
Villers-le-Lac F 42 Ka42
Villers-sur-Mer F 20 Fc35
Villerupt F 24 Jc34
Villeseneux F 23 Hd36
Villesèque F 54 Gb51
Villes-sur-Auzon F 65 Jc52
Ville-sur-Illon F 34 Jd38
Ville-sur-Tourbe F 23 Ja35
Villetrun F 31 Gb40
Villeurbanne F 48 Jb47
Villevallier F 32 Hb39
Villeveyrac F 63 Hc54
Villiers-Charlemagne F 29 Fb40
Villiers-en-Plaine F 44 Fb45
Villiers-Saint-Benoît F 32 Hb40
Villiers-Saint-Georges F 32 Hb37
Villiers-sur-Beuvron F 40 Hc42
Villon F 33 Hd40
Villotte-sur-Aire F 23 Jb36
Villuis F 32 Hb38
Villy-en-Auxois F 41 Ja41
Vilvoorde B 16 Hd30
Vimont F 20 Fc36
Vimoutiers F 20 Fd36
Vimy F 15 Ha32
Vinay F 49 Jc48
Vinça F 71 Ha57
Vincelles F 32 Hc40
Vingrau F 71 Hb56
Vinkeveen NL 12 Ja25
Vinon F 40 Ha42
Vinon-sur-Verdon F 65 Jd53
Violay F 48 Ja46
Violès F 64 Jb52
Viols-le-Fort F 64 Hd53
Viré F 29 Fb37
Viré F 41 Jb44
Vireux-Wallerand F 16 Ja32
Virieu F 49 Jd47
Virginin F 49 Jd47
Viriville F 49 Jc48
Virollet F 45 Fc46
Vironchaux F 14 Gc32
Virton B 23 Jb34
Viry F 49 Jd45
Visé B 16 Jb30
Vissec F 63 Hc53
Visseiche F 29 Fa40
Vitré F 29 Fa39
Vitrolles F 65 Jc54
Vitry-en-Artois F 15 Ha32
Vitry-la-Ville F 23 Hd36
Vitry-le-François F 33 Ja37
Vitry-sur-Seine F 31 Gd37
Vitteaux F 41 Ja41
Vittel F 34 Jc38
Vy-lès-Lure F 34 Ka40

Viviers F 56 Jb51
Viviez F 54 Gd51
Vivonne F 45 Fd45
Vix F 44 Fb45
Vizille F 57 Jd49
Vizzavona F 73 Ld58
Vlaardingen NL 11 Hc26
Vlagtwedde NL 9 Jd22
Vledder NL 9 Jc23
Vleuten NL 12 Ja26
Vlijmen NL 12 Ja27
Vlissingen NL 11 Hb28
Vocance F 56 Ja49
Vodable F 47 Hb48
Vœu F 39 Gc43
Vogüe F 56 Ja51
Void-Vacon F 34 Jc37
Voiron F 49 Jc48
Voise F 31 Gc38
Voisines F 33 Jb40
Voiteur F 42 Jc43
Volendam NL 8 Ja24
Volgelsheim F 35 Kc39
Vollenhove NL 8 Jb24
Vollore-Montagne F 47 Hc47
Vollore-Ville F 47 Hc47
Volnay F 30 Fd40
Volonne F 65 Ka52
Volvic F 47 Hb46
Vonèche B 16 Ja32
Vonnas F 48 Jb45
Voorburg NL 12 Hd26
Voorschoten NL 12 Hd26
Voorthuizen NL 12 Jb25
Voray-sur-l'Ognon F 42 Jd41
Vorden NL 13 Jc25
Voreppe F 49 Jd48
Vorey F 56 Hd49
Vorly F 40 Ha43
Voudenay-l'Église F 41 Ja42
Voue F 33 Hd38
Vougécourt F 34 Jd39
Vougeot F 41 Jb42
Vouhé F 44 Fb46
Vouillé F 45 Fc45
Vouillé F 38 Fd44
Voulx F 32 Ha38
Voussac F 47 Hb45
Voutenay-sur-Cure F 40 Hc41
Vouvant F 37 Fb44
Vouvray F 38 Ga41
Vouzailles F 38 Fd44
Vouzeron F 39 Gd42
Vouziers F 23 Ja35
Vouzon F 39 Gd41
Voves F 31 Gc39
Vrécourt F 34 Jc38
Vresse-sur-Semois B 23 Ja33
Vries NL 9 Jc22
Vriezenveen NL 9 Jd24
Vrigne-au-Bois F 23 Ja33
Vrizy F 23 Ja34
Vron F 14 Gc32
Vroomshoop NL 9 Jd24
Vught NL 12 Ja27
Vuillafans F 42 Jd42
Vulaines-sur-Seine F 32 Ha38

W

Waalre NL 12 Jb28
Waalwijk NL 12 Ja27
Waarschoot B 15 Hb29
Waben F 14 Gc32
Wachtebeke B 15 Hc29
Waddinxveen NL 12 Hd26
Wageningen NL 12 Jb26
Waimes B 17 Jc31
Walcourt B 16 Hd32
Walferdange L 24 Jd33
Walincourt-Selvigny F 22 Hb33

Wallers F 15 Hb32
Waly F 23 Jb36
Wangenbourg F 35 Kb37
Wanssum NL 13 Jc27
Wapenveld NL 9 Jc24
Warbomont B 16 Jb31
Warcq F 24 Jc35
Wardin B 17 Jc32
Waregem B 15 Hb30
Waremme B 16 Jb30
Warffum NL 9 Jc21
Warga NL 8 Jb22
Warluis F 21 Gd35
Warmenhuizen NL 8 Hd24
Wasigny F 23 Hd34
Waskemeer NL 9 Jc22
Waspik NL 12 Ja27
Wasselonne F 35 Kb37
Wassenaar NL 12 Hd25
Wasserbillig L 24 Jd33
Wassigny F 22 Hb33
Wassy F 33 Ja38
Waterloo B 16 Hd30
Watervliet B 11 Hb28
Watten F 14 Gd30
Wattrelos F 15 Ha30
Wavre B 16 Hd30
Wedde NL 9 Jd22
Weerselo NL 9 Jd24
Weert NL 12 Jb28
Weesp NL 12 Ja25
Wehe-den Hoorn NL 9 Jc21
Wehl NL 13 Jc26
Weiswampach L 17 Jc32
Wekerom NL 12 Jb25
Welkenraedt B 17 Jc30
Wellin B 16 Ja32
Wemeldinge NL 11 Hc28
Wemmel B 16 Hd30
Werentzhouse F 35 Kc40
Werkendam NL 12 Ja27
Wervershoof NL 8 Ja23
Wervik B 15 Ha30
Wespelaar B 16 Hd29
Westende B 15 Ha29
Westerbork NL 9 Jd23
Westerhaar-Vriezen-veensewijk NL 9 Jd24
Wester-Koggenland NL 8 Ja24
Westerlo B 16 Ja29
Westkapelle NL 11 Hb28
Westmalle B 12 Hd28
West-Terschelling NL 8 Ja21
Wetteren B 15 Hc29
Weyersheim F 25 Kc36
Wezep NL 9 Jc24
Wierden NL 9 Jd24
Wieringerwerf NL 8 Ja23
Wiers B 15 Hb31
Wieuwerd NL 8 Jb22
Wijchen NL 12 Jb26
Wijhe NL 9 Jc24
Wijk bij Duurstede NL 12 Ja26
Willebroek B 16 Hd29
Willemstad NL 12 Hd27
Willer-sur Thur F 35 Kb39
Willerzie B 23 Ja33
Willgottheim F 25 Kb36
Wiltz L 17 Jc32
Wimereux F 14 Gb30
Wimmenau F 25 Kb36
Wimy F 22 Hc33
Windesheim NL 9 Jc24
Wingene B 15 Hb29
Wingen-sur-Moder F 25 Kb36
Winschoten F 9 Jc22
Winsum NL 8 Jb22
Winsum NL 9 Jc21
Winterswijk NL 13 Jc26
Wintzenheim F 35 Kc39
Wissant F 14 Gc30
Wissembourg F 25 Kc35
Wissenkerke NL 11 Hb27
Witmarsum NL 8 Ja22
Witry-lès-Reims F 23 Hd35

Wittelsheim F 35 Kb39
Woël F 24 Jc36
Woerden NL 12 Ja26
Wognum NL 8 Ja24
Woippy F 24 Jd35
Wolphaartsdijk NL 11 Hc28
Wolvega NL 8 Jb23
Wommels NL 8 Jb22
Workum NL 8 Ja23
Wormeldange L 24 Jd34
Wormerveen NL 8 Hd24
Wormhout F 14 Gd30
Woudenberg NL 12 Jb26
Woudsend NL 8 Jb23
Woumen B 15 Ha29
Wuustwezel B 12 Hd28

X - Y

Xermaménil F 34 Jd37
Xertigny F 34 Jd39
Ychoux F 52 Fa52
Yenne F 49 Jd47
Yerseke NL 11 Hc28
Yerville F 20 Ga34
Ygos-Saint-Saturnin F 60 Fb53
Ygrande F 40 Hb44
Ymonville F 31 Gc39
Yrouerre F 32 Hc40
Ysselsteyn NL 13 Jc27
Yssingeaux F 56 Hd49
Yvetot F 20 Ga34
Yvignac F 28 Ec38
Yvoire F 42 Ka44
Yvré-le-Pôlin F 30 Fd40
Yzeron F 48 Ja47

Z

Zaamslag NL 11 Hc28
Zaanstad NL 8 Hd24
Zaltbommel NL 12 Ja27
Zandt, t' NL 9 Jd21
Zandvoort NL 12 Hd25
Zaventem B 16 Hd30
Zeddam NL 13 Jc26
Zedelgem B 15 Ha29
Zeebrugge B 11 Hb28
Zeeland NL 12 Jb27
Zeewolde NL 12 Jb25
Zegerscappel F 14 Gd30
Zeist NL 12 Ja26
Zele B 15 Hc29
Zelhem NL 13 Jc26
Zelzate B 15 Hc29
Zevenaar NL 13 Jc26
Zevenbergen NL 12 Hd27
Zicavo F 73 Ld58
Zierikzee NL 11 Hc27
Zieuwent NL 13 Jd26
Zoetermeer NL 12 Hd26
Zomergem B 15 Hb29
Zonhoven B 16 Jb29
Zonza F 73 Ld59
Zottegem B 15 Hc30
Zoutkamp NL 9 Jc21
Zoutleeuw B 16 Ja30
Zuid Beijerland NL 12 Hd27
Zuidhorn NL 9 Jc22
Zuidlaren NL 9 Jd22
Zuidwolde NL 9 Jc23
Zundert NL 12 Hd28
Zurich NL 8 Jb22
Zutphen NL 13 Jc25
Zuydcoote F 14 Gd29
Zwaagwesteinde NL 8 Jb22
Zwanenburg NL 12 Hd25
Zwartemeer NL 9 Jd23
Zwartsluis NL 9 Jc24
Zweeloo NL 9 Jd23
Zwevegem B 15 Hb30
Zwevezel B 15 Hb29
Zwijndrecht B 16 Hd29
Zwolle NL 9 Jc24